Public Access to the Internet

Public Access to the Internet

edited by Brian Kahin and James Keller

A Publication of the Harvard Information Infrastructure Project

The MIT Press, Cambridge, Massachusetts, and London, England

This book was printed and bound in the United States of America.

Library of Congress Cataloging-in-Publication Data

Public access to the Internet / edited by Brian Kahin and James Keller
    p.   cm.
  Includes bibliographical references and index.
  ISBN 0-262-11207-8 (hc : alk. paper). — ISBN 0-262-61118-X (pb : alk. paper)
  1. Internet (Computer network) I. Kahin, Brian. II. Keller, James.
TK5105.875.I57P83 1995
384.3—dc20   95-8808
                                          CIP

Contents

Preface

The Harvard Information Infrastructure Project began five years ago with a small workshop on "Commercialization of the Internet" (summarized in the online document RFC 1192). Held right after the first commercial Internet services were announced, that workshop asked how the subsidized Internet should evolve toward commercialization. The Project's first book, *Building Information Infrastructure* (McGraw-Hill Primis, 1992), was an early effort to scope out the broader vision of a digital infrastructure. In September 1993, the National Information Infrastructure initiative was officially launched. Throughout this period, the Internet has continued its extraordinary growth, becoming for the first time accessible not just to universities and high-tech companies but to the general public. The Internet has often been cited as a prototype for the NII, but it is also increasingly seen as a direct path and platform for the networked applications of the NII.

This volume looks at the Internet in the process of becoming broadly accessible. It examines the Internet's potential for transforming communities and institutions as well as issues in the transformation of the Internet itself. Most of the papers were first presented at a conference held at the John F. Kennedy School of Government on May 26–27, 1993, and subsequently revised and updated.

The conference and this volume were made possible by a grant from the John and Mary R. Markle Foundation of New York. Additional support was provided from the operating funds of the

Harvard Information Infrastructure Project, which during this period was supported by AT&T, Bellcore, Delphi Internet Services, GM Hughes Electronics, IBM, and the MITRE Corporation. We want to thank the contributing authors, especially for their efforts to refine and update their work in a time of rapid change. We thank those who helped in the production of the workshop and this volume, especially Nora Hickey O'Neil, Miriam Avins, and Janet Abbate at the Science, Technology and Public Policy Program. We also express our appreciation to Bob Prior and Larry Cohen at the MIT Press.

A collaborative effort between the Harvard Information Infrastructure Project and the MIT Press has made possible this series of volumes on information infrastructure issues, of which this is the first. A second volume, entitled *Standards Policy for Information Infrastructure,* is forthcoming, and others are planned. It is our intention to create volumes that reflect the judgments and research of practitioners and scholars from a wide range of areas and fields. We hope that they will collectively make a contribution to both policy and practice.

Lewis M. Branscomb
Director
Science, Technology and Public Policy Program

The Public Access Agenda

The Internet and the National Information Infrastructure

Brian Kahin

On September 15, 1993, the Clinton Administration formally launched its National Information Infrastructure initiative, an initiative that, in rhetorical terms if not in dollars, ranks with the space race as a major technology-centered policy initiative. The blueprint for the initiative, the *Agenda for Action*, defines the NII as the aggregate of the nation's networks, computers, software, information resources, developers, and producers.[1] While it makes the point that the NII is not limited to networks, for most observers the NII remains the "information superhighway"—much like the "highways" we have now for telephones and cable television, only bigger and faster.[2] However, the highway metaphor skews popular understanding of the NII toward a low-level infrastructure of right-of-ways and pipes, rather than the higher levels of intelligently ordered and functionally enriched information.[3]

This high-level infrastructure is embodied in the Internet and the constellation of services, applications, and resources that have been built upon it. In the year since the *Agenda for Action* appeared, it has become broadly apparent that the Internet is not only a model for the future but a rapidly evolving platform, already widely implemented and based on mature, affordable, and adaptable technologies.

Ironically, the association of information infrastructure with high-speed networks stems from the extraordinary success of the Internet. In the late 1980s, the success of the networks funded by the National Science Foundation (which were then the heart of the

Internet) inspired calls for a National Research Network and then, more broadly, a National Research and Education Network (NREN).[4] The NREN, in turn, has been subsumed in the broader NII vision.

The superhighway metaphor and the high economic stakes in facilities-based infrastructure initially focused public discussion on the competition between cable and telephone companies. Then the mergers fell apart. The case for switched broadband into the home has not been effectively made, either as a business model or as a new level of "universal service." Legislation to promote competition has again failed. Meanwhile, the Internet continues its dramatic exponential growth, now connecting perhaps 15–25 million users worldwide, with the majority in the United States.[5]

Often cited as a model for the future National Information Infrastructure because it is based on open standards, the Internet is open to attachment by suppliers, users, and new networks. Although the Internet has been built from LANs and leased lines, its protocols can be implemented over virtually any transport technologies, present or future. It has spawned higher level protocols (WAIS, gopher, World Wide Web) that have become global standards for managing access to distributed information. Unlike cable television, where the local operator packages the services available to the end user, the Internet allows end users to choose and access services directly. There are no gatekeepers: Although Internet service providers are unregulated, they generally operate as common carriers in the classical sense, publishing tariffs and providing access to all comers on nondiscriminatory terms.[6]

But the openness and explosive growth of the Internet obscure characteristics that fly in the face of traditional public telecommunications policies. These contradictions have gone unnoticed, in part because certain networks within the Internet have been subsidized and because it is still widely assumed that the Internet as a whole is dependent on, and therefore shaped by, public subsidy. In fact, the Internet is shaped primarily by the economic characteristics of the technology, especially by dramatic economies of scale.

The Evolution of the Internet

The technology of the Internet derives from the ARPANET protocols developed for the Department of Defense in the 1970s. The Internet itself came into being as the term for the set of interconnecting networks, including the ARPANET, that used the ARPANET's TCP/IP protocol suite. The upper-case "Internet" served to distinguish the interconnection of the large wide-area TCP/IP networks, such as the ARPANET and CSNET, from local internets.[7] Unfortunately, the name contributes to the impression that the Internet is a single system owned and controlled by somebody somewhere.

In 1986, the NSFNET was launched, initially to connect NSF-funded supercomputer centers, but it quickly became a utility for many forms of resource sharing and communications. Like the Internet as a whole, the NSFNET is actually a collection of autonomous interconnected and interoperating networks.[8] Because NSF adopted TCP/IP protocols for the NSFNET backbone network, the NSFNET immediately became part of the Internet. In fact, the NSFNET backbone, which soon had dozens of connected mid-level networks, became, in important respects, the unofficial center of operations for the greater Internet.

The success of the Internet drove visions of greater networks. In 1987, the National Research Council issued a report, *Towards a National Research Network*, which called for a high-speed data network available to all the nation's researchers.[9] EDUCOM, speaking for the academic computing community, advocated a "National Research and Education Network,"[10] a vision eventually embodied in the Bush Administration's High Performance Computing and Communications initiative[11] and in the High Performance Computing Act of 1991, sponsored by Senator Gore.[12]

As a practical matter, the NREN was not an all-new network to be launched at some future date (as it was sometimes described) but the evolution of the portion of the domestic Internet funded to support research and education. Technically the NREN became a program within the HPCC initiative, a program with two parts: research on high-speed networks and the "Interim Interagency NREN," which was no more than the set of interconnected agency research networks. H.R. 1757, "The National Information Infrastructure Act of 1993," which passed the House in August of 1993, made it clear that the NREN Program did not contemplate a new National Research and Education Network. The September 1993

Agenda for Action did not once mention the NREN. By the end of 1993, the IINREN had become simply the Interagency Internet. The idea of a special network dedicated to research and education has been subsumed into a vision of a general-purpose infrastructure that will serve a vast spectrum of social, institutional, and economic goals. This generalization of the political vision reflects the fact that the Internet has progressed from a few special-purpose networks to a constellation of networks used in a growing variety of ways for an infinite number of purposes.

Universal Service and Access to Information

At the end of the 1980s, the networks of the Internet were all noncommercial and, if not directly subsidized, were indirectly subsidized by virtue of their free use of the cross-country NSFNET backbone. Most of the mid-level networks were set up as or operated out of nonprofit organizations. They were typically styled as membership organizations, although many were in fact projects of particular institutions or existing educational organizations.

Commercial Internet access was first offered by PSI and AlterNet beginning in early 1990. Some commercial services were developed by nonprofit networks, either directly or through for-profit subsidiaries. Some commercial providers, including PSI and AlterNet, originated as spin-offs of nonprofit networks.[13] A few of the networks that make up the Internet are still subsidized, but most are not. Nonetheless, the assumption that the Internet is government-subsidized lingers.[14]

In late 1989, the Internet was still viewed as a experimental, special-purpose network, the precursor of an National Research and Education Network that would serve roughly the same constituency. Five years later, the Internet is seen as a principal pathway to a future National Information Infrastructure, and the NREN is all but forgotten. The new focus on general-purpose information infrastructure sidesteps the issues associated with advancing a special infrastructure for a privileged special community of users. It raises instead the problem of "universal service" for the new infrastructure—how accessible is the new infrastructure in terms of ubiquity, affordability, and usability, and how is this accessibility paid for? The problem has been voiced not strictly as an issue of simple connectivity, as it was with the telephone system, but as explicitly linked to *access to information.*[15]

Access to information has historically been addressed by public libraries, not by telecommunications carriers. In certain respects, it is addressed by copyright law and, in the case of government information, by a variety of instruments and institutions.[16] Indeed, intellectual property and government information are the subject of two of the three Working Groups of the IITF Information Policy Committee.[17] However, the Working Groups are concerned with matters of federal law and policy, while public libraries in the U.S. are locally funded and managed. Public libraries are subsidized on the order of $83,000,000/year through Library Programs in the Department of Education, but this funding has not been used as policy tool.[18] Although digital information in a networked environment flows instantly across the nation and the world, the library remains a creature of local policy.

"Access to information" encompasses a host of factors that do not figure in "universal service" as it has historically been applied to telephone service.[19] The latter is relatively easy to define in consistent terms. All users have essentially the same low-bandwidth analog connection to the network, a connection that terminates in a simple, eminently usable $10 handset. Special features are available, but except for fax machines and modems, which are entirely the responsibility of the user, they add little to the base functionality of the network.

In the emerging digital environment, there are many dimensions to service beyond simple connectivity. Connections may vary in bandwidth—from a dial-up line with a 2400 baud modem to a leased T-3 line at 45 megabits per second. The relative availability of local storage determines what messaging activity and information management is possible. The capabilities of the local computer and software determine what applications are available, how well they function, and their ease of use. Much depends on the user's skills and knowledge of available resources. Finally, of course, "access to information" depends on the price of the information and the user's ability to pay.

Access to the Internet

The present Internet illustrates the difficulties in defining universal service and access to information in a multifunctional digital environment (see table 1).

As noted earlier, a user with only email access to the Internet (or access to the Usenet for that matter) is not properly "on the Internet." For a user who wishes only to access information, occasional links (e.g., dial-up service) may be adequate. However, SLIP or PPP service[20] is necessary to exploit the full functionality of graphical user interfaces such as NCSA Mosaic. If a user wishes to act as a publisher or another kind of service provider, a dedicated connection is necessary. Such users normally secure their own domain-style address, not just a name (or worse, a number) on a commercial host.[21]

There are over fifty networks providing Internet services and perhaps several hundred hosts offering public access to the Internet.[22] The networks range from state networks to supercomputer center networks to interexchange carriers. However, many offer a limited variety of services or serve only certain categories of customers, such as educational users. Many large commercial providers have little interest in serving small customers and provide no dial-up service.

The number of public access hosts has been growing rapidly, and some retailers have enjoyed assistance from major network providers, notably Sprint and ANS. There are a few noncommercial public hosts, often provided through universities, such as CapAcess at the George Washington University. Delphi, the smallest of the consumer on-line services, began providing Internet connectivity in early 1993 and was subsequently acquired by Rupert Murdoch's News Corp. CompuServe and America Online have announced that they will offer full Internet connectivity by the end of 1995. Even Prodigy, the most conservative and "family-oriented" of the on-line providers, has announced that it will start a separate Internet access service.

The cost of an account on an Internet host, including email and basic Internet functionality, varies but is remarkably inexpensive for anyone in a major metropolitan area with flat-rate local telephone service. Costs at the margin are typically $1–$2 per hour.

Table 1 Levels of Access to the Internet

email	enables exchange of mail with Internet sites through mail gateways
Usenet	access to the Usenet, the massive global distributed bulletin board with over 3,000 newsgroups
indirect	access to basic interactive services through a host on the Internet
dial-up SLIP/PPP	direct Internet access over dial-up lines (when connected, user's computer operates as an Internet host)
dedicated	user's computer always connected as an Internet host over a leased line

Netcom, which started as a single host in the Bay Area and now serves 13 metropolitan areas nationwide, provides unlimited dial-up service for $18.95 per month and with dial-up SLIP as an option for an additional $2/hour. It is a very different story outside the major metropolitan areas. The cost of access to an Internet host by long distance or through an 800-number is likely to be $8–12/hour or higher—6–8 times the cost of Internet access through the host. In short, for the general public, access to the Internet is hostage to the costs, pricing, and regulatory environment of the underlying voice network.[23]

At the low end, as we shall see, the equivalent per-user costs at a large company or university may be only a few dollars per person per year for unlimited use. Such enormous disparities appear far greater than the disparities in the pricing of telephone service. Why? And why, with such inequities in the cost of access, should the Internet be touted as a model for the future?

The Underlying Economics

Unlike telephone networks and cable systems, which are both facilities-based, the networks of the Internet are overlay networks assembled from leased lines and routers (see table 2). The price/performance ratio of routers, like other computing equipment, continues to decline dramatically each year. (A frequently cited figure for microprocessors is 30% per year, or a halving of price/performance every two years.) While some recent firming has been seen in the pricing of leased lines,[24] they still afford dramatic

Table 2 Three Models for the "Information Superhighway"

	Telephone	Cable	Internet
Type of infrastructure	facilities-based	facilities-based	overlay (using leased lines)
Predominant use	voice	video	text and data
Capacity	narrowband	broadband	indeterminate
Signals	circuit-switched	broadcast	packet-switched
Directionality	two-way	one-way	two-way
Business model	carrier	vertically integrated	carrier
Regulatory status	regulated	partially regulated	unregulated
Annual sales	$150B	$20B	$200–300M

economies of scale, especially compared to tariffed use of the public switched network. The relatively low cost of leased lines in the U.S. has been cited as critical to the rapid growth of the Internet in the United States relative to Europe and Japan, where line tariffs are typically three to five times higher.[25]

Just as the dominant use of cable systems is for video and the dominant use of telephone networks is for voice, the dominant use of the Internet has been for text. That is, although some uses of the Internet, notably remote visualization, generate large numbers of packets or bytes, the bulk of the transactions on the Internet are electronic mail consisting of text in ASCII code.[26] This will change as higher protocols and tools enable greater access to images, sound, and video, but for the present, text dominates.

ASCII-coded text provides for extraordinarily efficient communications. A voice version of 4-page ASCII text requires roughly 100 times the number of bits; a video version of someone speaking the text requires roughly 10,000 times the bits. This extraordinary difference in bandwidth and storage requirements between text, voice, and video illustrates the fundamental pricing problem faced by providers of integrated digital services. If video is priced to be affordable, then—assuming the technology allows for arbitrage— voice must be nearly free.[27] Likewise, overlaying an infrastructure designed for affordable voice traffic, the Internet offers nearly free

Table 3 Direct Cost of Sending Four Pages

	Local	Coast-to-coast	Trans-Pacific
Voice	.10	2.00	16.00
Fax	.06	1.00	8.00
Commercial email	.50	.50	.50
Commercial Internet	.02	.02	.02

transit of text. If we take the four pages of text and upload it at 9600 baud (assuming unmetered local phone service), then at $1–2/ hour for unsubsidized commercial Internet service, the cost is around $.01–.02 in connect time whether the message is going across town, across the country, or halfway around the world. Furthermore, by feeding in a list of email addresses, the same message can be sent to dozens, even hundreds or thousands, of recipients at the same cost. (However, this inexpensive multicasting can impose substantial burdens on receivers of messages, especially those who rely on a host to store their incoming mail.)[28]

Thus even at the retail level, the Internet offers a radical shrinking and restructuring of communications costs (see table 3). Internet service underprices telephone and fax, especially beyond the local calling area, and therefore works to undermine regulatory structures that disfavor calls beyond the local service area. It has great potential to erode the market for international telephone calls.

The cost of Internet access also contrasts dramatically with the pricing of commercial email services, such as MCIMAIL. Commercial email services have been value-priced (in which regard they compare favorably to fax and telex), whereas Internet costs are explicit and fixed.[29] Users pay for leased lines to the nearest network point of presence (POP) and provide their own premises equipment and in-house expertise. When universities and companies have spent millions of dollars on wiring and configuring local area networks and tying these networks into campus-area and enterprise networks, $50,000 per year for a T-1 connection to the Internet and the world looks like very small change for enormous added benefit.

The cost-based environment of the Internet offers dramatic economies of scale. Decreasing costs at the margin define a "natural monopoly," which in a provider context traditionally argues for regulatory oversight. In the development of the Internet, however, these economies of scale (plus the availability of NSF support) induced the formation of cooperative-style networks, where costs continued to be transparent, and encouraged the acquisition of excess capacity. Excess capacity, in turn, has allowed experimentation and liberal access for new users within the organization.

Taking the costs of the leased line into account as well as connection fees, a T-1 connection is likely to cost only three to six times as much as a 56 Kbps connection, while providing 28 times the capacity. Similar economies of scale apply in moving from T-1 to T-3, which provides 45 Mbps. The representative prices shown in table 4 indicate a factor of two in the per-mile component (which represents the fiber) and a factor of nearly four in the base component (which represents the photoelectronics). The drop in marginal cost is dramatic. When NSF upgraded the NSFNET backbone from T-1 to T-3 in 1991–92, the incremental cost for each additional Mbps was, in theory, $1/12$ the cost for the initial 1.5 Mbps of capacity.

The technology of the Internet enables extremely efficient aggregation of traffic and sharing of network resources. Specifically, traffic from a large number of users can be combined, with the expectation that the uses will average over time through "statistical multiplexing."[30] Packets from different users representing images, text, sound, control functions, displays, or file transfers can be mixed together and sorted at their separate destinations.

All these factors combine to drive down the costs of Internet use. Indeed, the retail costs cited in table 3 are high compared to what the bulk of Internet users face. For example, Harvard University pays $46,000/year for its 10 Mbps connection to NEARnet, the New England Academic Regional Network.[31] (Although many schools pay for the cost of a leased line to the nearest network point of presence, Harvard's microwave links are treated as part of NEARnet's backbone.) When the direct annual cost of the Harvard's connection is spread across what is now approximately 12,000 users, the per user cost figures at $4/year for unlimited access to the Internet worldwide! Of course, this figure does not include the cost of local

Table 4 Representative Costs of Leased Lines, July 1994

	Capacity (Mbps)	Base $	$ per mile
DS-1 (T-1)	1.54	1150	1.60
DS-3 (T-3)	45.	7162	19.36

computers, routers, fiber and wiring, management and support, etc. Still, the figure is quite remarkable when contrasted with annual university-wide expenditures for telephone usage of $6.8 million (which similarly does not include internal costs). The Internet connection allows for unlimited use worldwide for students as well as faculty and staff, whereas the telephone figure does not include student telephone use.

The retail price of Internet access through a public access host includes many costs equivalent to a university's internal costs: acquisition and maintenance of the host computer and software, modem pools, telephone lines, and user support services. On the other hand, access through a dial-up host does not provide the functionality available to a configured workstation on a university's LAN. A small business seeking equivalent functionality with a 56 Kbps leased line is likely to confront costs many times higher. A firm with ten users on a LAN is likely to face costs of $600–1000 per user per year—roughly 100 times as much as a large company or university![32]

A Middle-Up Infrastructure

Of an estimated 15 million Internet users in the U.S. in mid-1994,[33] probably no more than 300,000 were accessing the Internet through third-party hosts. Since some of these are small businesses that could not justify the cost of full Internet connectivity, it seems reasonable to conclude that as of that time only around 2% of Internet users made use of public access Internet providers as individuals. (This figure is changing rapidly as America On-line and CompuServe start providing full Internet connectivity for their customers.) Here is the remarkable paradox of the Internet. Despite its reputation as a network created by users and a haven for hackers and other eccentric individuals, the Internet was and still remains primarily a network of large entities—of private networks linked together. The unaffiliated public enjoys access only through a small number of commercial hosts at a relatively high cost.

The Internet is sometimes touted as an example of bottom-up infrastructure,[34] but this is misleading. It is true that the technology for the Internet has been developed by a community of expert users based in research universities and high-tech companies. But as infrastructure, the Internet has developed from the middle up, driven by large-entity investments in distributed computing and local area, campus-level, and enterprise networks. In this regard, the Internet contrasts dramatically with Teletel (sometimes known as Minitel, the name of the end-user terminal). Teletel is a top-down service provided by France Telecom as a public service monopoly. Unlike the Internet, Teletel was intended for the general public from the beginning. And unlike the Internet, where users pay not only for premises equipment but also for the local loop, Teletel owns the terminal and rents it to the user at subsidized rate.

Internet service providers are classed as "enhanced service providers" by the FCC and are therefore exempt from federal regulation. At one time, the FCC considered imposing access charges on use of the public network by enhanced service providers, but the proposal was decried as a "modem tax" and defeated, in part by a letter-writing campaign of bulletin board operators and users. While the tax would have served the ideal of universal service for the voice network, it would have worked against the leveraging of new computer services from the voice network, and it would have further raised the barriers to public access to the Internet. The arguments made against the modem tax were not that the transactions were of such social value that access fees should not be imposed. The arguments were that use of computers and related technology should be encouraged as a matter of national technology policy. On the other hand, from a traditional universal service perspective, why shouldn't someone who can afford a computer and modem contribute to the fixed costs of infrastructure needed to provide basic voice connectivity?

A few state regulators have shown an interest in regulating enhanced services (especially when offered by local exchange carriers),[35] but regulators have generally shied from what quickly becomes a boundless problem, as seen in the difficulty of defining universal service and access to information. It is hard to define the scope of the service or the information at stake and to come up with paradigmatic uses (analogous to telephoning for help in an emergency) that justify some form of cross-subsidy or subvention.

In the policy context of broadening public access to the Internet, the computer and modem now appear as barriers to participation in a new infrastructure. But what are the uses to justify policies supporting access to this new infrastructure? And how do these weigh against what some might see as abuses, such as access to graphic pornography, a problem that invariably crops up in efforts to provide public access to the Internet through Free-nets and other subsidized programs?

One approach to the problems of universal access is to subsidize access through institutions, such as libraries, schools, and extension offices. These institutions can marshal and manage those diverse resources that are needed to make effective use of the infrastructure: computers, software, storage, high-bandwidth lines, skills, and knowledge. In theory, they can mediate access in ways that will at least minimize the potential for abuse. However, these institutions are not set up to manage electronic information. They have other priorities and established modes of operation and do not normally have the financial resources to undertake new activities.

The opportunity and the problem are addressed by the new Telecommunications and Information Infrastructure Assistance Program administered by NTIA. Initially funded at $26 million for FY 94 and then at $64 million for FY 95, this program offers matching funds for projects in education, community networking, health care, and public libraries that support interconnectivity and interoperability. Here the government is providing leveraged investment in infrastructure that serves a traditional public purpose, as it has done in the case of NSFNET.

Another approach is investment in the government's own infrastructure. Here the Administration has made very palpable progress in promoting agency use of email and getting agencies on the Internet.[36] Previously only research agencies were regular users of the Internet. Now many agencies have implemented gopher servers and World Wide Web servers for disseminating government information to the public.[37] Whereas government investments in information technology normally only help stimulate the market for technology, investments in communicating and publishing beyond the government stimulate the growth of the public infrastructure by increasing the value of and demand for the infrastructure.[38]

Intelligent Infrastructure

The *information superhighway* offers pipes for delivering large objects, such as television programs, on demand. *Intelligent infrastructure* enables users to navigate access to an infinite variety of objects from many different sources, generating context and meaning in the process. It provides interactivity and enables learning and decision making at an infinitely fine level.

The burgeoning use of the higher-level gopher and World Wide Web services (see figure 1) demonstrates the changing nature of "access to information" and the significance of the Internet for development and deployment of intelligent infrastructure. Gopher provides menu-oriented access to resources, including the ability to move the user seamlessly from server to server. WWW, which has surpassed gopher in popularity, provides links among servers at the object level, essentially creating a universal hypertext environment known as the Web.[39]

Although the FCC does not regulate intelligent infrastructure, intellectual property laws do. In fact, intellectual property laws regulate at several levels, by setting up the ground rules for direct competition, for balancing different interests along the distribution chain, and for enabling the creation and maintenance of privately regulated environments.

Because intellectual property is inherently unique and frequently intangible, it is difficult to analyze with the traditional tools of telecommunications policy. Yet content and functionality (which can be intellectual property) are now on a continuum along with conduit. The extent to which intellectual property behaves like a conduit bottleneck depends on issues such as the scope of patentable subject matter, the permissible breadth of patents, and the

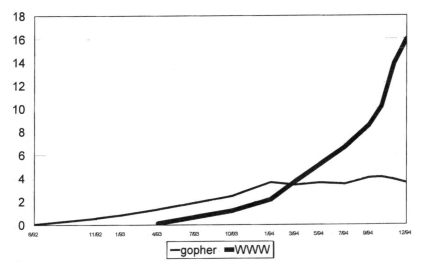

Figure 1 Growth of Gopher and WWW (percent of traffic on NSFNET backbone, June 1992–December 1994).

degree to which copyright protects "total concept and feel" or "structure, sequence, and organization." These are extremely complex, controversial, and unsettled issues, which are addressed almost exclusively by lawyers and in terms of traditional intellectual property principles rather than economic analysis. The concept of universal service is totally alien to these debates. Even the common carrier principle of open access on reasonable, nondiscriminatory terms smacks of compulsory licensing, which is anathema in intellectual property circles. However, the vision of an interconnected and interoperable information infrastructure puts the issue in a different context, ultimately a telecommunications context. In addition, Microsoft's dominance in microcomputer operating systems and, in particular, the company's control of the Windows application programming interface (API), has raised concerns, even among normally protectionist companies, about the limits of proprietary control.

Beginning with hearings in January 1994 before Congressman Markey's Subcommittee on Telecommunications and Finance, a new debate is underway on the proper role of proprietary standards in the National Information Infrastructure: Are there essential interfaces in the NII that should be "open" or "non-proprietary"? Which interfaces? How open should they be? Under what circumstances can proprietary interfaces qualify as open? Should the government encourage the development of nonproprietary interfaces? And, if so, how? Alternatively, how can open, nondiscriminatory access to proprietary interfaces be ensured? And what are reasonable rates?

Conclusion

The Internet is a primary path to the future information infrastructure, at least for structured digital formation. It is openly accessible public infrastructure, competitively provided, and based on nonproprietary technology. The small federal subsidies for certain parts of the Internet have been designed to stimulate the development of technologies, infrastructure, and markets—not to support universal service. Technology push and market growth are driving down many of the direct costs. High-level protocols and user-friendly software like NCSA Mosaic are reducing less tangible barriers to public use. But great disparities remain. In fact, the disparities will grow as those on the cutting edge leave the trailing edge farther and farther behind. Households without computers, keyboard illiterates, unaffiliated individuals, rural residents, the elderly, and small businesses are all disadvantaged in different ways and likely to remain so.

Difficult to quantify and assess, these disparities are not readily susceptible to solutions like the Universal Service Fund. Rather they challenge policy-makers to rethink and possibly recapitalize critical social institutions, while leveraging off institutional abilities to pool and manage information resources, network use, support personnel, and subject-matter expertise.

If the goal is indeed "access to information," then we need to reinvent the public library, clearly the institution most vitally affected by the digital revolution. This must be undertaken on a scale equivalent to Andrew Carnegie's efforts to institutionalize the "free library" a century ago. The new challenge is more subtle and elusive than building collections behind brick-and-mortar walls. It requires building on mass-market commercialization of technology, exploiting economies of scale, and attending to transaction costs. It means recognizing the remarkable ability of information technology to both penetrate and reconstruct walls—and turning such remarkable characteristics to strategic advantage in a principled policy framework.

Notes

[1] The National Information Infrastructure: Agenda for Action, September 15, 1993, pp. 5–6.

[2] Al Gore, whose understanding of information and technology issues has been essential to the NII Initiative, bears some responsibility for popularizing the highway metaphor. His father, also a Senator from Tennessee, was a leading proponent of the Interstate Highway System in the 1950s, a popular program with visible and lasting achievements, which his son frequently invoked as an exemplary infrastructure initiative. However, since the Interstate Highway System was funded entirely by the public sector, the metaphor misleadingly suggests that the government will actually fund the deployment of high-speed networks.

[3] See the author's description of the three principal aspects of information infrastructure (telecommunications infrastructure, knowledge infrastructure, and integration infrastructure) in "Information Technology and Information Infrastructure," in *Empowering Technology* (Lewis M. Branscomb, ed., MIT Press, 1993).

[4] The NREN was part of the Bush Administration's High Performance Computing and Communications initiative. See Committee on Physical, Mathematical and Engineering Sciences, Federal Coordinating Council for Science, Engineering and Technology, Office of Science and Technology Policy, *Grand Challenges: High Performance Computing and Communications, a Supplement to the President's Fiscal Year 1992 Budget,* Washington, DC, January 1991, often cited as "The Blue Book."

[5] As discussed below, the number is difficult to determine because most individual users are not themselves subscribers; rather they have access through their institutions or companies. The precise number also depends on how access to the Internet is defined. Additional millions have electronic mail access to and from Internet addresses, but email access alone is not properly considered being on the Internet.

[6] Even without oversight of a regulatory agency, it would be possible for a user to compel nondiscriminatory access, at least in states where the common law of common carriage survives the creation of regulatory agencies and laws. Of course, conduct that publicly violates common standards of behavior may be grounds to refuse service—for example, the posting of commercial notices indiscriminately to public mailing lists.

[7] Both the ARPANET and CSNET have ceased to exist. By some accounts, the Internet was initiated in 1981 when the new NSF-funded Computer Science Network, or CSNET, was connected to the DoD-funded ARPANET, enabling computer scientists at non-Defense-funded institutions to connect to resources and communicate with colleagues at Defense-funded institutions. See J. S. Quarterman and J. C. Hoskins, "Notable Computer Networks," *Communications of the ACM,* Vol. 29, No. 10, October 1986, pp. 932–939.

[8] And similarly, the umbrella created a misleading impression of central control. The National Science Foundation has had a limited involvement in the policies of the NSFNET backbone, which was funded under a cooperative agreement. NSF did not impose acceptable use policies on the grant-funded mid-level networks. It even allowed unfunded networks, including commercial networks, to use the NSFNET backbone for traffic that met the NSFNET policy on acceptable use (that the traffic support education and research). Under this loose arrangement, it was difficult to define just what the "NSFNET" encompassed.

[9] National Research Council, *Towards a National Research Network* (Washington, DC: National Academy Press, 1988).

[10] EDUCOM Networking and Telecommunications Task Force, "National Research and Education Network: A Policy Paper (April 1989; revised March 1990)

[11] See footnote 4.

[12] Pub. L. 102-194, Dec. 9, 1991, 105 Stat. 1594 (Title 15, Sec. 5501 et seq.) For a history of the Internet and the vision of the NREN see Jeffrey A. Hart, Robert R. Reed and Francois Bar, "The Building of the Internet," *Telecommunications Policy,* November 1992, pp. 666–689

[13] PSI was spun out of NYSERNET, the NSF-funded New York State network. AlterNet was developed as a for-profit of UUNET Technologies, which was originally a nonprofit corporation.

[14] There are certain central services that remain subsidized, notably the network number and domain name registries and some of the basic routing information. The InterNIC (Internet Network Information Center) is subsidized by NSF through three cooperative agreements: 1) to General Atomics for information services; 2) to AT&T for database services; and 3) to Network Solutions, Inc., for registration services.

[15] Agenda for Action, page 6. During 1993–94, the National Telecommunications and Information Administration held a series of hearings on universal service for the NII.

[16] These include: OMB Circular A-130; the Freedom of Information Act (5 USC 552 *et seq.*); the Government Printing Office, including the Depository Library Program; and the National Technical Information Service in the Department of Commerce. See Brian Kahin, "Information Policy and the Internet: Toward a Public Information Infrastructure in the United States," *Government Publications Review,* Vol. 18 (1991), pp. 451–472.

[17] The Information Infrastructure Task Force consists principally of three committees, including the Information Policy Committee with its three Working Groups: Intellectual Property, Government Information, and Privacy.

[18] The federal government also funds the National Commission on Libraries and Information Science (NCLIS), which could conceivably operate as a focal point for policy development. But the Commission's budget is less than $1 million per year, and it has not been effective in developing long-term policy leadership. NCLIS manages a White House conference on libraries held every ten years.

[19] See Milton Mueller, "Universal Service in Telephone History," *Telecommunications Policy*, July 1993, pp. 352–369. Mueller makes the case that "universal service," usually thought of as a construct of public policy expressed through regulation, was originally a business strategy of the early Bell System.

[20] SLIP stands for Serial Line Internet Protocol and PPP for Point to Point Protocol, the newer of the two. These protocols enable encapsulation of the Internet Protocol, which allows the local computer to act as an Internet host.

[21] There are roughly three levels of accessibility in domain-style addresses: 1) inscrutable addresses on host computers (the worst being CompuServe's use of 8–9 digit numbers); 2) logical and easy-to-remember addresses on Internet hosts, such as kahin@harvard.edu; and 3) personal domain names—e.g., brian@kahin.com. The registration of domain names has recently been the subject of publicity because of the trademark-like identity that they confer.

[22] See listing in April 18, 1994 issue of *Communications Week*. PDIAL, a more complete list of public access providers, is apparently no longer maintained. However, the last listing (December 9, 1993) is still available from the mail server info-deli-server@netcom.com by sending the command, "send PDIAL."

[23] In November 1994, MCI announced Internet MCI, which offered nationwide Internet access for a flat fee of $3/hour for dial-up access. The same service over an 800 number was priced at $7/hour. This remarkable pricing essentially provided nationwide long distance access for a premium of only $4/hour, a figure possible only because of MCI's enormous voice network. See Congressional Budget Office, *Promoting High-Performance Computing and Communications*, U.S. Government Printing Office, June 1993, pp. 40–41, noting declining per-mile component and rise in fixed component. See also George Gilder, "Into the Telecosm," *Harvard Business Review*, Vol. 69, No. 2, March–April 1991, pp. 150–161, on the reluctance of local exchange carriers and other leased line providers to tariff "dark fiber," i.e., optical fiber as basic transport without the photoelectronic activation normally provided by the vendor.

[24] Kenneth Flamm and Frederick Weingarten, presentation at Information Infrastructure Forum (John F. Kennedy School of Government), University Club, Washington, DC, April 7, 1993.

[25] If each link to a new item using World Wide Web is considered a separate transaction, then Web transactions are now more prevalent than electronic mail.

[26] See Robert M. Pepper, "Through the Looking Glass: Integrated Broadband Networks, Regulatory Policy and Institutional Change," Working Paper 24, Office of Plans and Policy, Federal Communications Commission, November 1988, pp. 46–49.

[27] The continuing decline in the cost of disk drives now makes storage capacity available for less than $.50/megabyte. However, many users must rely on limited capacity storage allotments on mainframes or minicomputers—limits that may have been established ten years earlier. These limits may preclude use of the network for multimedia messaging and other applications, even the transfer of Postscript files, since a single large file can clog a mailbox and disrupt incoming mail.

[28] Historically, MCIMAIL and other commercial services were much more user-friendly than public access Internet hosts with UNIX shells. This is changing as Internet providers have developed customized shells and as off-the-shelf client software including TCP/IP protocol stacks become widely available for Mac and Windows users. Mosaic and its commercial offspring have gone a long in addressing problem. The next version of Microsoft Windows, to be introduced in 1995, will allow users to connect directly to the Internet.

[29] This works very well, even with occasional congestion, for traffic such as electronic mail where delivery does not have to be instantaneous. It does not work well for interactive voice and video, where information must be delivered immediately and in proper sequence. This is one reason why telcos have been slow to take an interest in Internet technology. Reservation of bandwidth and service priorities are a major challenge for IPng—the next-generation Internet Protocol.

[30] Originally operated as a non-profit project by MIT, Harvard, and Boston University, NEARnet was recently acquired by BBN Systems.

[31] Even so the functionality is not equivalent. Although the small firm has 7–8 times as much capacity per user, it will (without incurring substantial additional costs of a higher bandwidth connection) always be limited to 56 Kbps per second and may experience degradation whenever more than one user is using the line.

[32] The Internet society currently estimates 25–30 million users worldwide, but this figure is easy to dispute for a variety of reasons. See *Matrix News*, June 1994, p. 1.

[33] Anthony M. Rutkowski, Executive Director, Internet Society, "The Present and Future of the Internet," Networld + Interop 94, Tokyo, July 29, 1994.

[34] Initially, the FCC sought to preempt state regulation of enhanced service providers, but this policy was overturned in *California v. FCC*, 905 F. 2d 1217 (CA9, 1991).

[35] Virtually all of the many agency personnel that the author has dealt with are accessible by mail over the Internet. As of late 1994, the only agencies where individuals dealing with information infrastructure issues do not have email

appear to be the Department of Justice, the Council of Economic Advisors, and the State Department.

[36] To some extent, this has been driven by the implementation of a White House Web server. The server lists the agencies of the Executive branch, indicating by color whether the agency has resources that the user can link to.

[37] For a discussion of government information as a driver for information infrastructure, see Kahin, "Toward a Public Information Infrastructure," *supra*, note 16.

[38] The popularity of the Web is attributable in part to NCSA Mosaic, a software program that integrates the functionality of World Wide Web, gopher, and other protocols under a graphical user interface. See New York Times, Dec. 8, 1993, p. C1, col. 3.

Balancing the Commercial and Public-Interest Visions of the NII

Lewis M. Branscomb

Introduction

The promise of an information-rich society, supported by a digital electronic infrastructure, is both very compelling and disappointingly elusive. With every information technology innovation, visionaries have identified the potential for using information services to reform public education, enhance participation in democratic processes, make government more accountable, and improve the quality of working life. Many people have worked very hard to bring to reality this dream of citizen access to both public and private information sources and efficient public services delivered over a network. At the same time the business sector, pressed by foreign competitors, has been restructuring firms internally and the way firms relate to each other. Vertical integration is giving way to corporate alliances; end-product manufacturers are relying more on fewer suppliers with whom they exchange technological information. Economists refer to this new industrial paradigm as "industrial networks."[1] Throughout the manufacturing and service industries, computer networks are being used to reduce transaction costs and support Total Quality Management.

The Internet, the largest collection of interconnected networks in the world, grew out of the needs of the research and education community for inexpensive communications and facilities for distance-independent collaboration. Internet has created a community of millions of computer-literate professionals in over 100 countries. Anthony Rutkowski estimates that at least 10 million people have access to the Internet world wide, and the traffic level has been growing at over 10 percent per month for a number of years. In the U.S. some 28 million personal computers, or 56% of all PCs installed in the US, will be attached to others through local area networks (LANs) by the end of 1995.[2]

Much of the technology to realize these public and private visions is in hand.[3] There are experiments and limited services in fulfillment of the dream available not only on the Internet, but on emerging commercial services sharing the same facilities. The Internet, however, remains primarily the province of computer-literate people who are able to tolerate its unfriendly interfaces and whose institutional connections give them low-cost access to Internet's resources. What is now required to realize the vision—both of the new applications and the new communications and computer services?

Two Policy Challenges

Two challenges face the administration. The first is to bring three diverse service environments together into an information infrastructure that integrates three different worlds:[4]

(a) *Knowledge Infrastructure,* symbolized by Internet, knitting together the research, education, and professional communities dedicated to generating and sharing knowledge;

(b) *Integration Infrastructure,* today reliant on Internet but expected to evolve to more expensive, reliable, and secure commercial computer networks, tieing the economy together through inter-firm alliances and business transactions;

(c) *Telecommunications Infrastructure,* driven by the technological revolution in broad-band, digital communications capable of delivering new multi-media services that open up enormous markets for public entertainment, as well as of more conventional communications services.

The issues here are: How can the openness, flexibility, interconnectivity, and low user cost seen by users of the Internet be preserved in networks that also serve the faster response times and higher reliability requirements of commercial information service? Will the entertainment-driven broad band capabilities emerging in the market also be able to support the needs of supercomputer applications in science and engineering? If the usage pricing common to many commercial services displace the access pricing of the knowledge networks, will the values that have driven the growth of Internet be lost to professional communities? How can the government leverage private investment and commercial markets in building information infrastructure and still achieve the goal of universal access to public services?

The second policy challenge is to provide the incentives that will stimulate the creation of the services, public and private, that are so promising for the nation's future. How will these new services be financed? What combination of public and private investments will be required? What incentives, standards, and regulations will best promote the establishment of the envisioned capabilities? Are policies needed to prevent the home-shopping and movie channels from suppressing or displacing these services (through inappropriate architecture or pricing policies) and merely expanding the scope of Newton Minow's "vast wasteland" of television?

Driving Forces for the NII

The National Information Infrastructure (NII) that is emerging is being shaped by two largely independent lines of market development. On the one side there are is the extraordinary growth of usage of digital networks such as the Internet, with exciting, innovative information distribution and retrieval services, many in support of the public interest. Many of them are stimulated by federal government science and technology agencies and focus on electronic access to public information sources and on service to the research, education, library, and health service communities. These are the services the National Telecommunications and Information Administration is exploring and promoting.

Internet also links industrial research and development laboratories to universities, government laboratories, and the independent sector. These links are very important to accelerated commercialization of U.S. research, and thus enhance competitiveness in our economy. Registration of commercial networks (much of it selling access to valuable information databases) now outpaces non-profit traffic on the Internet. :

The second development in the national information infrastructure arises from a totally different series of events—the emergence of new broad-band and interactive services into the home. New means for home access to video-on-demand—direct broadcast satellite, interactive cable TV, compressed video on telephone cable, CD ROM diskettes—seem likely to expand dramatically access to home-shopping and TV movies. Billions of dollars of capital are being invested in the new business combinations to exploit this consumer information market; the dollars completely swamp the modest investments being made in bringing public services to citizens and public institutions.

This revolution in telecommunications regulatory policy stems from the Modified Final Judgment in the ATT antitrust case. There are new technological possibilities for disseminating video over the twisted pair lines that bring phone service into the home, the possibility of interactive service on cable TV channels, including voice service, and emerging digital wireless services providing bypass into the home as well as mobile service. These new capabilities can evolve in either of two directions. They can provide the broad-band access to the "last mile"—the connection to the home— thus extending the Internet vision to broad-band access to anyone with a TV set. Or they can see the vision of a better informed, more efficient and democratic society overtaken by saturation of viewer attention by access to home shopping and a choice among 10,000 movies.

Balancing Commercial Markets and Public Interest Applications in the NII

Will these new entertainment and shopping channels push aside public services of great value to society? It seems likely that the enormous consumer markets for electronic entertainment and for voice communication will dominate the modest resources invested in the many networks that make up the Internet and the bulletin boards and other innovative information services accessible through the Internet.

Thus the first responsibility of the Information Infrastructure Task Force is to assign responsibilities and formulate legislation to set policies, regulations and standards that ensure that the vision of a wired, information-rich nation is not obscured by the much larger emerging electronic entertainment markets.

When television first appeared in the 1930s it was widely believed that its primary application would be to enrich public education. Educational broadcasting services were established, most of them at universities, to realize this dream. By the 1950s this dream was largely lost, overtaken by the sitcoms, games, and sports programs of commercial television. The educational channels were relegated the UHF channels, which few home owners could receive clearly, and little public funding was invested in educational programming and related curriculum development for the schools.

The computer industry made big investments in computer-based educational technology in the 1960's, only to realize that the technology was too complex for the schools and there was no source of investment in educational software and teacher training. Those early efforts were abandoned, and only to be revived in the 1980s; they are now beginning to deliver real benefits to schools. But they will still be a disappointment without huge investments in educational software, curriculum development and teacher training and assistance.

In the early days of cable television the Congress thought that by requiring local program origination, the power of television could put to the service of small communities, providing citizens video access to local government and to one another, but only a few communities have been able to realize this potential. Many local public access channels have fallen into disuse. The arrival of 500 more TV channels will not alter this situation.

Thus the Promise of the NII in section I of *The National Information Infrastructure: Agenda for Action* is surely an admirable vision, one which realizes the potential demonstrated in the Internet and takes advantage of the broad band capabilities being driven by entertainment. Unfortunately the nine principles of section III fall short of committing the Federal and State Governments and local communities to the realization of any of that vision save the sixth (access to your favorite movies and video games). The principles do specify essential elements of systems design: security, universal access, interconnectivity, universal service, protection of intellectual property, and technical innovation. They fail, however, to commit the federal government to leadership in ensuring that the architecture of the national telecommunications infrastructure, the policies for pricing of and access to both public and private services, and the generation of the public interest applications fulfill the Promise described.

A critical near-term issue is the preservation of the conditions that made Internet so successful. How will these values be preserved?

Preserving the Value of the Internet Culture[5]

NSF was the leader within government, in a position to assert those values and protect them, but is constantly narrowing its focus and backing away from asserting this leadership as the political and economic stakes rise.[6] Internet is egalitarian for those who are on it; it is elitist for those who cannot use it or do not have access to it. Who will guide the broadening of access to Internet, while preserving its special character? Who is going to protect the public values in the information infrastructure? Who will protect the culture built in the Internet by the users who created it? How should the federal agencies advance the NII, and what provisions of policy should be incorporated?

a) *Charging by access to communications capacity, rather than by end-user fees.* Charging by capacity makes network use feel like it is free. Admittedly, current practices do not encourage efficient use.[7] Charging by capacity keeps the price close to real cost, and minimizes administering a charge per use. The Regional Bell Operating Companies may prefer to apply the "telephony model" to networks.[8] Will they extend capacity pricing to digital computer networks? NETCOM and Delphi are two firms that are profitably offering Internet access for individuals on a flat rate basis.

b) *Maintaining distance-independent pricing.* International access through cooperating networks in other countries is a huge advantage for Americans seeking to compete and collaborate around the world. If international telephony rates were charged end-users this access would be severely restricted. But we must recognize that telephony prices are, in fact, only weakly distance based in the U.S., given the high intra-LATA prices, and increasingly competitive long distance rates.

c) *Network externalities: vital to both end-use value and to network economics.* The Internet needs to grow another two orders of magnitude before it is as economic as it could and should be. If the Internet becomes completely commercialized, will usage saturate at a level below that best capable of serving all society needs?

d) *Preserving the very low cost of information sharing.* Actual cost of information sharing, as demonstrated in non-profit bulletin boards and "gopher" services, for example, can be exceedingly low, and does not require a market incentive, according to Paul Ginsparg, who set up an electronic physics journal at Los Alamos National Laboratory. He does not charge for access, which runs thousands of queries per hour. We must distinguish between the price of information and price of access.

e) *The collective value attribute of Internet.* Internet is not used primarily for point to point communication: the sharing of information is a key value. This sharing (of queries, answers to queries, and shared information) lies intermediate between point-to-point communications and broadcast. There is a form of knowledge externality in knowledge sharing. There is a selflessness in the way people in the "Internet Culture" voluntarily collect and share information.

f) *International security value of international communication.* Many studies of the collapse of Communism and the disintegration of the Soviet Union point to the role of information technology as a democratizing (some might say revolutionary) force. Maintaining grass-roots communications to Americans around the world not only helps international collaboration among scholars, and the internal communications of multinational firms, but can make this a safer world.

g) *Preserving an environment for innovative new uses of networking.* The key to the success of Internet is that it was invented by its users. It is open to all manner of experiments, social as well as technical, and the technology is flexible enough to facilitate such experimentation. It is essential that as the NII develops federal regulation must not deny new styles of networking and new kinds of applications. It is not clear that a commercial entertainment driven NII will be able to offer such a flexible environment for innovation.

h) *A major value of the Internet culture, but possibly a transient value, is the absence of junk mail, advertisements, and oppressive commercialism.* If the policies for the development of NII are driven by commercial investment, how can this condition be sustained?

An Addition to the *Agenda for Action*

The Clinton-Gore administration came into office determined to understand the promise of information infrastructure, diagnose the barriers to its realization, and solicit the cooperation of Congress, states and communities, and the public realize this promise. This is still an attainable objective. However it will not be attained by leaving applications initiative to commercial firms and by leaving the architecture of the communications and computing services to the contention of carriers before the FCC. The *Agenda for Action* contains many of the action elements necessary to realizing the promise of NII. However, it would be a serious error to underestimate the importance of building both the institutional capacity and the software to support the public interest applications.

I recommend that a tenth Principle should be added to the nine in the *Agenda for Action*:

10) The federal government accepts responsibility for working with states and communities to develop and realize the many non-profit public service applications necessary for the realization of the "promise of NII." Appropriate responsibilities will be assigned by Executive Order to the departments and agencies.

To bring about the promise of Knowledge Infrastructure:

• *Department of Education, with the states and communities: Integrating electronic education materials into curricula and providing services to teachers to help them use them successfully.*

• *Department of Health and Human Services: Networking physicians, hospitals, clinics and insurance companies to reduce the cost and improve access to health care and ensure privacy and citizen control of their medical records.*

• *Responsibilities still to be designated: Information networks for the nation's libraries, community network services for participatory democracy, and other applications.*

To bring about the promise of Integration Infrastructure:

• *Department of Commerce's Technology Administration: Through NTIA, coordination and demonstration; through NIST, leadership of standards to facilitate Integration Infrastructure.*[9]

The issue that remains unresolved, in spite of much excellent work on the *Agenda for Action,* is the definition of the policy process that must be put in place at a high level of government that can identify the regulatory framework that best satisfies the needs of all these areas of promise. Thus policy process must embrace executive branch, congressional, and private sector participation, and must be capable of generating a consensus strategy that all can support. A major barrier to attainment of this most fundamental goal is the weakness of the NTIA as a leader of this consensus process, the complexity of relationships between the FCC and all three constituencies, and the enormous influence of emerging commercial markets for entertainment and shopping.

Notes

[1] See Christopher Freeman, *Networks of Innovators: A Synthesis of Research Issues* paper presented to the International Workshop on Networks of Innovators, Montreal Canada, 1990. Quoted in Michael Hobday, *Dyanamic Networks, Technology Diffusion and Complementary Assets,* October 1990, draft paper from the Science Policy Unit, Sussex University UK.

[2] Forrester Research's Network Strategy Report: *LANs for Free?* Nov. 1991.

[3] One exception is high performance computing, which has shown the most rapid progress of all the technologies in the NII, and is still in the early stages of an extraordinary revolution. All of the most advanced applications of the new multi-media world (virtual reality, interactive graphics, animation) stem from scientific developments based on high performance computing. The Agenda for Action contains a commitment to completing the HPCC plan; the most critical part of this plan is the public investment in High Performance Computing, still more promise than reality but an enormous opportunity for the U.S. economy and the platform for much of the brave new world of NII advanced applications.

See National Science Board, *From Desktop to Teraflop: Exploiting the U.S. Lead in High Performance Computing*, Report to the National Science Board, October 1993, by a Blue Ribbon Panel on High Performance Computing chaired by Lewis M. Branscomb.

[4] Brian Kahin, "Information Technology and Information Infrastructure" in Lewis M. Branscomb, ed., *Empowering Technology: Implementing a U.S. Policy* (Cambridge MA: MIT Press 1993) page 139.

[5] The following discussion is adapted from a report by Lewis Branscomb and Ken Klingenstein on discussions at the Telluride (Colorado) Institute's Ideas Festival July 25, 1993.

[6] NSF should be complimented, however, for funding some applications work of social significance—including rural "datafication" experiments.

[7] A study reported by Professor Kenneth Klingenstein found that 70% of file transfers at the University of Colorado are uncompressed, for lack of any direct incentive to minimize bandwidth use. Reported by Prof. Klingenstein, Telluride Institute Ideas Festival, July 25, 1993.

[8] It should be noted that the telephone companies do not employ usage-pricing in the local calling area, where most of the traffic is. These local calling areas are growing geographically in many parts of the country. Thus it is not quite fair to call the long distance pricing principles the "telephony model".

[9] Commerce must continue the emphasis initiated in the Bush Administration on standards to facilitate the use of networking in restructuring of U.S. industry—creating virtual companies, agile manufacturing, alliances between producers and their suppliers. A key element in this program are the industrially developed product definition standards (PDES-STEP) and their environment CALS (computer-based acquisition and logistics system).

Public Access Issues: An Introduction

James Keller

The Clinton administration has promoted information infrastructure as a powerful enabler that will leverage many of its program areas, support federal agency missions, and strengthen national competitiveness. This vision extends to anticipate a streamlining and rationalizing of communications, work, and educational processes at every level of our society. This is in strong contrast to the Bush administration, where the aim of federal policy on information infrastructure development was twofold: to support basic research in high-speed networking and to provide a platform to support the administration's science agenda. The Bush programs were targeted not only at specific industries but at a specific set of scientific research problems. As understanding of the value of a high-speed digital infrastructure has grown, policy concerns have moved increasingly from the strategic to the tactical, and the issue of public access has risen to the top of many agendas. Industry and government have both shown commitment to the development of an advanced national networking infrastructure. Concerns are now turning to how to make the network useful to and usable by individuals and institutions, while maintaining a business climate that is fair and attracts investment.

What We Mean by Public Access

The issue of public access is entwined in matters of technology, law, economics and, increasingly, sociology and organizational behavior. By public access we mean not only establishing physical connections to the network, but also ensuring that those connections are easy to use, affordable, and provide access to a minimum set of information resources. In particular, network use should not be limited to the passive receipt of information. Instead, the environment should be open, distributed and easily navigable. Even the most basic connection should enable users to act as information sources as well as destinations. In this way, development of the NII offers a potential paradigm shift in communications, publishing and human interaction comparable to that effected by the Gutenburg press.

Information infrastructure is an enabler of both free speech and efficient markets. It can help overcome barriers to information and create opportunities to convene regardless of geographic, physical or financial constraints. Disparate ethnic, economic, political, and other interests groups will find increased opportunity to organize and consolidate in the pursuit of their common interests.

Similarly, these enabling qualities can bring increased vitality to a market-based economy. While economists differ on the appropriate policy tools and ability of government to influence markets, there is common agreement on the set of conditions in which markets perform best. These conditions include perfect information and low (or ideally no) transaction costs, conditions best facilitated through information infrastructure. Access to market information allows easy aggregation of demand, which speeds the development of new products and markets. This has both near-term benefits of economic growth and job creation and the longer term competitiveness benefits that result from giving early adopters first-mover advantages in emerging markets.

The Internet as a Model

Development of the NII will go far beyond mere extension of the current Internet; it will be a product of both new technologies and resources and a newly defined Internet. Not a physical network, the Internet is best defined by a set of commonly supported applications. Historically, it has been defined as the set of voluntarily interconnected and interoperating networks that jointly support electronic mail, remote log-in and file transfer capabilities. Originally it was based exclusively on the TCP/IP suite of data communications protocols, but through use of protocol conversion and encapsulation it now encompasses networks running other protocols, including OSI, DECnet and X.25. Real-time, one-way and interactive packet audio and video broadcasts are implemented on the Internet multimedia backbone, the MBONE. While still experimental, these services have been improving rapidly. Also, standards are being developed for multimedia messaging, privacy-enhanced mail, and network accounting.

Much of the recent growth of the Internet can be attributed to the wave of publicity it has been receiving in the mainstream media and to the development and wide implementation of a powerful set of network search and retrieval tools.[1] Widespread use of the Internet beyond the networking and scientific communities had formerly been precluded by arcane commands and a lack of useful information resources. New application protocols such as Gopher, Archie, Veronica, WAIS, and World Wide Web, which are built on top of the existing file transfer protocol, create an easy-to-use interface typically based on point-and-click commands. These tools require virtually no training and make the resources of the Internet easily accessible from millions of connected desktops. In addition to making it easier to access information, these tools have made it easier to distribute information. Encouraged by the increasing ease of use and growing user population, a wide variety of organizations are now setting up public information servers on the Internet, including the White House, government agencies, the World Health Organization and MTV. All categories of information are available, from weather forecasts to Supreme Court opinions and restaurant reviews.

Growth in the number of users and in accessible information have fueled one another through a combination of demand pull and supply push, exemplifying the unusual economics of networks, where an increase in users increases rather than decreases the value of the service to connected users and institutions. This growth has challenged the culture of the Internet and drawn attention to the social aspects of participation in networked communities. These are explored further in the Issues section of this chapter and in

contributions by Lee Sproull and Samer Faraj and Cliff Figallo.
Figallo, former director of the San Francisco–based Whole Earth
Lectronic Link (WELL), describes the development of the WELL,
one of the first successful electronic communities. Figallo explains
how principles of openness, collaboration and community contributed to the continuing success of this commercial enterprise. In
their chapter, Sproull and Faraj examine patterns of network-
based human interaction and their implications for network policy
and planning. They identify the network as a social technology and
recognize users as social beings. These distinctions will be important ones as planners seek to design systems more broadly integrated into our daily lives.

The Internet is both the focal point of federal agency initiatives
and a working model of an open, distributed, non-hierarchical
environment for information exchange. Government initiatives
that will leverage the Internet include several National Science
Foundation initiatives; Digital Libraries; Information Infrastructure for Education; a project to distribute corporate financial
information collected by the SEC; the National Telecommunication and Information Administration's On-ramps program; and
new efforts to enhance the distribution of government information. These programs will of course further expand the information value and usage of the Internet.

Issues

The intent of this volume is to explore the issues around public
access to the Internet, both in order to elucidate public access
issues currently at hand and to present the Internet as a model that
can inform broader infrastructure development efforts. In exploring public access issues, we attempt to present a broad range of
stakeholder perspectives—including network users and potential
users and network operators—as well as more rigorous analytical
perspectives on pricing and architecture issues. Primary topic
areas addressed in this book are: organizational and architectural
models for network access; institutional perspectives on the benefits and requirements of access; the sociology and culture of
networks; and pricing. Several of these are considered briefly
below.

Pricing

Throughout much of the history of the Internet, pricing was a simple matter due to the relative homogeneity of network uses and users. Users purchased connections to regional networks, which in turn connected to the NSFnet backbone. In many cases, regional networks were established by users and could be viewed as co-ops. In Boston, for example, the New England Academic and Research Network (NEARnet) was created jointly by Boston University, Harvard and MIT. Connections to the regionals and other service providers have typically been sold at a flat monthly rate based on access speed. Now, a broadening user base and emerging applications are creating demand for multiple service classes. Quality of service, including low latency, is vital to creating an environment that will support mission-critical business applications. The viability of real-time interactive applications such as video conferencing will demand guaranteed bandwidth availability and the ability to synchronize packet delivery, requirements not necessary for e-mail or file transfer. At the same time, casual use is increasing, and many individual users are seeking low-cost access and will tolerate lower quality-of-service parameters. To achieve its growth potential the Internet will require a new pricing model that meets the needs of an increasingly diverse user community.

The evolution of Internet pricing poses an interesting problem. Flat-rate pricing is one of the conditions that has allowed the Internet to flourish. It has enabled low-cost dissemination, beta-testing and refinement of new tools and applications. As explained above, it is these tools that have turned the Internet into an enabling environment for the non-traditional users who are coming to dominate the network. The strength of many of these tools is their ability to operate in and rationalize a distributed and heterogeneous structure, making it easier to identify and retrieve information resources. Now the increased demand that has arisen due to the power and new resources these tools have brought to the Internet is creating a need for a new pricing model. One of the challenges of developing this model will be to maintain an environment that fosters application development and deployment, a condition vital to service providers as it contributes directly to the value of and demand for Internet connectivity. Usage pricing and service classes should make the Internet attractive to many new users. Some casual users will find it more affordable and business users may find a more stable environment on which they can trust mission-critical applications. However, one of the defining norms of connecting to the Internet will be changed, a fact that should be weighed into any decision to implement new pricing practices.

Another paradox of usage-based pricing is that its implementation may actually cost more on a per transaction basis than the underlying cost of the transport. In other words, counting a packet may cost more than sending a packet. However, this network accounting capability will also serve as a critical enabler for the provision of new information services and other entrepreneurial endeavors that will be built on top of the Internet. For the Internet to succeed as a fully developed information resource, value-added service providers must have an easy means of being compensated for their services. While larger, established services may be able to easily implement this accounting capability themselves, having this capability embedded in the network will lower barriers of entry for small, in some cases home-based, services. It can also provide a neutral source for billing verification.

Sociology and Culture of the Internet

As the Internet has grown, it has touched an expanding array of communities and institutions. The culture of the Internet is influencing the way these entities and the people in them operate and, in turn, the presence of these newcomers is beginning to challenge the culture of the Internet. The Internet has a culture of sharing that is unusual in the private sector. The technology that drives the Internet was largely developed in a voluntary and cooperative manner. The mere fact that it functions is remarkable. There is no administrative or authoritative hierarchy coordinating the interoperation of the 10,000 plus connected networks. An important and difficult question is how to capture the values of cooperation and shared experience in an increasingly commercial Internet.

Already, tacitly and overtly established modes of acceptable behavior are being challenged. The Internet began as a non-commercial entity. This was true in both the standards development process and in the use of the network. Use of the NSF-funded backbone has been restricted to research and education purposes by the NSF's Acceptable Use Policy (AUP).[2] The Internet Engineering Task Force, the de facto standards making body for the Internet, has maintained a policy that participation in the standards process precludes the pursuit of partisan commercial interests.[3] The AUP has now become less important due to the availability of alternative routing and will soon disappear when the NSF ceases to fund a production backbone.[4] As usage increases and commercial opportunities rise, it will be increasingly difficult to rely on informal rules of netiquette to maintain good citizenship. Debate, often of an acrimonious nature, on topics such as appropriate use, government subsidies and pricing models is ongoing on many Internet mailing lists. Today's Internet is a very dynamic environment and many traditional users appear anxious about changes in usage and pricing that are arising. Similarly, many entrepreneurs consider the Internet rife with business opportunities and are wary of the impact of government money on competition.

In many ways, the Internet as we know it is a fragile environment. Many discussion groups that serve as forums for social and intellectual exchange, technical development and policy debate are open and freely accessible. Within these fora the line between acceptable and unacceptable participation is often drawn very narrowly, causing newcomers to receive sharp responses for unwitting nonconformance. As the network grows, the culture of sharing is increasingly challenged. Servers supporting free information resources are becoming congested and in some cases virtually inaccessible during certain times of the day.[5] It is no longer clear whether it will continue to be viable for many institutions to support free public access servers. Due to the growth in users, a low-end PC is often no longer adequate to maintain a popular resource. Ironically, tools such as Gopher that have rationalized the distributed and heterogeneous environment of the Internet are now becoming victims of their own success.

While free services are a defining feature of the Internet, from an economist's perspective they may encourage inefficient use of resources. As there is no direct monetary charge for utilization of many information resources, their value will be reflected in the time users are willing to invest in waiting due to congestion: it can be assumed that users will invest time in trying to gain access to a service up to the point that their time plus the cost of the service equals the value of the service. Waiting is a non-productive investment of resources. Perhaps if this value was captured by information providers through fees, it could be applied to upgrading equipment. Until recently, due to the low cost of setting up information servers and the lack of network congestion, this was of little concern. We are just now getting to the point that congestion is causing significant consumption of resources; whether this becomes an increasing problem will be a function of both technology and pricing policies.

One of the defining characteristics of networks is their ability to transcend geographic and physical boundaries, enabling the establishment of virtual communities, work groups and organizations. In addition to the direct gains achieved through reduced communications and travel costs and quick turn-around, the informal, nearly real-time nature of these bonds results in intangible shifts in the dynamics of work-based and social interactions that often promote increased collegiality, productivity, commitment and accountability. While the dynamics of network-based inter-personal and interorganization communications are not always positive, they are uniquely different from other media and warrant increased understanding. The subtleties and unique qualities of this phenomenon make it a feature often not grasped by policy-makers lacking exposure to the Internet, yet these externalities are an important component for consideration in discussions of infrastructure development.

The question of what has promoted the cooperative nature of the Internet is an important one for planners and policy-makers. Even beyond the issue of maintaining this cultural component of the Internet, there may be a potential model for community development or organizational design. Clearly, several factors have facilitated this cooperation, including the ability for ad hoc interconnection, low (or no) marginal costs of sharing information and resources, and common interest in expanding the usefulness of the network. Some factors that have contributed to the culture of the Internet will surely change; an example will probably be the pricing structure. One characteristic that will help maintain the village-like character of the Internet after it has expanded far beyond its original close-knit membership is the ability to define and redefine virtual places and entities. Just as many corporations have realized the importance of promoting a work environment characterized by pride and shared responsibility, planners must pay careful attention to maintaining the many positive elements of Internet culture.

Access Models

In this volume the question of how to connect users to the network is addressed two ways. First is the question of organizational models for access. This includes a look at the experience of Big Sky Telegraph, a rural cooperative network, and at the public library and K-12 communities. Second is examination of network architecture and technology.

Historically, connection to the Internet has been based on a simple model. A large institution, often a university, purchases a high-speed connection to the Internet from a regional service provider and provides access to hundreds or thousands of users. This system works well for several reasons. The statistical properties of demand aggregation allow more efficient bandwidth utilization; bandwidth is much cheaper when purchased in bulk; and internal resources, such as network operations, maintenance and support, can be leveraged across a large user base. For a large institution, the annual cost of Internet connectivity is roughly $5–$10 per user.[6] This is an almost incidental cost when measured against total information technology expenditures within the organization and when considered in light of the value it brings via increased access to information, minimized delays of information transfer, and reduced postage and telephone costs.

Individuals and small institutions connecting directly to an Internet service do not benefit from any of the cost saving conditions available to large traditional users. Individual accounts on a commercial service can now be purchased for roughly $20 per month, in many cases not a prohibitive cost. These services are quite adequate for running many traditional applications, but they do not put a user directly "on" the Internet. Instead, they provide dial-up access, allowing a user's computer to act as a dumb terminal on the service's host. With this type of configuration, traditional Internet applications, e-mail, remote log-in and file transfer are enabled, but many emerging applications will not be. With a typical dial-up connection, the user is able to transmit character-based key strokes back and forth to the host machine on which their account resides. This allows the user to remotely manage the host's session on the network. The limitation is that during an Internet session, all mail, files, images, etc., must originate and terminate at the host, rather than at the user's computer. For traditional applications this merely introduces a second, typically slower, step of moving files between the user and the host. This is a more cumbersome process than working directly on a host machine, but quite manageable. However, the distinguishing feature of many of the new applications that are coming to redefine the Internet is the introduction of a more friendly and robust interface. This includes graphical and icon-based screens and audio and video communications capabilities. MOSAIC is a simple but powerful search and retrieval tool, offering users a common front-end to tie together the variety of distributed search tools that have recently proliferated (Archie, Gopher, Veronica, WAIS and World Wide Web). Using intuitive point-and-click and word-based commands it provides access to the latest satellite and other images as well as text files. To run MOSAIC, the client workstation must be an Internet host. Similarly, real-time interactive applications, such as audio and video broadcast and conferencing, will typically require direct network access. The technology is and has been available to establish an Internet host over an ordinary dial-up phone line,[7] but this type of connectivity is not widely available, and when it is typically costs over $100 per month.

To respond to the increased demand for Internet service among small and individual users, a number of new access models have arisen. In some cases these models are attempts to recreate the conditions under which large institutions are able to achieve scale economies through the aggregation of demand. These can be in the form of value-added resellers or buying cooperatives. Two examples of this approach are the Cambridge Entrepreneurial

Network (CENTNet), a non-profit, and PI-Net,[8] a commercial entity. Both of these networks use one high-bandwidth connection purchased from the regional service provider to serve a number of local organizations. Also, both benefit from a high level of technical sophistication among their members. Reliance on member sophistication will limit the extensibility of these models. In the case of CENTNet all network management is done on a shared, voluntary basis by members.

The FreeNet model, originally developed and advocated by Tom Grundner of Case Western Reserve University, has been implemented successfully in about 20 communities in the United States, Canada and New Zealand. Each FreeNet provides free dial-up e-mail service and access to a variety of local and national information, through voluntary labor and donated equipment and operating funds. The FreeNet model demonstrates the low cost at which BBS type access can be provided as a means of distributing community information. Like many aspects of the Internet, however, it is unclear how it will hold up in the future. Volunteer and philanthropic support may not be able to meet increases in demand. Also, in some cases commercial Internet service providers have been unwilling to allow customers to use their connections as access points for FreeNets, perceiving them as threats to the market for fee-based services.

The Future

We are now entering the most difficult part of the public access debate. There is wide agreement on general principles, but not on how these principles should be applied or implemented. Universal service, privacy, and government information are all areas of confusion and rancor. This is a function of rapid change in both technology and markets. Universal service is widely embraced as a critical feature of a national information infrastructure. However, even if it were possible to reach agreement on what level of service should be provided at what price, the variety of technology platforms over which this could be provided would make it difficult to determine a successful implementation scheme. Introducing regulated prices would likely skew competition between platform technologies and create disincentives for investment and innovation.

The Internet appears to be fueling its own growth. It is becoming increasingly rich in connectivity, interoperability and content. However, the same tools and applications that are expanding the enabling character of the Internet and attracting new users are pushing the network beyond the bounds of its current architecture. To maintain the growing usage and usefulness of the network and to fulfill the visions of connectedness described in later chapters will require the adoption of new operating regimes and systems. These will include new access methods, pricing schemes, and network architecture. The intention of this volume is to expand understanding of the current Internet environment and of stakeholder interests in and alternative models for the further development of the Internet.

Notes

[1] See Jonathan Kochmer, *Internet Passport: NorthWestNet's Guide to Our World Online,* 4th ed. Bellevue, WA: NorthWestNet: Northwest Academic Computing Consortium, 1993.

[2] The formation of the Commercial Internet Exchange in 1991 allowed internetwork traffic to pass between CIX member networks without transiting the NSFnet, and thus free of the AUP.

[3] Anthony Rutkowski, Vice President, The Internet Society, MIT Communications Forum, November 4, 1993.

[4] Under the current solicitation for the next generation NSFnet, NSF will fund very high-speed backbone network services (vBNS) exclusively for support of advanced scientific research. An even more restrictive AUP will apply to this service.

[5] *New York Times,* November 3, 1993.

[6] Brian Kahin. Information technology and information infrastructure. In Lewis M. Branscomb, ed., *Empowering Technology.* Cambridge: MIT Press, 1993.

[7] Serial Line Interface Protocol (SLIP) and Point-to-Point Protocol (PPP) are two commonly used protocols.

[8] PI-Net serves the Prospect Innovation Center, an office park in Waltham, Massachusetts housing primarily high-tech businesses.

The Sociology and Culture of the Internet

The WELL: A Regionally Based On-Line Community on the Internet

Cliff Figallo

Introduction

The rapid development of communications and computer technologies, combined with the adoption of computer networking by an exploding population of consumers, is forcing rapid change on the Internet. As increased popular usage and commercialization radically redefine the Internet's original purpose and alter the course of its development, there is widespread concern about its future and how that future will affect our society. Many of us have visions of how this network could serve the public at large and segments of the public in particular, and we wonder how (and if) those visions can still be realized.

My experience over the past twenty years has been centered around community-building. I see the Internet serving as the link between regionally-based electronic communities and as an information resource conduit for those communities, just as the interstate highway system serves as a link between geographic localities in the physical world. As a systems manager, I have witnessed the formation of one small but widely known electronic community; based on that experience, I am convinced that computer networking involving group dialogue (sometimes referred to as the "many-to-many" model) has a value to our society far beyond what can be measured by economics alone.

I believe that public electronic networking offers society an important new forum for the practice of democratic principles and

First Amendment rights to free speech and assembly. Its value to the nation and the world may be critical at this stage in history, when cumulative problems abound and faith in the accountability of central government is at a low ebb. The possibility that the future "Internet" (or whatever replaces it) will turn out to be a monolithic corporate-controlled electronic consumer shopping mall and amusement park is antithetical to the idea that the individual in the electronic communications world is a producer as well as a consumer, desires to interact freely with other groups and individuals there, and is the most qualified director and creator of the medium. A future centered around a one-way entertainment model would effectively gag those who would use networks as forums to exercise the freedoms that define our democracy.

The most effective platforms for these forums are regionally-based, Internet-connected electronic communities, where the motto "think globally, act locally" can best be put into practice. These systems may be self-contained in that they pay for their own operations and Internet connections, handle all administrative tasks for their users, and develop their own local community standards of behavior and interaction. Their users may "travel" out through their Internet gateways to other regional systems or search for information in the myriad of on-line databases. Other Internet travelers can visit these communities and experience their unique qualities—the local flavor, focus, and individuals who inhabit the systems. The main attractions of these local Internet "towns" may prove to be their characteristic on-line conversations and social conventions and their focus on specialized fields of knowledge or problem solving. The on-line system that I managed for six years, the Whole Earth Lectronic Link (known as the WELL), is an example of the kind of small diverse service providers I believe should exist in profusion on the Internet, all with open channels to each other.

The remainder of this paper will describe the history and function of the WELL to show how a small on-line system with limited funding and a regional base became a profitable enterprise and a contributing citizen-system on the Internet. Not all of the WELL's experiences will be applicable or relevant to other locales and situations, but certainly some will. Indeed, much of the WELL's story is about following ideas as they come up in group interaction, rather than sticking with long-range planning; that may be an important part of its lesson.

A Brief History of the WELL

The WELL is an 8,000-member computer-mediated public conferencing and e-mail system linked to the Internet. The WELL's primary attractions have historically been its users and the conversations between them. These conversations are spread among more than 300 "conferences" whose subjects range from the intimately personal to the very technical. There are WELL conferences on current events, parenting, telecommunications, poetry, sailing, UNIX, sexuality, gardening, and everything in between. Most conferences are public, open to all WELL subscribers, but an increasing number are private, with membership limited by the "host" of the conference. Each conference consists of a large collection of user-initiated "topics," many of them with hundreds of responses.

The WELL was founded in 1985 by Stewart Brand and Larry Brilliant as a partnership of Point Foundation and Brilliant's computer software company, Networking Technologies International (NETI). Brilliant and Brand agreed to have their organizations cooperate in establishing and operating a computer conferencing network that could serve as a prototype for many regional (as opposed to national) commercial systems. "Let a thousand CompuServes bloom," Brilliant put it. It came on-line in February 1985 and began taking paying customers April 1, 1985. By 1992, its initial staff of one full-time and one part-time employee had grown to 12 paid employees and well over 100 on-line volunteers. The WELL now runs on networked Sun workstations located in a small office building in Sausalito, California. It is now a property of Rosewood Stone, a financial investment company owned by the former owner of Rockport Shoes.

Initial funding came from NETI, which provided a leased VAX 11/750 computer and hard disks, UNIX system software, a "conferencing" program called Picospan, and a loan of $90,000. Point Foundation, the non-profit parent corporation of *Whole Earth*

Catalog, contributed the name recognition of "Whole Earth," the personal attraction of having Stewart Brand to converse with on-line, and the modest but important promotional value of constant mention in the small but influential *Whole Earth Review* magazine.

From its inception, business goals for the WELL were left flexible. But the idea that interesting discussion would attract interesting conversationalists was at the core of the enterprise's strategy. Initially, many free accounts were offered to people who had at some time been associated with Whole Earth publications and events, or who were thought likely by Whole Earth staff to be productive and attractive participants (referred to, tongue-in-cheek, as "shills"). In April 1985, the WELL began offering subscriptions at $8 per month plus $3 per hour.

The WELL has full Internet connectivity: its users can log into or search other Internet-connected systems from the WELL, and users of other such systems can log into the WELL. This "outgoing Internet" capability is offered to WELL subscribers at no additional charge to their monthly and hourly fees (currently $15 per month and $2 per hour). Most users call the WELL over regular phone lines and modems, and most long-distance customers reach the WELL using an X.25 commercial packet network[1] for an additional hourly fee. An increasing number of users are logging into the WELL via the Internet, many using Internet accounts on commercial gateway systems as a money-saving alternative to calling through packet networks. Those logging into the WELL through the Internet pay monthly and hourly subscription fees.

One of the WELL's most notable achievements is that it has survived for nine years while so many other startup systems, though much better funded, have failed. Its freewheeling and provocative on-line interaction has indirectly given rise to some noteworthy byproducts. The Electronic Frontier Foundation, a Washington, DC–based non-profit organization founded "to shape our nation's communications infrastructure and the policies that govern it in order to maintain and enhance First Amendment, privacy and other democratic values,"[2] was born largely out of the free speech ferment of the WELL and out of discussions relating to the new legal and regulatory predicaments that confront users, managers and owners of systems in this new communications medium. These discussions about telecommunications also attract a growing population of journalists, who find that cutting-edge ideas and concepts arise constantly in the WELL's forums. Many formal and informal organizations and collaborations that are affecting the world today also call the WELL home, some having their own public or private conferences.

Initial Design and Rule Making

The WELL presented its first users with the single disclaimer: "You own your own words." The owners of the WELL sought to distance themselves from liability for any text or data posted or stored on-line by WELL users, while at the same time providing a free space for creative, experimental and unfettered communication. An alternative interpretation of the original disclaimer (now referred to as YOYOW) held that rather than simply laying responsibility for WELL postings at the feet of the author, the phrase also imparted copyrighted ownership of postings to the author under the implied protection and enforcement of the WELL. Management and ownership resisted the onus of serving as legal agent for the WELL's users, recognizing the potential expense and futility of pursuing people who electronically copy and use customers' words. Thus, the evolving interpretation of YOYOW provided fuel for years of discussion on the topics of copyright, intellectual property, and manners in electronic space.

A general aversion to the making and enforcement of rigid rules has continued at the WELL, although incendiary incidents and distressing situations have occasionally brought calls from users for "more Law and Order" or absolute limits on offensive speech. The WELL management has consistently rejected these calls, avoiding the role of policeman and judge except where absolutely necessary, espousing the view that the medium of on-line interpersonal communication is too immature and unformed to be confined by the encumbrances of strict rules. We have realized that the imposition by management of limitations on language and speech, aimed at protecting the feelings or sensibilities of minority or even majority groups, would not protect the feelings and sensibilities of all. We do not want to lose the chance to discover what kinds of interaction really worked in the medium by stifling free and open dialogue. Interaction in public access systems seems to us to be much more productive, innovative, educational and entertaining where there are fewer prohibitions imposed by system management. In a medium where all can participate, continued dialogue has proved to be a better remedy for disagreement than repression. If limitations needed to be imposed and enforced, they could best be handled from within the user population on a "local" forum-by-forum basis, rather than on a system-wide one. The creation of private forums, where local rules can hold sway, has allowed public forums to retain their openness while providing more regulated "retreats" for those who felt they needed them.

The Interface

Immediately after opening the system to public access, the small WELL staff and the original participants collaborated to design a more friendly interface from the raw Picospan software. Picospan included a toolbox of software customization utilities that could be used to make system-wide changes or changes at the user's option. Picospan was tightly integrated with the UNIX operating system and could provide transparent access by users to helpful programs that operate in the UNIX environment.

The author of Picospan, Marcus Watts, had a direct effect on the WELL's culture through his conferencing software. Picospan prevented unnoticed censorship (the hiding or deleting of postings) by forcing hidden or deleted postings to display a conspicuous label reading <censored>. This feature prevented conference hosts (who are empowered to hide or delete any response posted in their forums) from exercising too much control over the flow or content of topics in their forums. Picospan also allowed topics (discussion threads) to be "linked" into several forums at once so that, for example, a topic on the future control of the Internet could be included in the Telecommunications, Politics and Legal conferences at the same time, and all three interest groups could participate. Obviously, such a feature aids in the cross-pollination of ideas and groups throughout the system. Picospan's method of displaying topics as continuously-scrolling documents (rather than as collections of separately-displayed responses) is one reason that WELL conversations are so coherent and able to draw users so deeply.

Staff Influence

The background of four of the WELL's non-technical senior managers who worked there during its first seven years is another significant factor in the formation of the WELL's open and independent culture. Matthew McClure, the first director of the WELL, and I, his successor, both lived in a commune of some renown called the Farm during the 1970s, as did the WELL's first customer service manager, John Coate, and his successor, Nancy Rhine. The experience of living cooperatively in multi-family situations in a community that reached a peak population of over 1500 adults and children had a tremendous influence on the style of management of the WELL. Carryovers from the experience of communal living included the principles of tolerance and inclusion, fair resource allocation, distributed responsibility, management by example and influence, a flat organizational chart, cooperative policy formulation, and acceptance of an ethos that was libertarian bordering on anarchic. John Coate was integral to setting the tone of the WELL, where users and staff mingled both on-line and at the WELL's monthly office parties. He has written a network-distributed essay on "Cyberspace Innkeeping"[3] based on lessons learned in dealing with customers during his time at the WELL.

Maintaining a History

An important component in the establishment of a community in any setting or medium is the keeping of a historical record of its environs, its people, their works, and the relationships and organizations that define the direction of the collective entity. For a variety of reasons, besides the security of backups, the WELL still keeps a significant portion of its past on-line interaction archived on tape and on its "live" disks, which are accessible to its users. Many of its conference hosts have also made a practice of backing up topics on their home machines before retiring them from the WELL. WELL users championed the idea that a history be kept, and went so far as to create an Archives conference where topics judged by them to have historical significance were linked from other conferences on the WELL and saved for future reference. This "history" of the WELL contributes to its depth and feeling of "place" and community. New users and veterans can refer to these archives for background to current discussion and to sample the character of the WELL from its early days. Having a historical record of groundbreaking discussions and debates also helps to avoid the constant replowing of old ground and the beating of long-dead ideological horses.

Connections

Originally, only direct-dial modems could be used to reach the WELL, but by the end of its first year of operation an X.25 packet system allowed long distance users to reach the WELL at reasonable cost. The WELL kept its San Francisco focus—local callers had cheaper access and could stay on-line longer for the same cost—but national and international participants were now more encouraged to join.

In 1986, the WELL took part in a beta-test of a regional packet-switched network run by Pacific Bell. For nearly a year, users from most of the San Francisco Bay Area were able to call the WELL with no phone toll charges. This fortunate circumstance helped boost the WELL's subscription base and connected many valuable customers from the Silicon Valley area into the growing user pool.

The percentage of users from outside of the Bay Area climbed slowly but steadily through the years. As word spread through frequent articles in the press, the WELL became known as a locus for cutting-edge discussion of technical, literary and community issues, and it became more attractive to long distance telecommunicators.

On January 2, 1992, the WELL opened its connection to the Internet through the regional Internet service provider, BARRNet. After much debugging and adjustment and a complete CPU upgrade, full Internet access was offered to WELL customers in June 1992. Staff and users opened an Internet conference on the WELL; users discuss services and information available through the Internet and can ask each other questions about the use of the Internet and its tools. As elsewhere on the WELL, users share their knowledge and their discoveries with each other in a variety of topics, ranging from best software tools to public access Internet sites to the future of the Internet. The Internet conference keeps users up to date and serves as a "living manual" to the resources, news and usage of the Internet.

Community

In a medium in which text is the only means of communication, trust is difficult but essential to build and maintain. There are no audible or visual clues to go by in one's on-line interpersonal communication. There are, though, ways in which trust can be built even through the small aperture of telecommunicated text.

System owners and managers can eliminate one of the major barriers to trust by being consciously non-threatening. One of the most menacing conditions experienced by new users of public conferencing systems is that of hierarchical uncertainty. Who holds the power? What is their agenda? What are the rules? Who is watching me and what I do? Do I really have any privacy? How might a "Big Brother" abuse me and my rights? The WELL's Whole Earth parentage brought with it a reputation for collaboration between publisher and reader. Whole Earth catalogs and magazines were well known for soliciting and including articles and reviews written by readers and for publishing unedited letters to the editors; indeed, they paid readers for their letters. Whole Earth customers trusted that the publications had no ulterior motives, were not owned and controlled by greedy corporations, and did not spend their revenues to make anyone rich. Readers supported the publications and the publications engaged in open dialogue with the readers. At the WELL, we strove to continue that kind of relationship with our customers even though the immediacy of feedback through public conferencing and e-mail often made open dialogue tricky.

Operators of multi-user computer systems hold a position of ultimate power; they are able to create and destroy user accounts, data, communications at will. More threatening is their power to violate the privacy of users by reading private files and e-mail. This is a simple fact of on-line life in almost any public access system. We realized that it was incumbent on us to make clear to all users our assumptions and the ground rules of the WELL in order to minimize any concerns they might have had about our intentions. Our aim was to be as candid with users as possible. John Coate and

I did our best to narrow the distance between ourselves and our customers by posting long autobiographical stories in the True Confessions conference soon after assuming our managerial roles. As we did not have technical backgrounds in the telecommunications or computing fields, we invited our customers to join us in problem-solving discussions about the system and the business around it, and we actively promoted the users themselves as important creators and developers of the WELL's product.

Staff members were encouraged to be visible on-line and to be active listeners to users' concerns. The staff took part in discussions not only about technical matters and customer service, but also about interpersonal on-line ethics. When on-line quarrels surfaced, staff members participated with users in attempts to resolve them. Over time, both staff and users learned valuable lessons and we recognized that a "core group" of users had begun to coalesce. These were users who seemed to have a strong commitment to each other and to the system that had brought them together and supported their regular interactions. Together, we realized that a viable community was forming, able to withstand periodic emotional firestorms and learn from them and strong enough to anticipate and soften their effects in the future. The ethical construct that we adopted was that one could say whatever one wanted to on the WELL, but that things worked best if it was said with consideration of others in mind. This became ingrained in enough peoples' experience to constitute a community standard. This standard was not written down as a rule, but is noted conspicuously in the WELL's User Manual and is mentioned on-line as an observation of how things work best.[4] Communication through a network can be most productive and effective if it is done with care.

Beginning in 1986, the WELL began sponsoring monthly face-to-face gatherings open to all, WELL user or not. Initially, these Friday night potluck parties were held in the WELL's small offices, but as attendance grew and the offices became even more cramped, the gatherings moved to other locations. These in-person encounters have been an important part of the WELL's community-building. They are energetic, intense, conversation-saturated events where people who communicate through screen and keyboard day after day can refresh themselves with the fuller experience of in-person interaction. Often, when attempts to communicate through text have reached an impasse, an in-person meeting at a WELL party has served to resolve the difficulties.

Collaboration in Technical Development

The WELL had to bootstrap its operation from the initial investment of 1985. As a business venture it was undercapitalized, and it struggled constantly to stay ahead of its growth in terms of the capacity of its technical infrastructure and its level of staffing. During this time, it continued to charge low fees. The undercapitalization of the WELL and the low user charges combined to force management to practice creative frugality. From the first days of operation, the expertise and advice of users were enlisted to help maintain the UNIX operating system, to write documentation for the conferencing software, to make improvements in the interface, and to deal with larger problems such as hardware malfunctions and upgrades.

Over the years, many tools have been invented, programmed, and installed at the suggestion of or through the labor of WELL users. In an ongoing attempt to make the interface a comfortable environment for any user, the WELL has become, if not a truly user-friendly environment, a very powerful tool kit for the on-line communications enthusiast. One of the basic tenets of the WELL is that "tools, not rules" are preferred solutions to most people-based problems. Menu-driven software tools were created to give control of file privacy to users, allowing them to make their files publicly-readable or invisible to others. The "Bozo filter," created by a WELL user, allows any user to elect not to see the postings of any other user. Some WELL veterans, after years of teeth-gritting tolerance of an abrasive individual, are now spared any encounter with that individual on the WELL.

Other tools have been written to facilitate file transfers, to allow easy setup of USENET group lists, to find the cheapest ways to access the WELL, and to extract portions of on-line conversations based on a wide range of criteria. These tools have all been written by WELL users, who received only free on-line time in exchange for their work, or by WELL employees who once were customers. Free time on the WELL has always been given liberally by WELL management in exchange for services. At one time, half of the hours logged on the WELL in a month were uncharged, going to volunteers or staff. Hosting conferences, writing software, consulting on technical issues and simply providing interesting and provocative conversation have been services that justified free time on the WELL. Much as we would have liked to pay these people for their services, almost to a person they have continued to contribute to the WELL's success as a business and public forum, demonstrating to us that they considered the trade a fair one.

Conclusion

What has been learned at the WELL can certainly be of value when planning new systems. The WELL experiment has demonstrated that high funding, elegant interfaces, optimum hardware, and detailed business plans are not essential to a thriving on-line community and a successful for-profit business. It is more important that the owners and managers of the system openly foster the growth of on-line community, and that there be a strong spirit of open collaboration among owners, managers and users in making the system succeed. With the right attitudes and relationships, a lack of strong capitalization and technical background can be overcome.

As a small town on the Internet highway system, the WELL shows not only how a regional system can offer public access to the greater network, but also how the users of the system can be a creative resource for the network, bringing to the greater networked population new ideas, lively and coherent discussion, and eloquently-stated public opinion. The open debate and dialogue of the WELL have had effects far beyond its relatively small user base. Almost every press story describing the Internet or the new on-line culture mentions the WELL or features one of its outspoken users. The WELL's informed population keeps itself up-to-date with the rapidly changing world of which it is a part. For democracy to work, the populace must be so informed and involved. The Internet is the group communications matrix that must support this involvement so that our wavering democracy can survive these problem-filled times.

By encouraging the formation of regional civic and commercial networks where local as well as national and global issues can be discussed, the government can help stimulate citizen involvement in the solving of problems, from the very local to the planetary. Such systems should provide affordable access to all economic levels of society, so that the discussion and debate can include more than just the affluent, white, well-educated population that now makes up the vast majority of network users.

The WELL is a good prototype, but it is not a definitive model of what full public access to the Internet might be. It has become known for the high level of discourse that takes place in its public conferences because its founders, its managers and a core group of it users wanted it to be that way. Facing the uncertainty and fear of what legal liabilities might threaten system operators and users alike in this new communications medium, we held steadfast to the idea that solving local problems could be done most effectively through public discussion rather than through blanket prohibitions of feared behaviors. The WELL has demonstrated how a system with few rules and regulations can become a lively and innovative on-line meeting place where the user-citizens are free to express their ideas and create their own communities and standards.

Notes

[1] X.25 packet networks allow one to call a local number with the modem and connect to the destination system for a lower cost than calling the system through direct long-distance.

[2] Electronic Frontier Foundation, 1001 G St. N.W., Suite 950 East, Washington, DC 20001. The telephone number is (202) 347-5400.

[3] Available from John Coate via e-mail at tex@well.sf.ca.us.

[4] From the WELL User's Manual: "The WELL, as a community, functions on mutual respect and cooperation. . . . Remember that words you enter in a burst of inspired passion or indignant anger will be there for you (and everyone) to read long after your intense feelings are gone. . . . You may, from time to time, find yourself in disagreement with someone on the WELL. At times like this, please remember that it's safer, more polite, and more persuasive to take issue with that person's comments, rather than attacking them personally."

Atheism, Sex, and Databases:
The Net as a Social Technology

Lee Sproull and Samer Faraj

Introduction

Discussions about network access and use are based on assumptions about people who use the net—who they are, what they want, what they do.[1] Assumptions about users and their motivations influence what metaphors are evoked in planning for change. These metaphors in turn suggest users' behaviors, tools and services to support those behaviors, and policy mechanisms to provide access to those tools and services. A familiar example from personal computing is the metaphor of the "desktop;" it implies that people do "deskwork" and want tools and services to support that work.

Current discussion about network access is dominated by a view of people as individual information processors who are motivated to contribute to and benefit from the explosion of information found on the net. The first section of this paper explores that view, with its metaphors of the electronic highway and electronic library. The remainder of the paper offers an alternative approach based on a view of people as social beings who need affiliation as much as they need information. We explore the metaphor of an electronic gathering, offer illustrations of electronic gatherings today, and suggest some technical and policy issues that follow from this alternative view of people on the net.

The Net as an Information Technology

The dominant view of people on the net is that they are individual information processors, looking for and manipulating information. They are continually motivated to find new information, and the net always offers more new information for them to discover. The net is viewed fundamentally as a technology for providing access to information and information tools. For example, a popular description of the National Research and Education Network (NREN) notes:

The Network will give researchers and students at colleges of all sizes—and at large and small companies—in every state access to the same:
• high performance computing tools
• data banks
• supercomputers
• libraries
• specialized research facilities
• educational technology
that are presently available to only a few large universities and laboratories that can afford them (CNREN, 1989, p. 9).

An assessment of the changing role of computers suggests, "By the mid-1990s, people can be expected to view personal computers as knowledge sources rather than as knowledge processors. . . . gateways to vast amounts of knowledge and information" (Tennant and Heilmeier, 1991, p. 123). Indeed, the workshop preceding the preparation of this volume described the Internet and NREN as an "efficient communications platform and increasingly rich data environment" (Kahin, 1993).[2]

The metaphors evoked by this information-centered view are the electronic highway and the digital library. People are said to "cruise" or "browse" the net. The pursuit of information—the cruise or the browse—is implicitly solitary; hundreds or thousands of people may search at the same time, but each is independent and unaware of others. The goal is to discover information. These discoveries can range from mildly amusing to enormously helpful, but their value is always determined by the individual searcher. (See column 1 of table 1 for a summary of the dominant view.)

This view of people on the net as individual information searchers and processors underlies ideas about tools to improve informa-

Table 1 People on the Net: Alternative Views

	Information Processors	Social Beings
Unit	Individual	Group
Place	Highway	Gathering
	Library	
Behaviors	Cruising	Chatting
	Browsing	Arguing
Consequences	Individual knowledge	Affiliation
Tools	Telnet/FTP	Listserv
	WAIS/Gopher	Usenet group visualization
Policies	Information ownership	Support for group
	Fee for access	Fee for membership

tion search and manipulation. Early tools relevant to this perspective include the Telnet protocol, which allows users to remotely log onto geographically distant computers, and the File Transfer Protocol (FTP), which allows users to start a session on a remote computer and to transfer files between their machine and the remote one. More recent tools provide a common interface to access large numbers of databases and services on the net. These include: archie, a sort of global file location catalogue; gopher, a utility that organizes access to Internet resources through a hierarchical menu system; WAIS, which acts as an electronic reference librarian by searching inside files for requested information; and WWW, a hypertext-based virtual information searching and browsing tool.[3]

This dominant view also influences policy discussions about net access and use. If people are primarily searching for and manipulating information, then charging them for accessing and transferring information is sensible. It is appropriate to propose pricing schemes in which people pay varying amounts depending upon the value of the information.[4] Protecting intellectual property rights is also important in this view.

A version of the dominant view is found in discussions about extending and increasing network support for scientists (see, for example, National Research Council, 1993.) In this view, individual scientists want to find or discover information in databases, journal articles, or other literature that can be made available on the net; they also want to gain access to scarce scientific instruments or apparatus. Increasingly, scientists will gain access to these resources through the net. Extending network access and services will let scientists work at a distance from their colleagues, their apparatus, and their data to create and leverage shared knowledge. The metaphor invoked is the virtual scientific laboratory, and it points to the need to develop tools for locating and sharing data, software for analyzing shared data, tools for controlling remote instruments, and tools for communicating with far-away colleagues (NRC, 1993, p. 56). It also suggests the need for policy mechanisms to ensure that scientists make data available to others on the net, to ensure that claims of priority for discovery can be registered, and to certify the quality of electronic information, much as peer review processes do for journal publications.

The dominant view of people on the net as information seekers and processors is sensible and productive. However, it is also incomplete and misleading in some important ways. An alternative view of the net as a social technology suggests different technical and policy issues.

The Net as a Social Technology

People on the net are not only solitary information processors but also social beings. They are not only looking for information; they are also looking for affiliation, support, and affirmation. Thinking of people on the net as social actors evokes a metaphor of a gathering.[5] Behaviors appropriate at a gathering include chatting, discussing, arguing, and confiding. People go to a gathering to find others with common interests and talk with or listen to them. When they find a gathering they like, they return to it again and again. (See column 2 of table 1 for a summary of this view.)

If we view people as social actors, then we should view the net as a social technology. Any technology combines artifacts and procedures to apply knowledge for practical ends. A social technology does so to allow people with common interests to find each other, talk and listen, and sustain connections over time. Dinner parties, bowling teams, college reunions, coffee houses, 12-step programs, neighborhood pubs—all are examples of social technologies. Oldenberg (1989) has called these "great good places" that provide a neutral meeting ground where social conventions are democratic and conversation is the main activity. They keep long hours, accommodate people when they are free from their other responsibilities, and are easily accessible. Great good places can be found not only in the real world but also on the net, in the form of electronic groups.

Just as a pub or coffee house is recognizable by its exterior decor and sign, so an electronic group is recognizable by its name. At a most basic level, a group name identifies people who share their common interest using electronic communication.[6] Beyond the name, group structure comes from membership control (whether it is private or public) and editorial control (whether it is moderated or unmoderated). Private groups are open only to people admitted by the owner of the list; public groups are open to anyone with access to a network over which the group can be reached. In moderated groups, all messages are sent to a moderator, who may organize or summarize them before posting them to the entire group. In unmoderated groups, each message sent to the group is directly posted.

Electronic gatherings are characterized by three noteworthy social attributes not found in real world gatherings. First, physical location is irrelevant to participation; if a person has network access, electronic gatherings are accessible. Physical distance has no influence on the size or shape of gatherings and is no longer a barrier for effective participation.

Second, most participants are relatively invisible. If people attend a real-world gathering, their physical presence matters even if they say nothing. They take up space; their movements and nonverbal noises can be interpreted by the speaker and other participants. In an electronic gathering, those who only read messages are entirely invisible because there are usually no reminders or cues to signal how many people, or which people, read a message.[7] In electronic group argot, readers who never post are sometimes called "lurkers," a term with more sinister connotations than is perhaps warranted.

Most electronic groups have a very high proportion of lurkers: for example, on the WELL, a network known for high levels of interaction, about 80% of its 6,600 members posted no message during a one-month period (Smith, 1993, p. 37). People who do post messages are visible only through the text they write. There is no accompanying visual or aural information about physical appearance, emotional state, social status, or personal situation.[8] People may personalize their messages through typographic conventions for emotion, such as the smiley face,[9] or through pithy sayings or stylized drawings in the signature block that can be automatically appended at the end of a message. Generally, however, signals and cues are limited to ascii text.

The third characteristic, which stems from the first two, is that the logistical and social costs to participate in electronic gatherings are quite low. For the most part, people can participate at their own convenience, often from their own office or home. They don't have to get dressed up, drive across town, worry about time zone differences, or schedule a conference room. They can participate for five or ten minutes at a time, logging in to check group mail or to read a newsgroup in the interstices between real-world events. People can participate in great social comfort, too. Invisible readers feel no social pressure to justify their presence or to contribute; passive participation impedes an electronic gathering not at all. Posters, who cannot see or be seen by their audience, have few overt reminders that others may be scrutinizing their text and feel secure that only their text can be seen by others. Because they are less aware of their audience, people who "speak" electronically are relatively unbound by social convention. This can result in startlingly intimate revelations that are posted to thousands of people. It can also result in rapid escalation from mild annoyance to "flame wars."

Scope and Instances of Electronic Gatherings

Electronic gatherings flourish on all networks. Corporate networks, which are justified for business reasons, support thousands of business-related electronic groups and hundreds of extracurricular electronic groups as well.[10] One large computer manufacturer, for example, supports more than 1,200 business-related groups devoted to such topics as computer-aided manufacturing, specific products, and computer languages. It also supports more than 350 extracurricular groups devoted to such topics as Celtic culture, diet support, religion, and four-wheel drive vehicles. Commercial networks support thousands of groups. The WELL, with about 6,600 subscribers, has more than 220 public conferences; America OnLine has about 350 organized special interest clubs and forums and "countless, countless 'grass roots' interest groups," according to an AOL source. Prodigy supports more than 400 discussion groups, Compuserve supports more than 200, and Delphi supports more than 50 "official" special interest groups and hundreds of personalized groups that are maintained by members. The number of dial-up Bulletin-Board Systems (BBSs) in the United States exceeds 45,000 and they are used regularly by 12 million users (Rickard, 1993) Recent estimates show that the Internet itself has about 2,500 public mailing lists, uncountable numbers of private mailing lists, more than 2,600 newsgroups or bulletin boards, and more than 200 real-time interactive groups.[11]

Usenet newsgroups illustrate the popularity and diversity of electronic groups. Usenet is a system of distributed electronic bulletin boards (called newsgroups) that are supported by more than 16,000 organizations and have more than two million subscribers. Usenet is not a computer network; rather, it is a network of bilateral agreements among system administrators to cooperate in managing bulletin boards. A site administrator or system administrator who subscribes to some or all Usenet bulletin boards receives all new messages for those boards and forwards them to another site. A person with an account at a subscribing site can read and post to bulletin boards available at that site. Typically, readers and posters are not directly charged for participating in Usenet groups. Newsgroups are not representative of all electronic groups on all networks, but do provide an easily accessible view of electronic group behavior that illustrates the function and potential of electronic groups. The Usenet community itself collects descriptive statistics and posts them to the newsgroup called news.lists.[12] Usenet groups are relatively accessible to anyone with Internet access.

More than 19,000 messages are posted each day to Usenet newsgroups (50 megabytes of text, equivalent to 20,000 hard copy pages of text). Newsgroups are organized in broad topic categories, such as "comp" for computer-related topics and "rec" for recreational topics. Each category includes as many groups as people wish to create and maintain. More than 100 of the most popular groups have memberships of more than 50,000 people. (See table 2 for descriptions of some popular Usenet groups.) Some of the largest groups function like subscription lists for special-interest daily magazines. They exhibit little interaction; messages rarely respond to previous messages. For example, rec.humor and misc.forsale both have more than 100,000 subscribers and receive more than 50 mostly-unrelated messages a day. But many large groups look more like gatherings than magazines—they have substantial social interaction with lively discussion sustained over time on many topics, including (among others) atheism, sex, and databases.

Table 3 displays data drawn from a study investigating the dynamics of electronic group interaction. It describes three groups that discuss social or political topics and three that discuss technical topics. Each group contains a daily mix of solo messages (postings to which no one replies), seed messages (postings that generate replies and thus a discussion thread), and replies. Over half the messages in each group show social interaction; that is, either they induce one or more replies or are themselves replies to previous messages. Like many real-world gatherings, these groups support more than one discussion (or thread) at the same time; threads last an average of three to five days. These groups exhibit some of the same social dynamics found in real-world gatherings: people take on different roles (for example, lurker, guru, keeper of archive files); there are comments about the true or intended purpose of the group and about what is or is not appropriate behavior; people give and get help; people come and go. But, unlike most real-world gatherings, these groups allow ongoing interaction for thousands of members.

Some Consequences of Electronic Groups

In the real world, groups benefit their members (and vice versa) by providing physical, economic, cognitive, and emotional resources. Electronic groups do not provide direct physical or economic

Sproull and Faraj

Table 2 Popular USENET groups[a]

Category # of groups[b]	Description[c]	Popular groups	Readers[d]	Volume[d] (messages per day)
alternative (alt) 778	Groups that discuss "alternative ways of looking at things"	alt.sex alt.sex.stories alt.activism	140,000 120,000 94,000	53 38 15
computer (comp) 457	Computer science and related topics	comp.windows.x comp.lang.c comp.graphics	120,000 94,000 93,000	29 38 30
recreation (rec) 276	Groups discussing hobbies, recreational activities, and the arts	rec.humor rec.arts.movies rec.music.misc	110,000 71,000 65,000	71 80 59
societal (soc) 90	Groups addressing social issues[e]	soc.culture.indian soc.singles soc.women	73,000 66,000 49,000	104 97 10
science (sci) 69	Groups discussing scientificresearch and applications (other than computer science)	sci.electronics sci.math sci.physics	67,000 57,000 53,000	50 31 42
miscellaneous (misc) 39	Anything that doesn't fit into the above categories, or that fits into several categories	misc.jobs.offered misc.forsale misc.consumers	150,000 120,000 59,000	37 59 37

a This figure provides an overview of highly popular groups in six domain categories. Groups were selected based on number of readers and volume of messages. Binaries groups, i.e., ones that post images coded in binary form, were excluded due to their specialized nature. Other categories exist but are not included here because of low volume or membership.

b Based on an analysis of a .newsrc file at acs@bu.edu on May 20th, 1993. This may understate the total number of groups active on the Internet; the numbers are based only on the groups received at Boston University.

c From Krol (1993, pp.129–130).

d Derived from Reid (1993).

e Here "social" can mean "politically relevant" or "socializing" or anything in between.

Atheism, Sex, and Databases

Table 3 Interaction in USENET Groups (6 sample groups)

	soc. culture. lebanon	soc. feminism	alt. atheism	comp. databases	comp. object	comp. c++
Group size	13,000	20,000	53,000	65,000	42,000	82,000
Messages/day (mean)	7.9	8.1	53.3	17.7	9.1	35.8
Message type:						
Solo (%)	30.9	24.8	19.0	41.2	31.7	41.7
Seed (%)	18.8	16.4	16.4	18.7	13.4	16.4
Reply (%)	50.4	58.8	64.6	40.1	54.8	41.9
Total lines of text per message	50.0	93.6	47.1	27.2	45.1	45.8
Percent of new lines per message	85.0	92.1	68.4	85.5	84.1	84.4
Percent of messages with embedded text	53.2	62.0	84.0	38.6	54.8	60.0
Average number of threads per day	4.3	4.9	31.4	10.0	5.0	14.8
Average time length of thread (days)	3.1	5.4	3.6	4.3	4.7	3.3
Number of authors posting per day (mean)	6.4	7.2	34.4	15.7	8.5	28.7
Domain of author organization (% of total authors):						
Educational	49.9	57.5	44.3	37.1	24.8	21.8
Commercial	16.9	18.6	23.8	24.1	31.4	31.2
International	26.8	15.4	21.4	31.9	34.2	32.7

Source: Faraj and Sproull (1994).

resources, but they frequently offer information that may lead to them, such as leads or advice about jobs or items for sale. Most electronic groups also offer information or cognitive resources for their members. For example, on "comp.databases," one can ask questions such as:

I am looking at products for pulling data from an Ingres database running on a VAX (VMS). We currently use PCLINK to get data to PC's but want to access this data through Ethernet instead of asynch ports. Does anyone have any advice on products from companies like IQ Software or Gupta?? What Ingres products on the PC do I need (Tools for DOS, . . .)? Any help would be appreciated.

The "comp." groups frequently offer technical advice. On "comp.databases," members exchange opinions about the technical merits of new database packages. On "comp.object," people struggling with trying to write programs using object-oriented methods appeal to the wisdom of more experienced members. On "comp.c++," members discuss the intricacies of the c++ programming language. They post portions of code, saying "they think it should work but it does not." These messages challenge other members to identify the problems and post a corrected version. In the technical groups some people expend significant effort to collect and provide technical information, while others maintain and circulate bibliographies. Members who receive many answers to interesting questions often publish a summary of them.

The social and political groups also offer information. "Soc.feminism," for example, provides impromptu reviews of new feminist books and movie reviews. These reviews are the catalyst for lively discussions regarding current cultural issues. On "soc.culture.lebanon," hard-to-find information is frequently posted: the text of U.S. travel advisories to Lebanon, the daily exchange rate of the Lebanese pound, news stories about Lebanon from the UPI and AP news feeds. People exchange advice about how best to prepare Lebanese dishes and suggestions for good bi-cultural baby names. Jokes, many in poor taste, are frequently posted and either enjoyed or disparaged by readers.

Many electronic groups offer entertainment, which can be an emotional resource. Three of the largest Usenet newsgroups, each with more than 100,000 readers, have entertainment as their primary purpose: "alt.sex," "alt.sex.stories," and "rec.humor." The technology policy community sometimes seems mildly embarrassed by such groups. They do not match lofty views of the net as a resource to elevate intellectual discourse; moreover, many people find the contents offensive. Nevertheless, they are extremely popular.

Electronic groups also offer affiliation. Despite the fact that participants in electronic groups may be surrounded by people at work or school, at least some of them feel alone in facing a problem or a situation. If their situation is problematic, it is easy for them to believe it must be their own fault, since no one else around them has the same problem or a similar perspective. Even though electronic groups are usually composed of strangers, because their members share a common interest, they are also likely to share common experiences. A result of finding others in the same situation or with the same problem can be the realization that "I am not alone!" Thus, electronic groups can provide emotional support to their members. Three examples follow.

In 1990, a postdoctoral physicist began a public electronic mailing list, the Young Scientists' Network, for scientists like himself who faced the prospect of being unable to find permanent jobs in physics. The Young Scientists' Network includes weekly messages from the founder on such topics as job tips, funding possibilities, and relevant news stories (Morell, 1992). Subscribers send in their own tips and scoops. Although it was created to provide information to unemployed or underemployed scientists, it rapidly became an informal support group. One physicist said, "The main value was in confirming the trouble I was having finding a job." Another offered, "It helps save your sanity, it helps to know that it's not because of a personal failing that you can't find research work." The Young Scientists' Network, which had about 170 members a year ago, has grown to 3000 members today.

In 1987, a computer scientist began a private mailing list, Systers, to share information with her colleagues about events and topics in the world of operating systems. Systers expanded to become a "forum for discussion of both the problems and joys of women in [computer science more generally] and to provide a medium for networking and mentoring" (Borg, cited in Frenkel, 1990: 36). There are messages about job openings, book reviews, conferences, and general conversations. One of its members says, "There's a feeling of closeness, so it's easy to talk" (field notes, 1/9/92).[13] She believes that the closeness was established early because the group was private and people were careful to show positive regard for others in their messages. She says that even today, when the interaction starts getting contentious, "somebody always sends mail that's soothing." Systers currently has over 1500 members in 150 companies, 200 universities, and 18 countries around the world.

"Misc.kids" is a Usenet group for discussing the joys and sorrows of kids and parenting. It's a mix of information, jokes, discussion, and debate, with topics ranging from diaper rash to corporal punishment. One reader describes misc.kids as "a support organization, a debate-team, an encyclopedia of information, and a social group all rolled into one. Even the people I never agree with, I care about" (field notes, 5/92). Another confided, "When I had problems in pregnancy (the baby had a chromosome abnormality), I posted about it and received support from all over the world—an amazing experience" (field notes, 5/92). Misc.kids sees about 60 messages a day and has about 48,000 subscribers world-wide.

These electronic groups do much more than provide information. They offer the opportunity to make connections with other people. They provide support and a sense of community. To be sure, they also provide information. But, as one group member said, it is "information with an attitude."

In the real world, mutual benefit is the social glue that sustains face-to-face groups over time; members who benefit from others reciprocate. Direct reciprocity is difficult if not impossible in the electronic context, but more generalized altruism is relatively easy to sustain. When one person asks for help, it is very likely that one or more group members will provide a helpful or supportive response. (A much larger proportion might be able to help but might be too busy, too diffident, or too selfish to respond.) With memberships in the thousands, the proportion responding can be extremely small and still yield one or more beneficial responses. Furthermore, responses can be seen by all group members, thereby helping others who had the same question or problem but did not post a message about it. With large groups, no one person need spend much time being helpful: a small number of small acts can sustain a large community because each act is seen by the entire group. Moreover, even people who receive no direct benefit from any particular helpful message see the process of helping behavior modelled in the group.

The benefits provided by electronic groups often extend beyond the direct participants when members act as conduits of information to people outside the group. Requests for information are frequently posted to a group "for a friend who doesn't have net access." Group members sometimes forward pertinent posts to friends or colleagues. In the case of technical groups at least, we hypothesize that employers benefit from their employees' group membership when information gleaned from the group is applied or passed on in the workplace. (Note in table 3 that users from commercial organizations represent a larger fraction of posters in the technical groups than in the social groups.)

Of course, the consequences of electronic group membership are not all positive, just as the consequences of affiliations in the real world are not all positive. Erroneous or poor information can be promulgated as easily as high-quality information. People can spend a lot of time reading group messages. Lively discussion can degenerate into frustrating conflict and rancor. But, for several million members, the benefits apparently outweigh the costs.

Technology and Policy Issues

Ideas about tools and policies for the net are influenced by one's view of people on the net. An information-centered view calls for tools to find and manipulate information and policies to protect it. People are currently building and using information tools such as gopher, WAIS, and World-Wide Web. As the amount of information increases and the number of people wishing to find and use it continues to expand, more and better information tools should be developed. An information-centered view leads to policy goals for limiting unauthorized access to information, for protecting the integrity of information, and for preventing the misuse of information. Access and use restrictions and legal restraints are important topics for current policy debate.

What tools and policies are suggested by viewing the net as a social technology?

Tools for Groups

Electronic groups have not been the major focus for network tool development to date, although a few helpful tools exist. DIGEST and DLIST help support moderated lists in digest format. Listserv programs help maintain and archive group membership lists. But for the most part electronic groups have flourished under conditions of benign neglect, much as email flourished in its early days with relatively low levels of technology support or policy attention.

Tools and services that help people find, join, participate in, and derive benefit from groups are important. Some tools might help people differentiate among groups and remind them of what group they are in. These could encompass tools for group visualization, group identity, and group memory—various ways to evoke the "character" and charter of a group. For example, some tools might represent different groups by using icons or graphics to display images of relevant places, people, or symbols. They might use behaviors (such as the number of messages a day) or attributes (such as the number of readers or posters with particular characteristics) to create representations that reflect the changing nature of the group.

Tools are also needed to help people offer services targeted to groups, rather than to individuals. Such services might include digesting or indexing group messages, matchmaking, toast-mastering, hosting, mediation, and conflict resolution. Nascent examples of these and other services can be found in some electronic groups today. But typically they are ad hoc efforts that are difficult to sustain, leverage, or generalize.

Electronic groups depend upon the talent and goodwill of thousands of support people: system operators, system administrators, Usenet site administrators, people who create lists and newsgroups, group moderators, and group archivists. Group maintainers also need better tools and services. Moreover, we need to understand how such people can be recruited, supported, sustained, and recognized. Economic analyses of networks that consider only equipment and transmission costs ignore the extraordinary value contributed by volunteers. Developing, sustaining, and recognizing the people who support the net is crucial.

Policy Issues for Groups

We have had relatively little experience with electronic group governance. The most important policy issue is how to balance people's rights and responsibilities in electronic gatherings. Every group creates and sustains a shared understanding of the rights and responsibilities of membership—a social contract. The social contract guides both individual behavior and collective response to that behavior. In the real world, social contracts take a variety of familiar forms: formal legal codes, professional codes of conduct, association bylaws, community standards. Their enforcement mechanisms are equally rich and varied, ranging from socialization of the novice member, to warning signs and signals, to gestures of solidarity, to penalties for noncompliance.

Social contracts in the electronic world are extremely problematic. Because electronic groups are both diverse and ephemeral, attempts to directly apply codes of conduct from the real world often go awry. Social influence is played out in a world that is rich in imagination and diversity and impoverished in its means of communication—ascii text.

Electronic groups currently lack subtle ways to convey expectations about behavior. In the real world, training, practice, and socialization are offered in probationary periods and sheltered environments such as driver's education class, moot court, and clinical internships; there are no electronic equivalents. In the real world, objects such as traffic signals, judicial robes and a raised bench, and party decorations remind people of appropriate behavior for particular situations; there are no equivalents in electronic groups. In the real world small transgressions can evoke small rebukes; in electronic groups, there is no easy equivalent of the raised eyebrow or "tsk-tsk" if someone misbehaves, so small transgressions typically go unremarked. But a large number of small transgressions can create an unpleasant environment.

Electronic groups currently have few ways to deal with blatant misbehavior. Sometimes people use a tool to filter out other people's messages that they deem obnoxious. Filters exemplify the consequences of thinking about people on the net as individual information processors—in this case, individuals who want to ignore messages with particular attributes. Although a filter may benefit the individuals who use it, it may be socially dysfunctional for the group; it does not inform the miscreant that his or her behavior has been identified as objectionable, nor does it inform the larger group that someone finds particular behavior objectionable. Thus it cannot educate either the individual or the group about objectionable behavior. It also gives people an easy technological way to avoid social responsibility.

Extremely disruptive behavior in electronic groups, often justified by the perpetrator in terms of freedom of speech, can generate endless debate over how to respond. Both the disruption and the debate can disenchant members who want to pursue the designated topic of the group, rather than issues of social control. Ejecting members from groups, removing groups from sites, or closing down groups are complicated and contentious undertakings.

It is much easier to suggest tools for groups than it is to suggest policies for how to balance people's rights and responsibilities. We need much more discussion within groups themselves as well as in the broader policy community about group governance. We also need research that documents implicit codes of behavior and social influence mechanisms across a wide variety of group types.

Conclusion

One might ask why it is necessary to attend directly to electronic groups and to the net as a social technology. The answer is that it is unlikely that social benefits will occur simply as a byproduct of information-centered technology and policies. As the number, size, and heterogeneity of groups continues to grow, so does the need for group tools and the need to understand group governance. Tools and policies directed at individual information processors are not necessarily responsive to group needs.

The human need for affiliation is at least as strong as the need for information. Often, both needs are met simultaneously in human association. Many electronic groups provide both information and affiliation, and the value of information received in groups derives, at least in part, from its being offered by people who have chosen to affiliate. The motivation to offer information also derives, in part, from the obligation and affirmation of membership. And, of course, the value of groups goes beyond information.

Even those who wish to design electronic highways and libraries for individual information processors can incorporate ideas about membership and affiliation. On a real highway, each vehicle carries few passengers. On the electronic highway we can run tour busses with hundreds of passengers and dozens of tour guides. People who like the people they meet on a tour can take another journey with them. In a real library, "no talking" is the rule. In the electronic library, we can have sociable gatherings around every document. People can give their opinions about something they have read; authors can rejoin or elaborate; readers and writers can become discussers and collaborators. If we remember that access to the net means not only access to information, but access to people, we can provide tools and policies to promote both.

Notes

[1] In this paper "the net" is broader than the Internet. It includes all interconnected, interoperating computer networks including commercial services such as Prodigy or Compuserve, and dial-up bulletin board services.

[2] See Lynch and Preston (1990) for a history and review leading up to NREN from this perspective.

[3] See Krol (1993) for more information on these tools.

[4] Peak load pricing schemes define value primarily in terms of timeliness of access (e.g., Varian and Mackie-Mason, 1993). Commercial vendors currently offer variable pricing based on time of day.

[5] In fact, some networks have created specific metaphorical places: for example, Larry's Bar on The Sierra Net or Roger's Bar on Big Sky Telegraph. Electronic Cafe (tm) makes the metaphorical gathering real by running real-time events simultaneously in two or more real places connected by electronic networks.

[6] The group name may be attached to an e-mail distribution list, in which case a copy of any message mailed to the group name is forwarded to every member's mailbox. Alternatively, the group name may be attached to a bulletin board or

newsgroup, in which case any message posted to the group is available to be read by anyone interested in that group.

[7] Some realtime conferences and games do signal the presence of readers. Habitat™, for example, displays a ghost icon if someone enters a room and does not announce his or her identity.

[8] The main activity in some network-based interactive fantasy games is creating and displaying identity through choice of name and persona, dress and other props, and interaction style. These identities often bear little relationship to their creators' "real" identities. (But see Turkle, 1992, for ways that role playing can help people work through issues of "real" psychological identity.)

[9] A smiley is a combination of two to four characters that approximates a human face when looked at with the viewer's head tilted to the left. A regular smiley :-) refers to parts of an article or a statement that are meant to be funny. Variations on the basic smiley run in the hundreds: they include ;-) a winky smiley expressing sarcasm and :-(a frowning smiley expressing unhappiness about something (see Godin, 1993, for a extensive list).

[10] See Finholt and Sproull (1990) for a description of electronic groups at work.

[11] Krol (1993: 91–154) provides an overview of email lists and newsgroups. See Hardie and Neou (1993) for an annotated description of more than 800 public mailing lists. See also "List of Active Newsgroups" and "Publicly-accessible Mailing Lists" on the Usenet group news.lists; both are periodic multi-part listings that are frequently updated.

The real-time groups are a marginal but fascinating piece of the world of electronic groups. They are called MUDs, for "multi-user dungeon games," or MOOs, for "MUDs, object-oriented." A person logs on to a MUD, creates an electronic identity, then moves from place to place in a particular electronic world, interacting with other people who are logged on at the same time. Most MUDs are based on adventure and fantasy games. See Curtis (1992) for more information.

[12] For a more detailed description of Usenet, see "What_Is_Usenet" on news.newusers.questions.

[13] Quotations whose source is "field notes" are from electronic group participants who preferred to remain anonymous.

References

Coalition for the National Research and Education Network (CNREN). 1989. *NREN: The National Research and Education Network.* Washington DC.

Curtis, Pavel. 1992. Mudding: Social phenomena in text-based virtual realities. Palo Alto: Xerox PARC. CSL-92-4.

Faraj, Samer and Lee Sproull. 1994. Interaction dynamics in electronic groups. Boston University: Unpublished paper.

Finholt, Thomas and Lee Sproull. 1990. Electronic groups at work. *Organization Science*, 1: 41–64.

Frenkel, Karen. November 1990. Women and computing. *Communications of the ACM*, 34–46.

Godin, S. 1993. *The Smiley Dictionary*. Publisher Group West.

Hardie, Edward T.L. and Vivian Neou (eds.). 1993. *INTERNET: Mailing Lists*. Englewood Cliffs, NJ: Prentice Hall.

Kahin, Brian. 1993. Public Access to the Internet Call for Papers.

Krol, Ed. 1992. *The Whole INTERNET*. Sebastopol, CA: O'Reilly and Associates, Inc.

Lynch, Clifford A. and Cecilia M. Preston. 1990. Internet access to information resources. *Annual Review of Information Science and Technology*, 25: 263–312.

Morell, Judith. May 1, 1992. E-Mail links science's young and frustrated. *Science*, 256: p. 606.

National Research Council. 1993. *National Collaboratories: Applying Information Technology for Scientific Research*. Washington DC: National Academy Press.

Oldenberg, Ray. 1989. *The Great Good Place*. New York: Paragon House.

Reid, Brian. 1993. USENET readership report for Feb 93. Article 2370 of news.lists.

Rickard, Jack. 1993. Home-grown BBS. *Wired*. September/October.

Smith, Marc A. 1993. Voices from the WELL: The logic of the virtual commons. UCLA: Department of Sociology.

Tennant, Harry and George H. Heilmeier. 1991. Knowledge and equality: Harnessing the tides of information abundance. In Derek Leebaert (ed.), *Technology 2001: The Future of Computing and Communications*. Cambridge: The MIT Press.

Turkle, Sherry. 1992. Reconstructing the self in virtual reality. MIT: Paper presented at the Conference on "Popular Cultures."

Varian, Hal and Jeff Mackie-Mason. 1993. Cost and pricing models for different levels of functionality and service. Paper presented at Workshop on Public Access to the Internet, John F. Kennedy School of Government, Cambridge, MA, May 26–27, 1993.

Establishing Network Communities

Learning and Teaching on the Internet: Contributing to Educational Reform

Beverly Hunter

Introduction

On the Internet, people contribute to each others' learning and to society's knowledge base. Internetworking[1] enables and accelerates changes in our educational system; many reforms sought in education are exemplified in the activities of learners, teachers and experts on the Internet. A growing number of students, teachers, and educational administrators, as well as people outside of formal educational institutions, are not only advancing their own education but are also contributing to each others' learning through their participation in network communities. Educational opportunities for all could increase as more people participate in the Internet, if networking infrastructure, services and applications develop in ways that help people contribute to the information infrastructure.[2]

The first part of this chapter provides a brief summary of reforms being sought by educational leaders, and how participation in internetworking contributes to these reforms. The second section provides examples of learning activities on the Internet; the stories illustrate ways people are contributing to each others' learning, to the information infrastructure, and to educational reform. In the third section, problems and processes for future development of the Internet and the National Information Infrastructure are discussed. The final section provides suggestions for policy-makers on how to "scale up" the infrastructure in a manner that maximizes the educational value for all participants.

Trends in Educational Reform

George Leonard said in 1968, "The highly technological, regenerative society now emerging will require something akin to mass genius, mass creativity, and lifelong learning" (Leonard, 1968). That vision of a quarter century ago is now sought by many reformers of our educational system. The SCANS report says, "Modern work is just too complex for a small cadre of managers to possess all the answers" (SCANS, p. 16). President Clinton said in a February 1994 speech to the American Council on Education: "Once the principal source of wealth was natural resources. Then it was mass production. Today it is clearly the problem-solving capacity of the human mind—making products and tailoring services to the needs of people all across the globe."

Reforms in education are driven by changes underway in society. The changing nature of the world's economic system, and the role of information systems in that change, is a pervasive factor driving educational changes for people of all ages (e.g., Reich 1991). The increasingly multicultural nature of our population is another (e.g., SCANS 1992 p. 16). Recent developments in our understanding of how people learn (actively, constructively, collaboratively, multisensorily, contextually) are a factor in the rethinking of schooling and instruction. The increasing complexity of the problems and challenges society faces places new demands on education, while technology advances afford new opportunities for learning. The pace of knowledge production is driving a reexamination of not only the curriculum content, but also the nature and roles of schooling. Unfavorable comparisons of U.S. students with their counterparts around the world, especially in mathematics and science, have also been driving reforms (e.g., IAEEA 1987, 1988).

Reforms, improvements, and transformations being sought in our educational system are diverse. Among the many groups defining these reforms are the National Center for Education and the Economy (NCEE 1991); the National Governors Association (NGA 1986); the American Association for the Advancement of Science, in its Project 2061 (AAAS 1993, 1989); the National Council for Teachers of Mathematics (NCTM 1991, 1989); the

Secretary of Labor's Commission on Achieving Necessary Skills (SCANS 1992); the U.S. Department of Education (e.g., OERI 1993); and the International Association for the Evaluation of Educational Achievement (e.g., IAEEA 1987, 1988).

Trends in educational reform might be summed up in the one word "authentic." Authentic means many things, including a closer relationship of learning to the real-world context of problems and projects; working collaboratively with peers and mentors; closer relationships between people inside schools and outside in the "real world;" working in a hands-on mode with the physical world, in addition to using symbols and words; learning something just at the time it is needed to solve a problem or complete a project, rather than in a preset curriculum sequence; learning in an interdisciplinary context, rather than always separating subjects into isolated topics; working on a problem in depth, rather than covering many topics superficially; teachers being guides and mentors and learners too, rather than only dispensers of knowledge; constructing one's own knowledge rather than memorizing facts from authorities; working on projects and problems of intrinsic interest to the learner or group of learners, rather than learning what everyone else of the same age is expected to learn at the time; building learning experiences on the learning one does throughout life, rather than only on "school" subjects; basing assessment on performance of real tasks rather than artificial tests; using the real tools for intellectual work that are used in the workplace, rather than oversimplified textbook techniques; working directly with people from other places and cultures, rather than only learning about other places indirectly through books. In addition, reform must be a collaborative effort or partnership among administrators, university faculty members, community, business, labor and political leaders, as well as parents, teachers, and students.

The central value of internetworking to support learning and teaching for our changing world is that internetworking can support or enable authentic learning experiences and cross-institutional collaborations needed for reform of education. When learners and teachers contribute to the information infrastructure by participating in virtual communities and by setting up information services on the networks, their experience has many of the "authentic" qualities summarized above. The key characteristic of internetworking that enables this kind of experience is that the people who use the Internet are creating and exchanging knowledge, rather than passively receiving someone else's information. This is a most important point to stress about education and the Internet, because there is a danger that the networks could be used to transmit and amplify traditional and outmoded elements of schooling instead of providing a mechanism for the transformation to lifelong learning needed by all citizens. Many well-intentioned efforts to apply technologies to schooling (often in the name of "reform") still assume such factory-era constraints as segregation of learners by age, a sequential curriculum, everyone learning the same thing at the same time, learning activities confined to the school or classroom, no participation of parents in the learning activities of their children, knowledge predigested by experts, teacher as authoritative knowledge base, memorization of facts today for use in later years, subjects isolated by disciplines, same roles for all teachers, right answers to all test questions, students following procedures written by outside authorities, class periods too short to think in, teacher as the only audience for students' work, and abstractions separated from experiential context.

The way in which we shape and engineer the technology, tools, organization of knowledge and virtual communities on the expanding Internet information infrastructure will directly impact on the potential productivity, roles, and equity of opportunity of young people in both the near and distant future, and thereby will affect the kind of society we evolve into.

Examples of Learning and Teaching on the Internet

Learning and teaching activities on the Internet are multiplying so rapidly that every day one could learn a hundred new examples. Out of the thousands of stories at our fingertips through the Internet, the examples in this section were selected to illustrate elements of educational reform discussed above. Our themes for these examples include the following: collaborative inquiry in networked communities; making collaborative learning more productive; involvement in world affairs; learning based on common special interests; contributions in simulated worlds; learning across ages and institutions.

Although individuals do use Internet resources simply to access information, most of the examples provided in this section involve people in virtual communities. Groups of people who work together on telecommunications networks are referred to as networked communities or virtual communities, to distinguish them from physical, geographic communities.

Conducting Collaborative Inquiry in Networked Communities

Collaborative inquiry in networked communities (Hunter 1993c) is a genre of learning, teaching, and knowledge-creative activity that embodies many elements of educational reform. Students in schools around the nation and the world gather data from their local environments, such as acidity of their rain water, quality of the indoor air, ozone levels, water quality in rivers and streams, biological indicators of changes in climate or pollution, effects of ultraviolet light on plant and animal life, species diversity, wildlife populations, or migration patterns. They work in teams, often engaging parents and other local community members (such as scientists or engineers from a local water department) in their investigations. Each team is also part of a virtual community of scientists, students, and teachers in other schools; each school contributes to a collective database. Thus, that database includes information from many different geographic locations. Through the networks, the students work together to aggregate, analyze, and interpret the data and share their discoveries and interpretations. The large database gives students the opportunity to recognize geographic patterns in the data, and provides a basis for comparing local data with data from other locations; data gathered locally now has more value because it is shared with a geographically distributed community.

There are hundreds of such collaborative inquiry projects and communities organized by teachers and experts and students. Global Rivers Environmental Education Network (GREEN), National Geographic Kids Network, and TERC's Global Lab are well known. Another example is the "Shadows" project: children from around the world measure the noontime shadows of a meter stick on their schoolyards, share their data, and use the collective data as a basis for thinking about the earth and its relationship to the sun, and for their own inquiry processes.

Such projects help students move between the concrete, physical world they can touch and measure and the electronic world of data they analyze to make and communicate powerful abstractions. By learning to observe and describe their local physical and social world in ways useful to people in other locations, they learn to create knowledge, a role that in earlier times was enjoyed by only the small minority of scientists, inventors, writers, industrialists, or statesmen.

Another of the "authentic" qualities of learning in such collaborative inquiry communities is that the learner has a real and responsive audience. This is highly motivating, just as it is motivating to any professional to get feedback from colleagues or audiences. The beneficial effects of this motivational aspect on learning have been studied in a systematic way by educational researchers including Margaret Riel, who has studied children's writing (Riel, 1990), and Nancy Songer, who is studying children's learning about weather and climate (Songer, 1994).

Making Collaborative Learning More Productive

Over the past several years, teachers and researchers have developed tools and standard methods that help make virtual communities more productive. In the Global Lab project organized by TERC, teachers, high school students, and research scientists around the world study local and global ecological change. They use low-cost instruments and sensors such as ozonometers, ion-selective probes for soil and water monitoring, and field data loggers. To make meaningful scientific comparisons with sites from around the world, students and teachers must ensure that all factors influencing measurements are identical; when students in Moscow and Boston establish uniform guidelines to compare data, they learn the rigors and excitement of research. Students learn to investigate trends, compare their findings with local regulations and standards, and report and analyze data. The use of common instruments and software helps establish a common basis for collaboration. A peer review system, scientists for on-line assistance, and collaborative research groups help develop quality research projects.

Similarly, in the FrEdMail network, teachers initiate networked projects in areas of their own and their students' interest and expertise. Over the years, FrEdMail has evolved an efficient and effective set of standard formats, operating procedures, and rules of participation for initiating, planning, organizing, structuring, documenting, scheduling, conducting, and managing teacher-initiated networked educational projects, and for publishing their results. Several other on-line educational communities, such as the AT&T Learning Network, have also developed rigorous standards (e.g., Riel, 1990; Riel & Levin, 1990).

Because schoolchildren are located all over the world, they can often monitor many more sites for environmental studies than the professional scientific community could support. Eventually, when large numbers of students and teachers have the appropriate tools and skills and network participation, they will fill an important role in areas such as monitoring atmospheric ozone, ultraviolet light, water and soil pollution, and bioindicators of global, regional and local change. The economic value of students' work has already been recognized by some of the companies that produce instruments and sensors. These companies value data collected in diverse circumstances and locations for testing their products; the companies provide the products to the community at reduced prices.

Such networked educational projects sometimes have direct and concrete benefits to the local school and neighborhood. One example is air quality studies conducted by Global Lab students in Pease Middle School in San Antonio, Texas, which resulted in improvements to the ventilation system of the school, and a new appreciation by parents and administrators of the contributions their young people can make (Berenfeld 1993).

Involvement in World Affairs

Driven by both a sense of national competitiveness and the increasingly global nature of economic, environmental and social issues, education seeks greater emphasis on working and learning with and about people in other countries and cultures. Educational networking projects facilitate interactions among people from different cultures, countries, or languages. A program called "Children as Teachers" brings native language expertise to schools. Russian children studying English and American students studying Russian help each other learn the second language. This year the students are testing a Russian-English editor and software designed to help students correct each other's mistakes. Teachers of foreign languages are some of the quickest to see the benefits of networking, because there is a vast untapped resource of young "experts" out there in other countries who can add value to a language class.

Students often contribute to the learning of others in distant places and different cultures by providing eyewitness accounts of historic events as they take place. Rachel Weston, a seventh grader in Washington DC, recently reported on her correspondence with an Australian child who lives in the path of the recent bush fires in Sydney. Rachel said, "All week long the information about the Sydney fires that I brought to my social studies class was more up to date than anything in the newspapers" (Weston, 1994)

Sometimes students go beyond description and communication to take action on a problem they learn about through the network. The Copen Family Fund has documented many examples of how teachers, students and their communities have used international networking to make a difference in the lives of others. The Nicaragua Water Pump Project to provide clean water to villages in Nicaragua is one example. It was developed on the educational network I*EARN by Mrs. Del Salza, I*EARN Coordinator in Boston. On a visit to Nicaragua she had learned that villages only 30 minutes from Managua, the capital, did not have clean water. As a result many people have diseases and some die. Del Salza also learned that for about $250—using a rope and parts from a bicycle wheel—a dirty well could be covered and would then provide clean water to a village.

In the first year of the project, schools on the I*EARN Network, including schools from the U.S. and Spain, raised over $2,000 for villages in Nicaragua. In the second year this project was offered as part of the PLANET Network, a consortium of six educational-telecommunications networks committed to humanistic projects.

More than $4,000 was raised from I*EARN schools and schools in TENET (Texas Educational Network). Kids raised money through a variety of endeavors such as T-shirt sales, jog-a-thons, and bake sales. A ten-year-old girl from one of the villages wrote to I*EARN and her message was sent to the schools by e-mail. She thanked all her friends for providing clean water to her village. Why? Because it meant that she did not have to walk 6 kilometers each day to fetch clean water and, therefore, she could go to school.

According to Peter Copen, the founder of I*EARN, the important aspect of this story is that the U.S. and Spanish children learned that they could make a meaningful difference in the world; they also learned about another culture as well as many other academic subjects such as geography, social studies, writing, and technology. The Nicaraguan child learned that she is part of a global village—she is not alone. She also contributed to the learning of the U.S. and Spanish kids.

The Copen Family Fund, in collaboration with the New York State Department of Education and the Soviet Academy of Sciences, launched one of the first international educational networking projects between schools in New York State and the former Soviet Union. This project ran from 1988-1991. It included 12 schools in New York State and 12 in Moscow at all grade levels. During those 3 years over 22 joint projects were completed between the U.S. and Russian schools. The projects included joint literary publications, environmental testing and analysis, studies of democracy, and a joint newspaper.

The program's impact on the New York schools was assessed by independent evaluators, who found that the project helped students improve their intercultural awareness and understanding; helped increase the amount of time students spent in intercultural-related activities such as discussions of social and/or political issues and discussions of international events; and helped to improve teachers' understanding of international events and their involvement with causes for the betterment of society.

Learning Based on Common Special Interests

Students and teachers with specialized interests can address unfamiliar and complex phenomena with the support of like-minded investigators in a virtual community. A teacher can more easily encourage her students to investigate a new subject if there are other resources available to her students through the networks.

For example, Community of Explorers is a high school science project organized by BBN in which science teachers work together to create new methods of teaching that take advantage of computer simulations of phenomena such as gravity, relativity, photosynthesis, and population ecology. It is usually difficult for teachers to begin working with tools and methods that are unfamiliar to them, so day-to-day collaboration is very helpful. Teachers in several schools across the country are able to share their simulation files and teaching experiences over the network. Electronic mail and bulletin board technology serve as a simple way to transfer files containing simulations of the experiments. More experienced teachers serve as mentors to less experienced teachers.

Sometimes, a topic is of interest to only a few students in a school, so the school cannot justify creating an entire "course" for them. This is the motivation behind "distance learning." In traditional distance learning, an instructor broadcasts lessons by satellite to distant locations, with limited interaction with students by telephone. While this model offers educational opportunities that students might not otherwise have, students' contributions to the learning community are limited, as are the number and kinds of resources they have access to. By adding other mechanisms for interaction and putting more responsibility on the students for creating and sharing knowledge, we can try a broader range of models for distance learning. Rather than one organization or person being responsible for all the teaching, responsibilities can be distributed among different groups and locations.

Recently, a handful of high school students at a Department of Defense Dependent School (DoDDS) in Seoul, Korea, worked long hours, with some all-night sessions, collaborating with students in two DoDDS schools in Germany and a school in Kentucky. The students shared their theories, interpretations and understandings about the formation of galaxies, based on simulations they conducted—via the Internet—on a Cray supercomputer in Illinois. They also taught each other how to use the various computer-based tools involved (Telnet to log on to the remote supercomputer, FTP to transfer the simulation output files, a file manager on their workstation, NCSA Collage for collaborative viewing of the output of the simulation, BBN Picture Window for video conferencing, and an e-mail program), all of which were new to them. They invented procedures for conducting the collaborations, which they accomplished through a combination of real-time audio/video, real-time text conversation, scientific collaboration tools, and electronic mail. In each school a teacher was available to provide advice, but did not necessarily have expertise in physics or the technology, and did not prepare lessons. The students and teachers were also able to obtain assistance via e-mail and sometimes telephone with experts at the supercomputing center and at BBN in Cambridge, Massachusetts.

Science teachers rarely have an opportunity to do scientific research. Networked communities make it possible for a teacher to locate other teachers, scientists, and students who are interested in a particular research topic. Some educational projects such as Global Lab support such teachers as initiators and leaders of a research strand (and get dozens or hundreds of young research assistants in the process!).

In the national agenda for reform and modernization of mathematics education, geometry is one of the highest-priority topics, yet few mathematics teachers are familiar with recent developments in this fast-changing field. The Geometer's Forum, an NSF-supported network of research geometers, college faculty, high school teachers and students, and mathematics education researchers, fosters the exchange of ideas and information among these very different institutions and groups that usually have no professional interaction. In a recent communication on the Forum, a high school mathematics teacher discussed the benefits of the Geometer Forum:

As winter approaches my students and I are working hard to create an internet Geometry classroom. We have begun relationships with other students, teachers, student teachers, college professors, a researcher, a publisher, and individual Geometers from around the globe; relationships which need constant attention and care. We are keeping on-line journals and using Geometers' Sketchpad software to solve problems posted on the Geometry Forum. Students' work is being posted on the Forum and emailed to individual Geometers in California, Georgia, Philadelphia and Pittsburgh. The relationships the students and I are forming provide excitement to the learning process and magnify our interests in Geometry. We are learning, among other things, to ask better questions. We have experienced enough to believe more deeply in the possibilities.

Contributions in Simulated Worlds

We have pointed out that active construction of knowledge, participation in learning collaboratives, and building on the learners' interests and experiences outside of school are major threads in educational reform. Children's worlds outside of school are increasingly the "simulated" worlds of television and video games. Children do not usually create the television shows or video games. As television, video games, telephones, newspapers, libraries, and computer networks begin to be connected and woven together, they will be seen and experienced as essentially a "virtual world" in which we spend much of our time living, learning, working, and playing. The Internet provides a model for the future information infrastructure in which children do participate in the construction of simulated worlds and learn to make connections between the physical world and simulated worlds.

Some insights into the virtual world of the future are suggested by a kind of on-line community called a Multi-User Simulation Environment (MUSE). A MUSE is a virtual "world" running on a computer attached to a network. Any number of people may be in the world at once, each connected through a network. The people can "see" and communicate with one another in real time, but currently only through text. (Some people consider the text-only nature of MUSEs to be an advantage for learning, because the participants must visualize in their own minds rather than being shown the visual images on a screen.) People can design and construct rooms and objects, and give them behaviors and interactions. Hundreds of people can interact within this programmable microworld simultaneously. Some objects respond to the actions of the participants. For example, a MUSE at MIT is a virtual science museum with interactive exhibits. Its Cryogenics Lab, for example, includes an interactive experiment with liquid nitrogen and a balloon. When the visitor puts the inflated balloon into the flask of liquid nitrogen, the balloon deflates as it cools, and a pool of pale-blue liquid oxygen condenses inside it. When the visitor removes the deflated balloon from the liquid nitrogen bath, it gradually warms up and reinflates as the condensed pool of liquid oxygen boils away into a gas at room temperature. Before long, objects in such MUSE worlds will be connected through the Internet to distant resources, such as remote telescopes that the MUSE visitor can use to see the real distant planets and galaxies that are simulated in the MUSE.

While most participants in the 200 or so MUSEs so far established have been undergraduate students, elementary school children have begun to join and contribute. For example, MariMUSE is a virtual college and a partnership between a community college and an elementary school intended to increase the number of inner-city Phoenix students who obtain a college education. By participating in this program, elementary children, characterized as "at-risk" by their schools, became part of a global, inter-generational community where reading and writing were key to interactions. Children communicated with each other and created objects. They built castles and mansions, botanical gardens and caves within their virtual world, showing that although they often do not perform well on tests, they can create. MUSE gave them a place to create, to see the results of their work, and to share what they did with others. The work became public, which led to pride in construction. Students began to carry around dictionaries and do library research because they wanted to do quality work.

The children also learn about ways of interacting with people. Often, the members of a MUSE community devote considerable effort to working out the rules of behavior and governance of the community. Such a caring, cooperative spirit in a virtual world can be a welcome alternative to children who live in violent, uncaring physical communities, and can teach them that alternatives are possible.

Contributions Across Ages and Institutions

Educational reform requires new kinds of collaborations across institutions, such as closer relationships between universities and public schools. MariMUSE is one example of how the networks make it possible for students of different ages, for example in elementary schools and graduate schools, to help each other learn. Another example is the Earth Day Treasure Hunt. Three doctoral students from the University of Illinois worked together to coordinate the Hunt. Participants included the graduate student project coordinators, local elementary schools, and elementary, middle and high school classrooms throughout the United States and several European countries. The coordinators sent and received e-mail messages, organized and verified the clues submitted, assembled the treasure hunts, responded to transmission problems, and sent certificates to the participants

Twenty sites participated. The children ranged from grades 3 through 9. Children in each school wrote sets of clues and sent them to the coordinators, including the reference that they used in formulating the clues so the coordinators could verify the accuracy of the information. The graduate student coordinators reviewed the accuracy of the information and categorized the hunts as easy, medium, hard, or challenging. More than 100 sets of clues were verified and assembled into treasure hunts in which all children participated, to the apparent benefit of all concerned. The graduate students benefited by having an opportunity to work directly with children from diverse backgrounds. This project also created a model that has been copied and modified by others.

Support for Colleagueship and Restructuring

Networking facilitates grassroots participation in educational innovation; every individual and group involved in educational change and research can be a direct contributor to the collective process of innovation (Hunter, 1993a). Currently, teachers, school administrators, and educational researchers on the networks contribute to each others' development and creativity by exchanging ideas, experience, and information on every conceivable topic in educational reform—specific curriculum innovations, absentee policies, cooperative learning strategies, connections between research and practice, parental involvement in schooling, and every other concern of educators. A common observation by teachers is, "What I like best about the Internet is that it requires minimal effort for me to share my lessons and ideas with my colleagues." Teachers and administrators find that the Internet provides a natural framework of support for their efforts at educational reform and school restructuring.

A good example of this is Common Knowledge: Pittsburgh (described later in more detail), which grew out of the on-line activities of teachers in the Pittsburgh Public Schools. As Common Knowledge: Pittsburgh has expanded, participating teachers have used the network to develop internal proposals through electronic mail within the school district, information servers maintained by the school district, and external resources and experts from all around the world. A remarkable feature of this process is the speed with which teachers move from being network neophytes to relatively sophisticated users of the resource.

Problems and Processes for Internet Infrastructure Development

These examples of learner and teacher contributions to the current Internet provide a glimpse of what is possible with today's technology, infrastructure, and organizational arrangements. However, the value people can contribute to the infrastructure, and the value they get from it, is limited by the local networking infrastructure, the tools and services on the Internet, and the free-for-all nature of most current virtual communities' interactions. Most contributions wind up as flotsam and jetsam on a vast chaotic sea of e-mail and newsgroup messages—with little order, discipline, structure, retrievability, review, or aggregation.

There has been considerable recent progress in developing software that makes it easier to get onto the networks and discover information from personal computers. As more people attempt to participate and more virtual communities are formed, we are gaining more insight into the kinds of tools and services needed for full participation, including user construction of information services. The Clinton-Gore Administration's National Information Infrastructure (NII) plan recognizes the importance of broad-based participation in the development of the Internet and the evolving nature of the NII:

The NII will be of maximum value to users if it is sufficiently "open" and interactive so that users can develop new services and applications or exchange information among themselves, without waiting for services to be offered by the firms that operate the NII. In this way, users will develop new "electronic communities" and share knowledge and experiences that can improve the way that they learn, work, play, and participate in the American democracy (NTIA, 1993).

Current User Tools for Internetworking

Several tools are currently used by learners and teachers to provide information, knowledge, advice, technical assistance, and project collaboration to others on the networks. The most common is electronic mail, either personal or to mailing list groups. KIDSPHERE is the oldest and most popular Internet mailing list for educators. Founded as KIDSNET by Patt Haring in New York in May 1989 and maintained since September 1989 by Robert Carlitz of the University of Pittsburgh, it is frequently used by newcomers to the network to help them get oriented. The KIDSPHERE archive contains thousands of messages, and the list currently serves about 10,000 people, primarily teachers who provide information to each other. Newsgroups, bulletin boards, file exchanges, and Gopher and MOSAIC servers are also common mechanisms.

Users invent new mechanisms, too. For example, NEWSDAY is a multi-curricular project of the FrEdMail network, in which students at each participating school produce a local newspaper based on the news dispatches submitted to the NEWSDAY newswire by student correspondents. Students become news gatherers and reporters, editors, layout and graphics artists, and publishers. This involvement with national and international news leads to an understanding of broad issues that transcend local concerns. Schools produce their papers in various ways, ranging from simple cut and paste to desktop publishing. Participants receive the newspapers produced by all other participants in the project.

A small but growing number of schools and school districts publish their work through Gopher servers or World Wide Web servers. For example, elementary school students in the Ralph Bunche school in New York City publish their discussions and theories about shadows, the earth, and the sun (Newman et al, in press; Newman 1993a). At Gonzaga High School in Washington

D.C., students and their teachers are creating an Internet World Wide Web server on the subject of earth system science. Students use systems modeling software (STELLA II), data visualization tools (NCSA Image and NCSA Collage), and data from NASA databases to research earth system science topics. In each project the students conduct background research; create hypotheses; develop a strategy for data search, investigation, and testing; model the system qualitatively and quantitatively; and communicate their findings through a hypermedia document using NCSA Mosaic on the Internet. The teachers, Mike Keeler and Farzad Mahootian, are collaborating with teachers in other D.C. schools to form an exchange of such models and course materials through their Internet server.

Learning from Testbeds for Educational Networking

To help base decisions about investment in information infrastructure on a more informed and empirical basis, in 1992 the National Science Foundation funded the pilot phase of four consortia to develop infrastructure and applications of computer and communications networks to support innovation in science and mathematics education (Hunter, 1993b). These consortia, involving industry, higher education, K-12 schools, and other institutions, establish a set of conditions—institutional, technical, educational—that enable teachers, students, scientists, engineers, educational researchers and educational administrators to determine benefits and costs of using the Internet to support innovations and reforms in education. The innovations address most key aspects of education: professional development for teachers, classroom science and mathematics instruction, informal science education, teacher preparation, assessment of student learning, project-based science learning, curriculum development, school restructuring, and state systemic initiatives. Findings from these testbeds are intended to help decision makers in government, the community, and industry make better decisions concerning investments in networking technology and information infrastructure for education.

Each testbed is developing and testing a different approach to building a cost-effective infrastructure to support educational networking applications. Each is encountering limitations in the existing school and Internet infrastructure technology and services.

Building Local Networking Infrastructure

Currently, few teachers and students in elementary and secondary schools have access to the Internet. Those who do have some form of connectivity typically have only electronic mail—which, though extremely useful, is the lowest level of access. Furthermore, it is rare to find a teacher's or student's computer that is connected both to a local area network within the school and to the Internet. In fact, most teachers who use e-mail find it easier to do so from home than from school because they do not have a telephone at school. Therefore, Internet-based learning activities are not an integral part of curriculum or school culture; rather, they are a supplementary kind of activity, usually initiated by one or two innovative teachers in a school.

The National School Network Testbed led by BBN focuses on three main ideas: first, that the benefits of the Internet will not be apparent in a school until all students and teachers have ready and easy access to both their local network and the Internet from their desktops or laptops; second, that students, teachers and others can learn by constructing knowledge and sharing that knowledge on their local network and the Internet; and third, that the combination of universal access and user construction of knowledge will result in a transformation of the school culture. The testbed is developing and testing an approach to school networking that would support a wide range of applications for teachers, students and administrators in a school or school district. They are testing system architectures intended to enable cost-effective "scaling up" of the infrastructure, with a focus on the local (e.g., school or school district) infrastructure and how it interfaces to the Internet. They have designed and developed a family of technologies called "Copernicus" that move away from the "telecomputing" paradigm that depends on a central computing resource or host computer to which classroom computers connect as terminals. The technologies feature:

- *Distributed network technology.* "Distributed" means that the computing power of all the users' computers is used, rather than all of the computing power being centralized in a host computer. "Distributed" also means that functions such as initiating and offering information services are decentralized organizationally. Distribution, in contrast to centralization, supports local initiative in development of and access to resources.

- *Client-server model of computing.* In a typical client-server configuration, a client program runs on the user's personal computer, providing a familiar and appropriate interface to the applications and information. The client program knows how to interact with its corresponding server software to exchange information and operations. The server software may reside on a computer anywhere in the network (including the user's own computer). The client-server arrangement has numerous advantages over the host-terminal configuration, in which the user's computer acts as a dumb terminal and the user interacts directly with a remote, centralized host computer. Because the client and server operate with agreed-upon protocols, functionally equivalent client software can be implemented on different makes and models of user computers— thus a person can participate comfortably in a network service using one of a variety of personal computers, and the server can serve people using many different personal computers.

- *Open* software and hardware platforms that all developers can use and extend using the public *standards* for network communications (TCP/IP, the Internet protocol suite).

The schools, school districts and state education agencies in this testbed are investigating whether this family of technologies can live up to its promise as a basis for scaling up the network from the current very low level of participation within a school or local community to universal participation. The term "participation" is used here instead of "access," because the educational purpose is to enable all learners, teachers, and others such as curriculum specialists and administrators to participate in the construction of knowledge, services, and communities. The promise of these technologies includes the ease-of-use afforded by the client-server model and the smooth transition from a single computer to multiple computers at a school site afforded by Internet protocol connections. These technologies may also increase the value of schools' network connections by permitting them direct access to multiple projects and resources, and help keep costs manageable by allowing schools to join the network gradually and flexibly— inviting incremental investment without dead ends (Newman, 1993b).

The Copernicus Internet Server uses the client-server model for all the services it supports, including the management function. This easy-to-use software allows non-technical people from their desktop computers to manage resources on the Copernicus server— for example, to create and modify personal e-mail accounts, mailing lists, and newsgroups (bulletin boards), a task that normally requires the technical abilities of a Unix system administrator. Versions under development add management of Gopher, World Wide Web, and WAIS databases, and other system housekeeping tasks. They are also extending the functionality of several public-domain user (client) programs to make them more suitable for a classroom and school environment—for example, allowing several children or teachers to have their own private accounts and files on the same personal computer.

Evolution of District-Wide Infrastructure

Individual schools are not autonomous: they are part of a school district, a local community, and a state education system. If internetworking is to support educational reform, the infrastructure must encompass the entire school district and community. Another testbed project, known as Common Knowledge: Pittsburgh (CK:P) has been pioneering Internet support for curriculum reform and restructuring of a large city school district. CK:P is a collaboration involving the Pittsburgh Public Schools, the Pittsburgh Supercomputing Center and the University of Pittsburgh. It aims to develop networking activities with a curricular focus and to gradually institutionalize the use of networking technology throughout the Pittsburgh Public Schools. The project's long-range goal, once connectivity is provided for all students and teachers in the Pittsburgh Public Schools, is to use this resource in support of curricular activities in all subject areas and at all grade levels. This evolution of networking is taking place in the context of a major restructuring of the school district that places more responsibility on local schools for management and curriculum innovation than the previous organization did. The project brings to bear the technical resources of the Pittsburgh Supercomputing Center and uses those resources not only to design and implement a network for the school district but also to foster within the school district the expertise necessary to maintain this facility and use it in the ongoing process of curriculum development and revision.

The history of the project explains how this process can work. Beginning around 1990 a number of network access accounts were created on computers at the University of Pittsburgh. A simple menu system patterned upon one developed for the Texas Educational Network was used to guide people to a set of Internet resources. Teachers were encouraged to use the KIDSPHERE mailing list to contact other teachers around the world and begin to develop activities for classroom use. This stage of activity attracted the interest of many innovative teachers in the school district, and this group began to show network resources to other teachers and to school administrators. Their experience formed the substance for a successful proposal to the National Science Foundation to fund the CK:P testbed.

With the availability of formal funding, the project moved to support projects at individual school sites through the installation of local area networks with connectivity to the Internet. To compensate for the low speed of the inexpensive dialup routers used for Internet connectivity, each site was equipped with a local information server. An internal grants program encourages competition among schools for expansion sites and has proved extremely successful in stimulating school-based initiatives around the city. At the time of this writing, proposals were under review from more than 40% of all the schools in the city; future implementation will be limited only by the availability of funds for hardware.

While pursuing an essentially grass-roots approach to implementation, CK:P has taken care to involve administrators throughout the district, particularly the regional principals to whom all school principals in the school district now report, as well as the support staff central to the district's school restructuring efforts. During the competitive grants process teachers from sites wishing to join the project have visited the project's beta test site, allowing them to see the sort of hardware that will be available under the competitive grants and to see examples of Internet resources currently in use in school district classrooms. Information about CK:P is disseminated internally and externally through the project's Internet gopher. This facility is maintained by school district personnel.

The whole process has been designed to introduce new technology to the district gradually, allowing teachers and administrators to gain enough familiarity with the technology so as to be able to claim ownership to it and apply it in their own way in their schools and classrooms. The attitude is to use the technology as a tool for teaching and learning and to provide teachers with the support necessary to master the use of these tools and to apply them successfully in the curriculum.

Network Support for Virtual Communities

Because of the lack of local school, school district and community infrastructure for internetworking, most Internet learning and teaching has been among people in virtual communities. Thus far, it has been mainly the most adventuresome and innovative teachers who have participated in virtual communities. Virtual communities are different from groups of people who work in the same organization or who live in the same neighborhood, because their members are distributed geographically, culturally, temporally, or institutionally.

The testbed consortium led by TERC is developing software and learning activities to support collaborative inquiry projects in virtual communities of teachers, students and scientists (Hunter, 1993c). A major design goal is to make it easy for any teachers, students, and scientists to participate in networked educational projects, using whatever telecommunications capability is available to them. Information infrastructure will continue to evolve unevenly across the nation and world. People in some schools might call a local community-based telecommunications bulletin board that has an e-mail gateway to the Internet; other schools might have a statewide educational network with Internet access; while still others might be part of an advanced networking infrastructure with broadband capabilities exceeding those of the current Internet. The designers seek to provide equitable access to projects and virtual communities despite disparities in the overall infrastructure and to make it easy for people to do their work once they are connected. In the current state of the Internet, such a strategy is difficult to implement due to the diversity of existing "on ramps" to the information highway and the lack of technical skills in elementary and secondary educational institutions and the state and regional organizations that support schools. The metaphor of "on ramps" to the information highway encompasses many variables, such as the power and functionality of the users' personal computer hardware, system software, and tools; the nature of the local area network and storage capacities within the school or other organization; the methods used to make the connection; the bandwidth of the connection; the protocols for internetworking; and several others.

Scaling Up: Technical Infrastructure Services Needed to Encourage Broad-based Contributions

From a technical standpoint, the Internet and the future NII consist of three tiers (each of which contains several layers not discussed here):

(1) *Bitways*—the physical-level transport that moves digital data such as text, numeric data, graphics, voice, and video. It is made up of diverse physical media, such as fiber optics, copper wires, satellites, cables, switches, local area networks and computers.

(2) *Services*—general-purpose services that are used by many different applications. Examples include electronic mail, file transfer, data security, data interchange and format conversion, directories.

(3) *Applications*—specific programs and end-user applications in different areas such as education, libraries, manufacturing, electronic commerce.

While much attention has been paid to the creation of the *bitways* that would allow physical access to the Internet, the development of *applications* has been severely hampered by the Internet's current limited repertoire of generic *services*. Developers of educational applications and tools such as those in government-supported educational networking testbeds spend a substantial proportion of their very limited resources inventing and creating such services. Progress could be much faster and more efficient if each project did not have to invent basic services but rather could build upon a common services infrastructure. For example, nearly all educational networking projects (as well as projects and applications in other sectors) involve people initiating and managing lists of participants in virtual communities; creating, accessing, managing, and archiving relevant distributed resources; and providing technical assistance to participants. If services to support such activities were as ubiquitous and standardized as electronic mail and file transfer protocols are today, the following benefits would be likely:

• Non-technical people would face fewer barriers to making contributions to the infrastructure

• The information that people do contribute to the infrastructure would be easier to locate and access

• The limited resources for educational innovation could be spent on application-relevant inventions rather than basic services

• There could be more rapid progress in developing standards at the application level, thereby increasing the value of individual contributions to knowledge

• The quality of educational applications could improve much more rapidly

• Educational publishers and other service providers would be more likely to invest in this market

• Educational reform efforts such as new curricula and assessment projects would be more likely to take advantage of the power of networked resources.

Investment in research and development and standards work to make the "services" tier more robust would benefit more people in the long run than would an investment in a "pilot project" in one particular application or sector. At the same time, such services need to be tested and evolved in the context of several application areas in order to ensure their generality and usefulness. A possible strategy for federal agencies is to fund work to advance the generic services tier and to test these services through use in other government-funded (as well as other) networking applications and pilot projects. Such a strategy would require greater coordination across agencies than presently exists.

Questions about Scaling Up

"Scaling up" is a term used to refer to a wide range of issues about participation in the Internet and the information infrastructure. Throughout this chapter we have considered some of the many factors that affect the value of contributions made by individuals and groups to the larger Information Infrastructure. Thus we can see that scaling up is not a simple matter of physically connecting more people to the Internet. Rather, scaling up has many dimensions—technical, organizational, educational, economic, social. What is to be maximized, overall? Is it the number of people who have access to the networks? Is it the ease with which these people can learn to take advantage of the resources? Is it the educational opportunities they have had, which make them competent managers of information and creators of knowledge? Is it the contributions they have an opportunity to make? Is it the accessibility of their contributions to others, within and outside of their own local and virtual communities? Is it the social creativity and solutions to problems that result from this synergy? Is it the effectiveness of a new economy based somehow on individuals' (or groups') contributions to knowledge?

If internetworking and the National Information Infrastructure are to support the kinds of educational reform and transformation discussed here, then "scaling up" has to mean all these things, and more. But if this is agreed to, then decisions made by government agencies, corporations, and communities about investment in the various NII components should take into account the mechanisms needed to make progress on all of these fronts. We must constantly update our thinking on these matters. The following principles may help to guide our decision making, particularly with regard to elementary and secondary education:

1) Responsibility for learning and managing information must be shared by all. The pace of change is too fast for individuals to depend totally on others to structure their learning and information for them; pre-planned courses, textbooks, teacher training programs, technical support staff, and the like may not always be available to meet an individual's particular learning need. New curriculum frameworks, instructional materials, assessment and testing schemes, and teacher training programs should take into account these increased responsibilities for information management. Similarly, software and networked information services for educational purposes should be designed with the assumption that users will be taking on these responsibilities. For example, "ease of use" is a commonly called-for characteristic of networks, information services, and software, but there is always a trade-off to be made between ease of use and complexity or functionality. In the quest for "ease of use" of information in the Internet, we must be careful not to exclude people from participation in the more complex and rewarding tasks of constructing knowledge. Students need to learn how to deal with phenomena that are new and more complex than they are "ready" for, and get opportunities to make sense out of situations before they understand all the first principles.

2) Responsibility for teaching and mentoring must be shared more widely than in the past. Classroom teachers can not be expected to have expertise in all the areas of knowledge their students are encountering. The Internet provides new opportunities for teaching by people whose primary work is not formally teaching, but who have expertise in industry and other public sectors. Incentives to perform these part-time and out-of-school teaching and mentoring roles need to be devised. Communities and school districts making an investment in new curricula or technology should not attempt to overlay such innovations on outmoded methods of operation of schools; rather they should look broadly for new opportunities to engage people in nontraditional roles.

3) Follow the "low threshold, open growth" principle when designing network services, applications, and projects. For the foreseeable future and maybe forever, different people will have access to different levels and kinds of functionality in their personal comput-

ers, local networks, servers, storage, software, bandwidth to the wide area networks, and so forth. We should design internetworked services, applications, projects, and virtual communities in such a way that people can join in at some very low threshold. At the same time, if we wish to make progress in the quality and range of services and applications, we must also design these such that participants can take advantage of greater functionality as it becomes available to them. For example, applications involving graphics or video images via World Wide Web should also wherever possible offer at least a subset of the application in text via e-mail, since text-only e-mail is the lowest common denominator for access around the world.

4) Evolve educational reforms in synchrony with the evolving information infrastructure. As a society, we are working hard on "educational reform" at the same time that we are evolving new information infrastructure. There is a great danger that enormous efforts now put into educational "reforms" will turn out to be irrelevant to the circumstances of learning and working in a networked, knowledge-creative society. Current investments in reformed curriculum frameworks, standards, assessments, teacher in-service programs, and the like should take advantage of networking to reduce industrial-age constraints; at the same time, they can contribute vitally to the evolving information infrastructure, to the learning benefit of everyone.

Conclusion: Information Infrastructure and Educational Transformation

In conclusion, it is important to appreciate the interdependence of education and internetworking. In shaping the evolution of the information infrastructure, we are at the same time shaping the future educational system and opportunities for learning. One of the world's first visionaries to articulate this relationship was Yoneji Masuda, author of *The Information Society as Post Industrial Society* (Masuda, 1980). He believed that the first and most important effect of the worldwide networked society would be transformation in the educational system. In his vision, the changes in education would be of five main kinds:

• The first change will be to lift education out of the restrictions of formal schools. The present closed educational environment will be replaced by an open educational environment, made up of knowledge networks. It will eradicate the educational gaps between town and countryside, and between industrial and non-industrialized countries.

• The second change will be the introduction of a personal type of education, suited to the ability of each individual, replacing the traditional uniform system of collective education with a system determined by individual ability and choice. . . . This means that the present education system, graded according to age, will be supplanted by a system that allows the people's abilities to move on to advanced courses, irrespective of age. . . .

• Thirdly, the system of self-learning will become the leading form of education. . . . When a system of self-learning is introduced, teachers will act as advisers or counselors. . . . students will be able to study by themselves, watching CRT displays and conversing with a computer and with other people by computer.

• The fourth change will be to knowledge-creative education. Education in this industrial society aims at cramming the heads of students with bits of information and training them in techniques. This will be replaced with knowledge-creative education and training, because the information society will develop through information values into a high knowledge-creation society.

• The fifth change will mean lifetime education. . . . greater importance will be attached to the education of adults and even older people, because this will be necessary to enable adults and elderly people to adapt themselves to the changes of the information society. . . . (Masuda 1980, p. 66).

Masuda's vision has much in common with the goals of current-day educational reformers. We now have a window of opportunity to shape the evolving Internet and the larger information infrastructure in ways that will help develop the abilities and contributions of all citizens.

Notes

[1] By "internetworking" I mean not just the physical connection and operation of telecommunications networks and computers, but also the software, information, standards, and people who participate in networked communities.

[2] The "information infrastructure" is an evolving concept that encompasses not only the networks, information, software, standards and people on the Internet, but also the seamless interconnection of all information and media such as television, libraries, and voice communication. The Internet is viewed as the model, or precursor, to the National Information Infrastructure.

References

AAAS (1989). *Science for All Americans: Project 2061.* Washington DC: American Association for the Advancement of Science.

Berenfeld, Boris (1993). A moment of glory in San Antonio. *Hands On!* Vol. 16(3), Fall 1993. Cambridge, MA: TERC.

Hunter, Beverly (1992). "Linking for Learning: Computer-and-Communications Network Support for Nationwide Innovation in Education". *J. Science Education and Technology,* Vol. 1, No. 1, pp. 23–33.

Hunter, Beverly (1993a). Internetworking: Coordinating technology for systemic reform. *Communications of the ACM.,* May 1993, pp. 42–46.

Hunter, Beverly (1993b). NSF's Networked Testbeds Inform Innovation in Science Education. *T.H.E. Journal,* October 1993.

Hunter, Beverly (1993c). Collaborative Inquiry in Networked Communities. *Hands On!* 16(2), Fall 1993. Cambridge, MA: TERC.

IAEEA (International Association for the Evaluation of Educational Achievement) (1987). *The Underachieving Curriculum: A National Report on the Second International Mathematics Study.* Champaign IL: Stipes Publishing.

Leonard, George B. (1968). *Education And Ecstasy.* New York: Delacorte Press.

Masuda, Yoneji (1980). *The Information Society as Post-Industrial Society.* Washington DC.: World Future Society.

NCEE (1991). *America's Choice: High Skills or Low Wages.* Rochester, NY: National Center for Education and the Economy.

NCTM (1989). *Curriculum Standards for Mathematics.* Reston, VA: National Council of Teachers of Mathematics.

NCTM (1991, 1989). *Professional Standards for Teaching Mathematics.* Reston, VA: National Council of Teachers of Mathematics.

NGA (1986). *Time for Results: The Governors' 1991 Report on Education.* Washington DC: National Governors Association.

Newman, Denis (1993a). School networks: Delivery or access. *Communications of the ACM.* May 1993, pp. 42–46.

Newman, Denis (1993b). Getting the NII to school: A roadmap to universal access. BBN Position Paper. Cambridge: Bolt Beranek & Newman Inc.

Newman, Denis, Paul Reese, and A. Huggins (in press). The Ralph Bunche Computer Mini-School: A Design for individual and community work. Chapter to appear in Hawkins & Collins, eds., *Design Experiments: Restructuring through Technology.* Cambridge: Cambridge University Press.

NTIA (1993). *The National Information Infrastructure: Agenda for Action.* Washington: Dept. of Commerce, NTIA.

OERI (1993). *Using Technology to Support Education Reform.* Washington, DC: Office of Educational Research and Improvement.

Reich, Robert (1991) *The Work of Nations.: Preparing Ourselves for 21st Century Capitalism.* New York: Vintage Books.

Riel, Margaret (1990). Cooperative learning across classrooms in electronic Learning Circles. *Instructional Science,* 19: 445–466.

Riel, Margaret, and James Levin (1990). Building electronic communities: success and failure in computer networking. *Instructional Science,* 19, 145–169.

Songer, Nancy (1994). Presentation at the National Science Foundation Invited Conference on Systemic Reform in Science Education, Washington DC, February 24, 1994.

SCANS (1992). *Learning a Living: A Blueprint for High Performance.* Washington, DC: The Secretary's Commission on Achieving Necessary Skills .

Weston, Rachel (1994). "Networks: Where have you been all my life?" National School Networking Essay Contest Winner (contest@lupine.nsi.nasa.gov).

Issues in the Development of Community Cooperative Networks

Frank Odasz

Introduction

For decades there has been the promise that one day low-cost, portable microcomputers linked to global networks would allow creative individuals the opportunity to engage in rewarding work regardless of their location or schedule. Such unprecedented flexibility could bring a new era of economic freedom for workers, and would provide a choice of lifestyle and residential location, freedom to travel, and freedom to innovate. This promise of individual economic freedom, job satisfaction, and mobility appears almost within reach given today's powerful notebook and home computers, which facilitate increasing citizen access to the global Internet. The federal National Information Infrastructure (NII) initiative has recently been reinforced by several announcements of major corporate investments totaling billions of dollars. This combination of public and private actions is moving us closer to the vision of public participation in widespread global networks, raising questions as to the potential economic benefits of networking.

Prominent among these questions is the extent of inconsistency between the corporate and individual visions of the potential benefits of an NII. Are these visions the same, or mutually exclusive? Is economic freedom for individuals the goal of the huge corporate initiatives? Or do they aim to secure billion dollar contracts providing entertainment services rather than services in support of individual and community economic benefit? What should be the leading vision?

Reflection on the history of cable television reminds us there is good reason for concern about these inconsistencies. In the 1970s, cable was promised as a new vehicle to provide education to the home. But today, far more shows center around the theme of murder than of education; corporations profit from "lowest-common-denominator entertainment" and have sidestepped cable's educational potential. We risk repeating this pattern with top-down implementation of the NII.

From the perspective of individual economic freedom, most of our informational needs are best served by textual, not visual, information. Most information that can really make a positive impact on individuals is textual; even that must first be finely honed. The prevailing assumption of federal NII discussions and corporate announcements, however, appears to be that expensive bandwidth with a video emphasis is what citizens need. These different assumptions or visions imply different implementations of information infrastructure, one consistent with the community and individual vision, one not.

Communities can avoid repeating the history of the cable example by implementing information infrastructure through grass roots efforts, focused on achieving local economic and social benefits in a cost efficient manner. The impetus for making economic freedom a reality for workers appears to be coming from the bottom, not the top. Distributed conferencing, combining bulletin board systems and Internet communities, has been shown to provide affordable global communications. An estimated 40,000,000 people worldwide use bulletin board systems (BBSs), a number only recently reached by the Internet.

While there are more than 100,000 electronic bulletin board systems in the United States, minimal governmental or corporate support has been demonstrated for the proliferation of these versatile systems in communities. Grassroots innovators have predominantly had to do for themselves what common sense dictates we should be doing as a nation. The industrial age blossomed through the diverse innovations of tens of thousands of garage tinkerers. Here at the emergence of the information age, the need

exists, nationally, for a similar renaissance of widespread inventive-
ness, spurred by personal global communications systems, home
PC's and communicating notebook computers, and local networks, beginning with the most affordable. Federal funding for
grassroots innovation is necessary to reach our national goal of an
NII based on practical applications: "Value-pull, not Tech-push."

The next section examines the benefits of networking to individuals and communities. This is followed by a discussion of what
is necessary in order to achieve those benefits. The paper then
presents various options for communities that wish to take advantage of networking, and briefly considers some of the barriers to
widespread network use. The last section outlines a plan that states
could follow to encourage the use of computer networks. This
paper argues that grassroots innovations demonstrate more potential for a truly beneficial NII than the visions of the corporate giants.
Federal funding of grassroots innovations is necessary to provide
the diversity of applications needed for a successful NII.

Benefits to Communities of Networking

The inconsistencies between the corporate and individual visions
of networking may be based in part on different definitions of
benefits. Do benefits to individuals motivate any part of the corporate vision? Are there unsubstantiated assumptions about what the
"obvious benefits" should be? The following is an attempt to
identify what people need for greater economic freedom.

Access to Global Niche Markets

Networking will enable citizens and their local businesses to create
and pursue entrepreneurial opportunities through global niche
markets. The Internet will accelerate the evolution of an electroni-
cally-connected global economy. For example, corporations with
offices in different cities and countries can use electronic communications to coordinate manufacturing, management and marketing. Global niche markets will become accessible even to individual
entrepreneurs. Small manufacturers will have the option to co-
contract with other manufacturers and to co-market products with

unprecedented flexibility. The emerging telepreneurial potential is limitless.

Rebuilt Communities and a New Sense of Purposeful Belonging

In a slower, perhaps more humane era, our communities were based on purpose. The baker provided the baked goods, the blacksmith worked the steel, the butcher prepared the meat, and everyone needed each other. Today, with the supermarket across the street from the drygoods discounter, we do not experience interdependence as we once did. We often do not know our next-door neighbors. We often do not have an identifiable reason to maintain a sense of community. Our schedules are so full that community socializing is becoming a rarity. We've lost our sense of place, of belonging. Because this is a vital human need, many are rediscovering a sense of purposeful belonging through on-line communities.

In the past, communities have formed to meet needs as a group that we cannot meet as individuals. Today, group protection from marauding animals or enemies is being replaced by group protection from the assaults of constant change and too much information. As information networking begins to enter mainstream society, each of us discovers new sources of data in our specific areas of interest, and suffers from the increasing pressure of information overload. We're finding we have a new purpose, a genuine need, to reestablish a support community. We're finding we need to ask those with the expertise, "What is it I really need to know about telecommuting, the Internet, electronic access to federal services, on-line distance learning, telepreneurship, and using my computer to get a better job?" Networking increases the opportunities for collaboration, which helps protect individuals from information overload.

Networks can also link people in "virtual" communities. Urban isolation can be every bit as real as rural isolation. Networking makes it possible to be "relationship-rich" even when one might feel isolated in one's local environment. Isolated individuals without access to supportive on-line communities are likely to continue to be "relationship-poor."

Home-Based Business and Social Action Opportunities

Home-based businesses are the fastest-growing provider of jobs nationally. Business development incubators should encourage the use of technology in establishing home-based businesses, instead of trailing the trend.

It is already technically feasible for individuals to collect highly specific information gleaned from the Internet for personal use or to be sold from a home-based microcomputer as a cottage industry. An on-line class, taught via modem from the home, on how to establish such a home business could be another enterprise. One community might create a support service for other communities attempting to start a community network by providing validating, inspirational stories or models of individual telepreneurial successes and step-by-step lessons on how to bring individual community members on-line to form a mutually supportive on-line community network.

Networking, by its very nature, leads away from rigid stratified structures and toward informal, lateral, socially supportive learning partnerships. All of us can learn enough to help someone else survive. Once this is understood by the goodhearted among us, the incredible power of networked, knowledgeable, caring people taking purposeful collaborative action may begin to effect worldwide change, transcending governments, cultures and religions.

Amnesty International's use of the Internet is but one example. Daily "Urgent Alerts" go out via the Internet to broadcast human rights violations and solicit letters of protest from Amnesty International members to government officials. Hundreds of political prisoners have been freed because of the pressure of this global publicity.

What Is Needed to Achieve These Benefits

Communities need to learn how to enhance their local information infrastructure, to rebuild and rehumanize from within through the many advantages of local telecomputing, and to use those same developed skills in a global context via the Internet. Communities will be better served if NII implementation places emphasis on assisting citizens to access that information proven to be beneficial, and not just on providing the physical connection.

Community Awareness and Action

Communities are beginning to realize they need to take a proactive stance toward raising local awareness of the opportunities created by telecomputing. The benefits of networking cannot be achieved without an awareness of what they are. Locally accessible low-cost community networks allow any community to provide training opportunities for its citizens that are targeted toward community strengths and the best potential economic opportunities. Each community must take practical steps to assure that citizens become aware of the maximum available benefits of connectivity at minimal cost. In contrast, training provided by the federal government would not be likely to have a local focus on a community's most promising opportunities or necessarily reflect a budget-sensitive approach.

Equitable Access

With low-end jobs disappearing, we can't afford to leave anyone behind as our nation's economy becomes more information-based. As networking becomes the highway to commute to work, we need to assure that everyone finds the means to travel. Thus, equitable access is an essential element of local networking implementation, and is discussed in depth in the outline of implementation options presented later in this paper.

Skills for an Information Economy

The abilities to glean specific information rapidly from global sources and to work collaboratively with others to mold that information into entrepreneurial opportunities through global niche markets appear to be the key skills required for success in the emerging global info-gathering society. As the rate of change increases, success depends more and more on an individual's ability to learn steadily, and to make decisions based on up-to-the-minute information.

Consider two visions of this future. First, an age of independent individuals in ruthless competition with each other on a global basis, with most people lacking the ability to compete. Now consider a second scenario: The competition of the industrial age is giving way to information-age collaboration as a strategy for success. While the key to success in the industrial age was to control and protect information, the key to success in the information age may be the ability to partner with those who represent sources of continually expanding expertise beyond one's own specialty. The ability to access sources of highly specific expertise and to manufacture this knowledge into unique information products and courses of action is likely to be key to future commercial success for individuals as well as businesses.

Perhaps those who collaborate best to share information with others will be the most successful entrepreneurs, a key national resource. The Internet offers many entrepreneurial opportunities in the global marketplace to individuals who combine telecommunications and collaborative skills with an entrepreneurial spirit. The nations that first establish a high degree of citizen "teleliteracy" may well become the new global economic leaders. Thus, successful implementation of the economic potential of networking must emphasize the development of these skills.

Support Communities

Collaboration is essential to achieving the benefits of networking, as it helps protect individuals from information overload. Very few of us are able to remain disconnected from the increasing pace of modern life. Information becomes obsolete ever more rapidly; none of us can keep up on all arenas of activity, but each of us does keep up on at least a few circles of activity and expertise. We need to learn how to partner with others who know more than we do, both within and outside our local communities, in return for sharing our own particular expertise and support.

Value vs. Volume

Many technologies are sold as solutions before they have proved their benefits. We need to assess the value of the connectivity options, rather than being dazzled by technological glitz, in order to not waste resources on technological options not necessary for achieving the benefits of networking. Local implementation increases the ability of citizens to make these comparisons.

Do we need really need hundreds of pages per second, or would five pages per minute suffice? It should not be assumed that faster transmission technologies will automatically result in increased access to the information that will make a significant positive change in our lives. Transmission speed does not automatically equate to value of information.

Information condenses to knowledge, which condenses to wisdom; economic value is added through this process. The highest-value information is typically condensed information that may not require more than the simplest of transmission technologies to deliver. Given this premise, perhaps the highest-value network service would be e-mail access to experts who provide condensed information and training targeted to individuals' specific needs. Equity of access to such human-mediated services must be assured.

Opportunities for BBSs as Means for Achieving These Benefits

Options for Internet and BBS Access

This section outlines a model for providing equitable public access to local and national networked information sources. Each community would have a BBS, accessible from home computers, schools, and public sites. Each community would customize its BBS so that users would be guided to those resources most valuable to them. In addition, these local networks would help to integrate communities by facilitating communication. These BBSs would connect to the Internet nightly, providing communication with those outside the local community and an affordable initial level of access to the vast resources of the Internet for all communities in the short-term.

How can a National Information Infrastructure be fairly implemented? Those who receive gigabit bandwidth services may enjoy disproportionate advantages over those, perhaps in the rural United States, who do not. How can we all move forward together?

Local electronic bulletin board systems offer a minimal-cost network server model to provide store-and-forward Internet e-mail services, as well as local free access to customized menus containing self-directed training and high-value information specific to the local community, gleaned from the Internet. These can be supplemented by SLIP access to full Internet only as needed, within local budget restraints.

Big Sky Telegraph

Big Sky Telegraph (BST) is an example of the kind of service provider that can provide equitable public access to the Internet, with an emphasis on e-mail. Eighty per cent of Internet use is for human communications; e-mail, combined with access to librarians with full Internet, can bring most benefits of the Internet to citizens using this most affordable, scaleable form of ubiquitous access. BST's prime goal is to demonstrate low-cost, high-imagination networking models that can run on either low-end or high-end equipment.

BST was founded in 1988. Its first project was to offer an on-line course via modem to rural K-12 teachers, many of whom were teaching in one-or two-room schools. BST has sponsored the creation of six community BBSs. A few of these are outfitted with Internet e-mail, Internet self-teaching lessons, lists of K-12 network projects, graphics, customized databases, and document libraries with carefully selected information on how networking can help K-12 education, entrepreneurship, and network literacy.

BST's internal network runs on a single personal computer (486 PC) with a gigabyte hard drive and 8 modems, with an additional 16 ports linked to 90 PCs on the Western Montana College campus. BST has full Internet connectivity, and the community networks can send e-mail to and from the Internet through BST. The BST network can be reached by long-distance phone calls and through the Internet. Internet e-mail is passed through BST to local bulletin boards and to specific individuals through off-line readers and "point disks." (More on off-line readers and point disks below.)

BST actively promotes and facilitates the use of community networks, offering free access and on-line lessons covering the basics of networking and modem use. BST also serves as a clearing-house of educational projects and community networking models and related information.

Networking in Action

BBSs such as those developed by Big Sky Telegraph are simple to put in place; once operating, they can be used for any number of projects.

Cynthia Denton, a teacher in Hobson, MT (Population 200), took the on-line course from Big Sky Telegraph and with BST's assistance established the Russell Country BBS on her home PC. Hobson residents now have free access to Internet e-mail and lessons, the state legislative information office, weather and travel reports, and interactive conferences from the Internet. Denton has created the nation's first Native American on-line computer art gallery and hosts graphic images of products created in Hobson and on Native American reservations for sale globally.

Denton taught her third-graders keyboarding skills by having them correspond with third-graders in Japan and Australia. Her high school students taught students in Kamchatka (formerly part of the USSR) how to sell their consulting services to an interna-tional travel business. The "K12net" conferences locally available on her system are exchanged among 300 teacher-run bulletin board systems globally through short automated phone calls each night. These same conferences appear as Internet newsgroups.

Denton's third-graders could potentially exchange lists of locally produced goods with other third-graders worldwide, and advise their parents about verifiable global trade opportunities among small businesses. Telepreneurship training could start as early as the third grade to teach the concepts and skills students will doubtless need to be successful. School-based community net-works could provide convenient interaction with the local business community as we all look toward what we need to be teaching our students and citizens about the shifting world of work.

BBSs as Network Servers

Internet access is not an all-or-nothing issue; there are different levels of access and benefit. For many Internet users, the key power of the Internet is the connection to other minds—the Internet as a community. Reliable, convenient, and purposeful communications with 40 million Internet users is possible without full Internet access.

Internet messages stored on a local BBS for nightly transfer via high-speed modems can bring e-mail benefits virtually identical in most ways to expensive full Internet access. Even with full Internet connectivity, we must wait for our mail to be read and answered. For the purposes of building global communities of learning or trading based on interacting regularly with experts, the global Internet is within reach for any community member on a shoestring budget. A community's choice of over 15,000 Internet discussion groups can be "echoed" on local BBSs with great economy. Newsletters and listservs on rural and community development are already being shared worldwide. The potential is limited only by imagination, and for this fundamental level of connectivity, costs and bandwidth are virtually non-issues.

For many, the power of the Internet is the ability to instantly search databases and archives, and to obtain direct access to nearly 1.7 million on-line systems. While this capability has obvious merit, similar results can be achieved with BBSs because it is possible to store and forward many types of search requests. Thus, while there is not immediate interactivity, well-targeted searches can often locate information within 24 hours. This is true for use of FTP ordering of files and the use of Internet mail to automatically search many different forms of databases.

Initially, the most efficient searching strategy is to e-mail a librarian with superior searching skills and request that search results, and their interpretation, be sent via e-mail. (Many federal and public offices could provide more assistance for more citizens through the efficiencies of electronic mail without an increase in staff or funding.) For individuals and communities without the option of full Internet access, these options represent very acceptable temporary alternatives compared with the only other economic choice—access to nothing.

Careful analysis of how full Internet access is currently used for many commercial applications will show that many serious needs can be adequately satisfied through the bulletin board store-and-forward model. For uses requiring direct Internet connection, it is possible to make a simple modem call via long distance lines for a temporary full connection. Alternatively, a BBS can be set up to allow a temporary full Internet connection (intermittent SLIP connection) whenever users need such access. When it becomes more economical for an individual or community to pay for 24-hour Internet access (compared to the pay-for-what-you-need model), then full Internet access is warranted. Economics suggest this progressive model is necessary to avoid paying for underutilized Internet access.

An assumption prevails that the Internet is self-teaching. In fact, the greater cost of the Internet is not the connection, but the training required to fully benefit. Friendly, responsive, on-line librarians and mentors will be key to the successful implementation of any community network. Public and federal employees must learn how they can utilize the efficiencies of electronic mail to provide such responsiveness to citizens. Public service participation in on-line interaction should be encouraged by all citizens and government employees.

BBSs Help Integrate a Community

With a BBS, community involvement suddenly becomes possible through local discussion conferences, community-wide e-mail, local posting of "gems" from the Internet, and distributed conferences. Self-teaching or mentored lessons could be accessible locally to teach the skills necessary to enjoy increasing benefits from local and distributed telecomputing and the various levels of Internet access. Menus customized for the local community can provide local "fingertip" access to the best resources on the Internet. CD-ROMs are now available with Internet archives costing $20 per 600 megabytes for access via local networks.

Community organizations with full Internet access but no bulletin board system may lack access to the Internet from homes and the ability to interact on-line with the local community. Important as global access may be, it is usually perceived as a poor second to local community interaction. The optimal combination is to have a local BBS as a user-friendly "front-end" for the Internet as well as a convenient local community communications tool.

An additional benefit would be that the community and parents could dial in for school-related information. Student-to-student, student-to-librarian, parent-to-teacher, or student-to-teacher communications would be available from the home via local phone calls. A loaner laptop program could provide initial home access experiences for local citizens. The community outreach potential for schools has many advantages, such as involving community expertise in making K-12 education immediately relevant to real-world community needs. E-mail allows 24-hour contact between students and the community, opening doors to many new levels of interaction. Successful K-12 educational reform hinges on linking classroom instruction to relevant problems and issues within the local community. Education need not be confined to 50-minute periods that end at 3:00 p.m. five days a week.

Community networks can benefit the government by providing the training necessary for citizens to access government information electronically. Local experts can assist the general public in accessing information and services through the convenience of e-mail. Those government services most important for a given community can be tailored through customized on-line menus for enhanced ease of access by the public. A community network can potentially provide a single point of access for local, state and national government services, accessible with the help of friendly local on-line public servants. Government information CD-ROM databases can be economically mass-produced and made locally accessible on multiple community networks. Regularly updatable, and potentially tailorable for the needs of specific communities, CD-ROM databases can provide gigabytes of government information mass-producable for $1 each.

BBSs as a Path to Full Connection

Distributed bulletin board systems are not a substitute for full Internet access, but rather are the logical pathway toward full Internet access. They are "training-wheel" systems for the Internet that will continue to provide an important local support function even after full Internet access is achieved. Bulletin board software has recently evolved to the point where an increasing number of systems can allow upgrading to full Internet capabilities while retaining the valuable local services and customized user-friendly menu-driven design. Eighty percent of Internet use is for e-mail, which can be handily served by BBSs at minimal expense.

Each community needs to validate the benefits of both local telecomputing and full Internet access, without a great initial expense. Local bulletin boards provide an economical first step that most communities can easily take. Valuable skills can be learned from a local bulletin board in preparation for eventual Internet access. These include use of e-mail, uploading and down-loading files, distributed conferencing, and use of menu-driven and/or graphical knowledge access interfaces.

The global Internet will soon be the commercial information highway for the entire planet; the National Information Infrastructure will soon be the national information highway system, with all the economic potential our national railway and highway system brought to communities a century ago. Each community must assess the benefits of network access against the costs for both the infrastructure and the community "learning-curve" challenges.

Summary of Successive Internet Access Options by Cost

Regional

Through a provider such as Big Sky Telegraph, Internet e-mail access is very affordable. Long distance prime-time rates of 25 cents per minute translate to a nickel-per-page cost at 1200 baud. At this low speed, a five dollar weekly phone budget can allow the transfer of over 80 pages of text in a twenty minute session. With a 9600 baud modem, costs drop to under a penny a page at prime-time rates! Internet accounts are offered for $120/year per individual account. Full Internet, with technical support and step-by-step on-line lessons, are included with a subscription. Customized Internet menus provide simplified access to the highest-value services and resources. While use of Internet e-mail is sustainable with minimal phone charges through use of off-line readers, full Internet browsing becomes cost-prohibitive for many citizens due to high hourly phone costs.

Local Model

A "Tinysky" community network server running on an IBM-com-patible PC, Macintosh or even an Apple IIe (with hard disk) can provide an entire community with free local access to Internet discussion conferences and vast amounts of information. Auto-mated single nightly phone calls can exchange whole conferences and individual messages with other community systems and the Internet. Through such a system citizens can access self-teaching lessons and experiment with local, regional, and global electronic mail, menu-driven systems, distributed conferences, Internet listservs, and conference discussions. Such a system can also be used for proprietary, encrypted, global trade communications with individuals using similar local community networks. A community system is as changeable as a document on an individual's word processor.

The most cost-effective Internet connection would be e-mail exchange through a local bulletin board system. Installation in a community would cost roughly $3,000 for hardware and software and $3,000 for initial training of the system operator and local trainers. The monthly cost for an entire community to use Internet e-mail through Big Sky Telegraph (and other providers) would be roughly $100. An additional nominal charge for the few minutes of Internet access required for message exchange should be added. The cost of operating a community BBS is roughly $50 per month per phone line and $50 per month for nightly automated calls, plus the cost of the time for a local system operator (4 hours per week). A monthly budget of $100 for remote technical assistance is recommended. These costs would be the same for both urban and rural communities. Costs depend on the number of systems being created and the number of phone lines per system; each phone line could accommodate about 1,000 callers who call the system twice a week using off-line readers and/or point disks.

Any school or community in the nation could raise locally the nominal funding necessary, for example through an aluminum can drive. Such a system could provide free local and global Internet e-mail access and successive self-teaching lessons to lead interested citizens of any age through the concepts, skill development, and on-line community-building to open the telepreneurship opportunities of the global info-marketplace.

Off-Line Readers and Point Disks

There are several ways to cut down on the amount of time that users are connected to the local bulletin board or the Internet. Among the most useful are off-line readers and point disks. An off-line reader is simply a computer disk that offers many customizable options to quickly retrieve messages from a BBS, either directly or via a modem phone call, for reading and responding to messages off-line. For example, each student in a class could insert his or her computer disk into the school-based BBS to quickly receive all new messages in their selected conferences. Students would then go to their microcomputer workstations to read new messages and write their responses. At the end of the period students would reinsert their disks and the BBS would hold their outgoing correspondence until midnight, when it would make its single nightly phone call to exchange information globally, costing under $50 per month. This model could serve an entire community through a public library or public office without requiring citizens to own computers.

A point disk is more automated than an off-line reader, and is particularly suited for introductory or more limited purposes for those initially intimidated by learning computers and telecommunications. A user inserts a point disk into a PC and types a single command. The disk initiates an on-line call, picks up all new messages in selected conferences, and sends any messages on the disk. Upon completion of the automated call, the user reads new messages, and responds off-line onto the disk, using the on-disk word processor. Then the user again initiates a single command to send and receive the next exchange of messages. Many types of similar automailer software programs exist.

A point disk allows a user to select one or more conferences listed on the local community network. With gateway software, point disks also allow access to Internet listservs and FidoNet conferences. Almost no telecommunications skills are required to use the point disk. Even via long distance, the cost for daily use of a point disk would average under one dollar per automated two-to-four minute phone call at daytime rates. Point disks can be set to automatically call network servers at night, when long distance rates are lowest.

Potentially any collection of textual or graphical resources could be requested through a point disk. The user would make resource selections from a listing retrieved by the point disk, and the files would appear on the disk after the next automated call. For example, the daily White House press releases, presently available on a gopher server on the Internet, could become conveniently accessible through local community networks. Minimal training and costs are required to use point disks, as opposed to the skills and time required to connect to a network and browse for desired information.

Intermittent Internet Access

The lowest cost for intermittent full Internet connectivity is roughly $19 per hour for long-distance dialup to a system or BBS with full Internet connections ($16 per hour for standard long distance charges and $3 per hour for Internet fees). SLIP software that allows use of specific client software Internet interfaces is another option. Long distance costs can be brought as low as $5 per hour with recent price drops in 1-800 telephone services. Delphi and Colorado Supernet both offer full Internet access for $3 per hour. This option can be cost-effective for limited access for specific purposes, such as retrieving Landsat satellite images for a science class.

If an economic development office or an individual from home needs only a few hours per week on the Internet, an occasional $19-per-hour charge is cheaper than $17,000 per year, the rough price of full connectivity. Capturing information via a high-speed modem can bring costs down to under a penny per page for Internet information.

24-hour Full Internet

Full Internet connections cost about $17,000/year for a dedicated 56kb line, plus a one-time charge of $10,000 for the router and initial connection (from Northwestnet.) A 56kb line will adequately meet the low-end needs of most schools and many colleges. Price wars should bring steadily dropping prices. Full Internet connection is the option of choice, but realistically, if we all had full Internet connections tomorrow, it would take months or even years for most of us to begin to tap their real potential, resulting in a major waste of money for underutilized full access. In addition, as the Internet currently stands, it could not handle the additional load of all 83,000 schools and their communities jumping on the Internet at once.

Integrated network solutions are rapidly evolving. One example is the LORA BBS, developed in Italy, which runs under the OS/2 operating system and is fully multitasking, allowing full Internet connectivity while retaining the easy maintenance and customizability of a typical BBS. LORA also allows a "connect as needed" full Internet menu-driven BBS SLIP option. LORA will allow whole menu structures to automatically be "echoed" on multiple systems, allowing centralized development of multiple distributed network servers. Point disks, off-line readers and other benefits of BBSs come as part of this integrated, plug and play package.

A LORA system on a single 386 PC could allow 8 full Internet users per minute using concurrent long-distance SLIP phone calls, costing under \$2/hour per student for temporary full Internet access. Voice-mail and voice databases can be running simultaneously on the same LORA system. For \$6,000 per school or community LORA system, this represents an affordable first step for most schools and communities.

Barriers to Community Networking

Community BBSs are already in use in rural areas, and FreeNets are proliferating in urban areas. However, there are some subtle but very real barriers to their widespread adoption.

Enlightened Self-Interest vs. Short-Term Profit Motives

Who will promote the practical use of community networking? If corporations do not see billion-dollar projects that promise large future profits, they may not support community innovation networks. Citizen input to federal decision making is necessary to assure that citizens' best interests are not forgotten as the National Information Infrastructure begins to take form.

Leadership Teleliteracy

With the increasing pace of technological advancement, our federal, state, and corporate leaders need to stay keenly aware of rapidly evolving low-cost, high-imagination networking options. Citizens need to assure that our leaders stay current in their knowledge of what practical networking options exist, so that they are able to lead us intelligently. To date, we have not held our leaders thus accountable, as demonstrated by the incomplete nature of most network-related legislation, which is oblivious to the practical alternatives already functioning at the grassroots level.

Fear of Technology

Many people older than 30 are not comfortable with the idea of learning computer skills, much less networking concepts and telecommunications technologies. We need to ensure that fearful citizens can receive all the human support they need to become comfortable with the use of computers. Local volunteers need to be encouraged to help citizens through this transitional period. Youth service programs could be tasked with this mission.

Acceptable Use Policy (AUP) Inconsistencies

Different interpretations by regional providers of the NSF Acceptable Use Policy have resulted in community networks being able to offer varying levels of free Internet e-mail and services to the public, and some being prohibited from offering any level of access without prohibitively high fees.

Testbed models are needed to identify economic approaches that provide verifiable citizen benefits at an affordable cost, while allowing Internet providers to sustain development of value-added Internet access and human mentorship.

Control of Information

Networking represents a cultural shift toward new communications behaviors. Existing management structures are threatened by the lateralization of information access. If control of information represents power, resistance to making information more broadly available is to be expected. Incentives and ongoing evaluations for strategic partnering among federal, state and local agencies are needed.

Every community stands on four basic legs: education, business, health, and government. The tendency has been for each of these separate communities to establish its own networking infrastructure, not connected to the others. These and other groups within the greater community need to work together to realize economies of scale and avoid wasteful duplication. Creating a successful strategy to achieve partnering among the different groups within each community is a challenge we all have a stake in.

A Bottom-Up Statewide Economic Development Program

This section outlines a minimal-cost action plan states could take in the short term.

A statewide model could be based on a menu-driven UNIX-based system that would share resources from the many state information providers. Much of the information on this statewide system could be easily "echoed" on an ongoing, updatable basis to hundreds of community BBSs. This central system would cost between $10,000 and $75,000. The biggest cost would be the staffing to maintain and develop the resource sharing collaborative partnerships and person-to-person support services.

The fastest way to proceed would be to establish a number of demonstration community bulletin board systems with Internet mail capabilities. These should include on-line training for citizens and teachers aimed at global citizenship, global entrepreneurship, knowledge access skills, how to teach on-line, and a primer on "grassroots innovations."

A "Grassroots Call to Action" flyer promoting the creation of similar community systems, funded by local money, could be disseminated statewide. A "Community Challenge" competition would be announced in which awards would be presented to those communities whose citizens' participation and innovations demonstrated a replicable vision for the state. Innovators should be given free Internet access in return for showcasing the value and benefits derived from such access.

Videos showcasing working community networks and grassroots innovations should be available for community presentations to begin building a shared vision of the possibilities. Packets for an on-line class should be made available so citizens can begin learning at their convenience the specific skills required to benefit from networking. Each new community network should be inaugurated with a major "Barn-Raising" event, with local and regional notables entering their names on the systems as a symbol of support.

Training for citizens is a major component, and would be "people-intensive." Trainers and presenters for community demonstrations of the potential would be needed. The additional training of citizens would be an added staffing cost. The scope and speed of implementation would determine how many trainers would initially be needed. A dozen individuals could get any state going at high speed within six months.

Conclusion

Federal, state and local governments need to develop programs for funding grassroots innovations and for sharing and rewarding successes.

Citizen participation on local networks is crucial to realizing the potential of a national information infrastructure. This will take an investment by the government in promoting teleliteracy. The government should be active in:

• Providing citizens friendly, low-threat opportunities to learn about verifiable networking benefits

• Broadly sharing success stories that demonstrate the economic value of connectivity

• Providing citizens free local access and mentored training in use of the on-line medium

- Providing global telepreneurship training to the home via modem or other media

- Providing public access computers and community learning centers to help all Americans in all communities prepare for survival in this transitional decade. Loaner laptop programs represent one feasible first step.

- Providing federal support for grassroots innovations to create the diversity of applications required for a successful NII

- Soliciting citizens' input regarding the NII to establish a sense of ownership, understanding, and a desire for participation

- Advocate through government leadership "a national mission for citizen teleliteracy centered on community networking for the national good."

Facilitating as many bottom-up innovations as possible by encouraging direct participation and evaluation by citizens has become necessary to define the verifiable benefits of the emerging National Information Infrastructure.[1] The future economic health of the United States lies squarely in our citizens' ability to use telecommunications for productive ends. Telecommunications infrastructure investments must be matched with investments in citizen teleliteracy training and support for citizen innovations.

The government's biggest benefit from community networks will be the national tap on local innovations. Widespread grassroots innovations will be necessary for the potential of electronic delivery of government services to become reality and for our nation to be an economic leader in the information age.

Note

[1] The Congressional Office of Technology Assessment has released an important report "Making Government Work; Electronic Delivery of Federal Services." Federal support for grassroots innovations is strongly encouraged. Free copies are available to all citizens while supplies last. Send your complete snailmail address to: elecdelivery@ota.gov or write to: Congressional OTA, US Congress, 600 Pennsylvania Avenue, SE, Washington DC, 20510.

Public Access to the Internet:
American Indian and Alaskan Native Issues

George Baldwin

This paper is a historical and sociological discussion about emerging computer-mediated communication networks used by Indian people and tribal organizations. It focuses on the policy implications related to Indian access to the emerging National Information Infrastructure. These issues are best understood in the historical context of the role of communication technologies (film, radio, press, television, and telephone) in the evolution of modern Native societies. The historical perspective will help readers better understand the attitudes of Native people toward the emerging national information superhighway, and what this means for survival of tribal cultures in the near future.

Communication Technology and Indian Culture

At the time of the European invasion, the native people of the Americas had developed several systems of communication. In North America, intertribal communication was based on the spoken word or sign language, and was transmitted by Indian runners, who carried news between tribes. The advanced civilizations of Central and South America had communication systems that included data encoded symbolically by various means. Delivered by runners over well-engineered roadways, the "moccasin telegraph" was a highly developed communication network. (The networks of the past were far more complex than the smoke signals portrayed in Hollywood movies!) Tribal networks were augmented in speed and range by the adoption of a radical new transportation technology, the horse. With the deployment of the horse, the moccasin telegraph was extended in speed and distance, but communication was still primarily word-of-mouth.

White expansionism, the Indian Wars, and the advent of the reservation system took their toll; restricted movement and rural isolation effectively limited the communication that Indians conducted between themselves as well as the information they received about the dominant society. As the 1800s progressed, the distribution of text-based communications within the dominant European culture accelerated. The media—generally newspapers—competed in specialized information markets and helped to create what we now recognize as a growing "culture of information." At the same time, the lack of newspapers and libraries on reservations combined synergistically with the low literacy level of Indian people to create a society characterized by its information poverty. This lack of information has contributed to the tribes' long-term dependency on the Bureau of Indian Affairs (BIA) for the management of their day-to-day relationships with the outside world. Poor communications, lack of information, and rural isolation have conspired to prevent tribes from effectively organizing to resist Western civilization.

Thus, one can argue that the European invasion of the New World was successful, in part, because of the rapid evolution of communication technologies and popular access to information among the invaders. Richard Brown noted that in the late 1700s, most information in Western society was communicated face-to-face: "public information and learning generally flowed from the upper reaches of society downward to the common people—a hierarchical diffusion pattern."[1] A change in the role of print and the way it was distributed improved Europeans' access to information. Advanced transportation technologies (the horse, sailboat, train, etc.) and the telegraph revolutionized the rate of information exchange across large distances. However, for Native people, face-to-face communication remained the primary mode of information exchange for several generations more than in the dominant culture.

One reason for this is that Indian adaptation of Western communication media was actively resisted by the invading society. For example, the first reported tribally-owned newspaper was begun in 1828. A story in itself, the *Cherokee Phoenix*, which served the eastern Cherokee, was more than just a newspaper; it became (like Sequoyah, the inventor of the Cherokee written language) a symbol of Cherokee literacy and cultural integrity. Cherokees' literacy rate in written and spoken Cherokee soon exceeded the English literacy rate of white settlers in the same region. It should be no surprise that the Cherokee press's political and civic messages of cultural unity were found threatening by the surrounding Anglo culture, which coveted Indian land. Under President Jackson's administration, the *Cherokee Phoenix* was destroyed by troops and Cherokee land was given away by lottery. Many Native Americans died during the forced march to the new Indian territory in Oklahoma, and literacy in spoken and written Cherokee has yet to return to its former level.

Radio and television came later to the reservations than to the rest of the country; the first "TV generation" of Indian children has only recently reached adulthood. Many reservation communities and homes now have cable or satellite receivers. One might think that in today's more politically correct world Indian children would have escaped the stereotypical images drilled into previous generations of U.S. society by western movies: Indian warriors attacking the workers who installed the telegraph wires; horseback attacks against steam locomotives and wagon trains; Wells Fargo and Pony Express riders racing from certain death at the hands of murderous savages. These made for exciting movies, but did little to promote positive personal identities for Indian youth—or to recommend career choices in the communication industries. Now satellite distribution and cable TV have immortalized these movies with the invention of the "Western Channel." These images symbolize the European concept that "the West was wild" (like the Indians), and that modern communications were the tools that civilized it.

In short, history shows that American Indians recognized that Western communication technologies were powerful weapons for cultural expansion. While tribes understandably resisted the deployment by the Western invaders of such communication technologies, they also made numerous attempts to assimilate them. As one Native communication professional commented, even "smoke signals were digital communication," though you won't hear it interpreted in that light.[2] Nevertheless, stereotypical images of Indian hostility toward communication technology persist in the public's mind.

Today we find that these images of Indian hostility to technology have been incorporated as political myth by the media campaigns of various special interest groups. Political myths are stories communicated by society that serve the purpose of conveying appropriate attitudes and behaviors to society's members. The political myth embodied in the traditional media image of Indians focuses on the unchanging nature of the Indian's culture. Special interest groups manipulate the political myth for their own purposes. For example, the environmental movement bombards the public with video images of traditionally garbed tribal elders who stoically cry (one tear) while reflecting on the pollution of our nation's rivers. As politically correct as this image may seem, like state-financed "Indian tourism," it fosters a view of tribal cultures that either died or became endangered species because they resisted technological change.

Such media campaigns perpetuate a popular image of technology-stagnant American Indians that may impede the development of progressive telecommunication policies for tribal people. The myth also helps to gloss over to a significant degree the repression experienced by native people who have attempted to control their own communication and information technologies. By focusing the public's imagination on Indians as archaic history, the myth discounts the significant social change that Indian culture has undergone and the role that communication technology has played in this transformation.

This stereotype clashes dramatically with the reality of the tribal councilmen who are now considering the use of reservation lands as a storage site for nuclear and medical waste. Or the tribal council that must choose which subcontractors should design software that will integrate casino and bingo operations with overall tribal budgets. Or the tribal planner utilizing a Geographic Information System to track development of tribal roads and industry, a satellite network of Indian-owned and operated radio stations, or a national satellite video network of Indian colleges.

Few of today's tribal leaders would disagree that the acculturation of Indian people continues; most of us working in the communication field might even be hard pressed to explain how Native
communications are "different" from the dominant media. Why
should computer communication networks or the National Information Infrastructure change any of this? Murphy and Murphy
write that "Indians have had to modify their culture by contact with
the white culture, but they have not become absorbed. The adaptation of the 'white man's media' to the Indians' needs is yet
another instance of such acculturation."[3] Computer networks, like
the communication media that preceded them, have been assimi-
lated by a growing Native population. As these user populations
grow, sociological questions arise from the dynamics of the media
and the cultural attributes of the native users.

A decade of research literature tells us that the very act of
watching TV or listening to the radio has influenced cultural
change in our society and the self-concepts of individuals. Native
communication professionals insist that the messages embedded
in our minority media are somehow culturally different than those
found in the dominant communication networks. These culturally
grounded messages are said to support Native culture and support
positive self-concepts for the native viewers or listeners. Is this true?

Native communication professionals assert that tribal people
must struggle to preserve media content that reaffirms cultural
values. Where this has been a critical Indian issue for mass communication professionals, there has been virtually no advocacy for
similar cultural concerns within the computer-mediated communication environment. The American Indian Radio Satellite Network, the Native American Public Broadcasting Consortium, and
the American Indian Higher Education Consortium's satellite
video network are all examples of Native communication projects
designed to incorporate tribal values into the media. The "electronic migration" of Indian people into our nation's growing
infrastructure of civic computer communication networks presents itself as the latest chapter in the history of Native assimilation
of communication technology—an area of telecommunication
policy whose limits are yet to be defined. Advocates for such
cultural concerns on computer networks are just now emerging.

Tribal Rights and Cultural Identity in Cyberspace

In stark contrast to the predominant image of Indians, today there are hundreds of tribally owned and operated newspapers, dozens of radio stations, and a growing number of Indian controlled communication companies.[4] Computer networks are only now being recognized by leaders in the Indian community as a communication medium useful to Indian people. One must desert the fanciful thinking fostered by the "Western Channel" and see Indian people and organizations for what they are: Readers must imagine Indian youths, academics, and scientists in locations all over the United States as they hover over glowing terminals, fingers flying on clicking keyboards.

Many Indian people communicate in this manner for hours each week. Some are collaborating with research teams, others are receiving in-service training for college credit, many are students simply chatting with their friends at other BIA boarding schools. Native networked communities include children of the First Nations attending Canadian schools[5] and Alaskan Native and American Indian junior high school students who attend reservation boarding schools. Graduate and undergraduate Indian college students and their professors from major colleges and universities are also on-line. Tribal members relocated in urban areas or even Europe can communicate with their rural or reservation cousins. Collectively they have become active in a worldwide electronic "virtual ethnic community."

Describing the boundary of this "virtual ethnic community" is difficult. The closest comparison is with the minority-owned mass media, particularly radio and press; listeners and viewers share the experience with others in their ethnic group, and this often assists in generating a sense of community. Tribally controlled papers and radio programs have been immensely popular with their audiences, but must struggle to avoid being absorbed by larger communication corporations. Advances in computer communications have challenged the tribes to master newer techniques for communication; absorption remains a problem.

Numerous listservs and bulletin board systems have developed distinct cultural and ethnic biases. The emergence of Jewish,

Hispanic, Latino, and Black, as well as American Indian and Alaskan Native computer networks was inevitable. Like radio and press, the owners and managers of computer-mediated communication (CMC) formats must strive to maintain their identities; this is difficult within the politically open forum of the Internet and BITNET newsgroups and listservs. The borders of these growing "virtual communities" are defined not so much by their geography but by the *interests of the participants*, which in this case is focused on the real, imagined, or socially constructed ethnicity of the network participant.

The line between who is and is not an American Indian can appear blurred, but the right to tribal identity is strictly reserved for Indian Tribes and nations under the U.S. Constitution and by right of treaty law. Ethnic fraud, i.e., individuals who present themselves as Indian but are not, has become a serious issue for tribal leaders. In *Santa Clara vs. Martinez*, the Supreme Court rendered a decision that affirmed that Tribes have the right to determine who a tribal member is. In the public data networks, however, anyone is free to claim that he or she is Indian. Randy Ross (Otoe-Missouri) writes that, "because of the virtuality of network information systems, a sysop, conference moderator, or user is free to claim that he or she is Indian. If a Tribe refuses the claim and says 'no, they are not a member of our Tribe,' data networks must respect the right of the Tribe to make that determination, even if the individual persists. As online moderated conferences become a common forum for public discussion, non-Indian moderators may attempt to control the spirit and direction of online discussions held for Indian people."[6] This is usually described as "giving help to Indians," whether we ask for the help or not.

Indian people who use the public data networks are now asking, "How do we implement the principles of *tribal sovereignty* and *self-determination* online?" Determining who has the right to an Indian identity is an important part of this issue. Information access and electronic cultural policy may contribute to strengthening tribal cultural resources and education among Indian communities. Sovereignty and tribal nationhood are being debated in court on numerous fronts, from bingo and gambling to automobile tags and tribal passports. When considering the electronic networks of the future, tribal sovereignty and self-determination should remain paramount.

Today information is the raw material of communication networks. It is treated as a marketable commodity. Like the myth of Indian resistance to communication technologies, there is a myth denying Indian ownership of property. For example, the popular misconception that "Indians don't own land" ignores the focus of the Indian wars. Like land, ideas are recognized by Native people as property. For example, intangible property played a significant role in Kiowa life: "In addition to tales of military exploits, individuals owned the rights to their creative products. A man would not sing a song another had composed without permission. The same principle applied to a woman's beadwork designs."[7] The Plains Indians were not the only tribes that recognized nonmaterial, high-status property. Today, stories about our ancestors, traditional myths, and particularly the cultural traditions related to protecting the environment have become products for sale. Not surprisingly, these stories are often written by non-Indian authors, scripted by non-Indian screen writers, and star non-Indians in Indian roles. Indian people, like Americans in general, have become consumers of information about themselves, with few of us actively engaged in the production end of the economic equation.

If one views computer networks as highways over which the commerce of ideas flows, one finds that the sale and distribution of Indian-related information invariably profits the non-Indian information economy. There is an overwhelming presence of non-Natives in the newsgroups and listservs of the Internet that were originally created to serve Indian interests. Outnumbered and out-typed, many Indian networkers have become passive viewers of conversations about themselves.

Indians and Educational Computing

The manifest function of the majority of the CMC networks has been to support education, research, and improved access to public data for tribal development. The latent function of these networks—as one "reads between the lines"—is to promote and defend native cultural beliefs and values. Both functions can be discerned from the content of the written conversations and their topics. The participants, as well as their audience, represent a fascinating component of pan-Indianism, the intertribal social movement where several tribes unite, usually to confront an enemy such as the federal government.[8]

The content of the on-line discussions suggests that there is a growing agreement that the enemy to Native cultural survival is the increasingly ubiquitous Western worldview promoted by the "transmedia intertextual phenomena of television, radio, press, and video games."[9] American Indian and Alaskan Native cultures have become commodities in this transmedia environment. The phenomena of CMC networks as transmitters of cultural beliefs and values has not been studied to the same degree as radio, television, and film, but within our nations it is clear that minority groups are organizing a growing computer communication infrastructure, in a manner similar to the way they used earlier media.

Contrary to stereotypical images, American Indians and Alaskan Natives are not strangers to computer technology. Several social and economic forces have actually encouraged the growth of computer use in Indian populations. Perhaps the major force was the growth of an extensive government bureaucracy on reservations. The government offices acquired personal computers and mainframes, which required trained clerks and managers to operate them. Federal funding supported both. As a result, tribes such as the Cherokee and Navajo have *several* mainframes each and dozens of personal computers. Numerous surveys of Indian organizations find that even our smallest groups invariably have a computer, printer, and telephone.

Indian boarding schools and reservation schools have a significant investment in computer hardware, primarily Apple IIs.[10] The 27 Indian colleges have even higher ratios of computers for student and faculty use.[11] These two studies tell us that the number of computers per person in Indian educational institutions is quite respectable in comparison to non-Indian schools. In many cases it is higher.

How these systems are used is generally not reported in the literature. As a consequence, though there are dozens of culturally supportive computer uses and projects nationwide, few Indian project directors are aware of the work that others are involved in. There have been a few published reports on the pioneering uses of *distance learning* technologies for Native education. Most of these have not been as well documented and have been published by non-Indian organizations and principle investigators who received grants for demonstration projects that included an Indian school or organization as part of the required funding formula. Most grant writers understand the process of getting "extra points" in a proposal by including the statement "American Indians and Alaskan Natives." This form of "electronic carpetbagging" generally benefits the non-Indian institution that manages the grant and the non-Indian schools that make up the majority of the audience. Rarely is the curriculum tailored to the Indian world view. While this has been especially true for the one-way mass media of television, film, and video, it has not worked well with the interactive media of CMC either. The audiences of CMC networks always have the opportunity to become participants; Indian applications of CMC distance education appear to have failed in the past due to their lack of interactivity.

Some observers have noted that in the past, policies that were intended to help Indian or Alaskan Native people purchase information and communication technology were subverted and used primarily to benefit non-Indians. This has been referred to as "information carpetbagging"[12] and "electronic colonialism."[13] One must wonder about the educational effectiveness of currently funded Star School Programs, the BIA's ENAN network, the Mansfield Transcontinental Classroom, the Internet listservs, and various private BBS networks, all of which have named Indians as beneficiaries of their projects. Without effectiveness evaluations conducted by unbiased researchers whose continued funding is not tied to the project's success, we have no real way of evaluating such networks except anecdotal accounts from participant observers.

Civic and Governmental Networks

As the National Information Infrastructure (NII) develops, a growing number of government services and information sources will be made available electronically. Like television, radio, and the telephone, computer communications will be necessary for commerce and timely access to government data. Will access to such networks be guaranteed to the tribal governments (of which there are over 500) under the proposed National Information Infrastructure Act? Just as important, assuming that tribal leaders accept such connectivity, will these systems benefit American Indians and their organizations?

There are currently several hundred BBS systems operated by federal agencies that carry information of interest to tribal governments. The Environmental Protection Agency, for example, has three BBSs. Like most of the federal BBSs, not only are these systems not coordinated (which could be accomplished through something as simple as a FIDOnet link), the different departments are not even aware that other departments have similar systems! The Indian Health Service has a small BBS system that even the department heads are not aware of. Is it any wonder that the tribes are unaware of the existence of these systems?

When government BBSs are available, it is questionable if they are of use to Indian people. For example, FEDIX is an easily accessible and usable (toll-free and Internet telnet) federal information service. Grants and funding sources are indexed for African Americans, Hispanics, and Women, but as in most public database systems on the Internet, nothing is indexed by the key term "American Indian or Alaskan Native." This situation is improving: several Internet Gopher servers have been constructed for Native users, and at least one federally supported project (INDIANnet) has started to organize information useful for Native people on both bulletin boards and Internet locations.

Funding for such projects has come from diverse sources. For example, the National Science Foundation has developed a tribal initiative called "Electronic Pathways," which has the mission of assisting tribes to get connected to the Internet. However, at this time only one federally recognized tribe has an Internet address. This may soon change: Both the Cherokee Tribe of Oklahoma and the Navaho Tribe are slated for Internet addresses through a program funded by the National Aeronautics and Space Administration (NASA). The National Indian Policy Center at the George

Washington University has also proposed to create an electronic clearinghouse of Indian information utilizing the Internet.

One can see that the transmission of civic information to Indian populations through CMC networks is underway, yet policy issues concerning tribal access and usability of the data have yet to be addressed. Federal legislation has been a tool to promote the use of communication technologies by minorities in a number of instances; for example, we have received grants supporting the Native American Public Broadcasting Consortium and Indian radio networks. The American Indian Higher Education Consortium was recently funded by the Department of Commerce to create a satellite video network. A pattern of subsidizing various forms of mass media to increase the Native presence on the networks has clearly been established. We can expect that with appropriate Indian political activism, bills that are being written to assure access to government information for the general public will be modified by attaching "American Indian and Alaskan Native" entitlements.

Such entitlements are often misunderstood by the American public. This is part of the political myth that Indians must struggle with. Entitlements are not handouts; they are earnings based on returns from historical contracts—that is, treaties. American Indians are the only minorities mentioned by name in the constitution, and Congress made treaties with the tribes that guaranteed health care, education, housing, and a range of other services. Many Indian leaders assert that these treaty-based earnings, broadly interpreted, must include electronic access to government agency databases and documents, which means access to computerized network information services. The U.S. government has a broad-based trust responsibility to Indian nations. If the interest of government trust under public policy and law is not extended to data networks and access to those networks, Indian activists today are asking, "How can we protect tribal autonomy and sovereignty?"

The phrasing of civic networking entitlements for American Indians is very important. The past decade has underscored that the Indian Nations wish to be considered separate governmental entities. Government information and connectivity to the tribes should be understood as a form of government-to-government communication, and this legal relationship should be codified.

The Clinton-Gore administration has stressed the need for a National Information Infrastructure that empowers our citizens with civic connectivity. Can our autonomous tribal governments promise any less to our Indian nations' citizens? Not only should federal data be supplied easily and openly to the tribes, but information related to the workings of our Indian Nations should similarly be mounted on-line for our people. This particular aspect of civic networking has not been addressed in any tribal forum. Some of these questions may soon be answered by the "Tribal Telecommunications Study" directed by the Office of Technology Assessment. This is the first federally funded study that has actually conducted site visits in an attempt to interpret federal policy in relationship to its impact on the telecommunication infrastructure that serves Native people.

Summary

Computerized network information services are the most recent communication technology to influence the direction of social change experienced by all Americans, including Indians.[14] These systems deliver text, graphics, audio, and video in digital form over various telecommunication carriers. At this time, only a few such systems are operated for, and sometimes by, American Indians. Like Indian newspapers, radio, and television broadcasts, they meet the special needs of Indians and those who are interested in Indian affairs. How will these systems affect Native culture?

Sociologists and anthropologists have long argued that exposure to media, be it print or electronic, can doing nothing but facilitate the assimilation of those who view it. The groundswell of enthusiasm for using communication technologies to promote the Native worldview seems to have ignored this sociological tenet. Projects currently funded or proposed such as INDIANnet (a civic network of government data), the American Indian Higher Education Telecommunication Network (for the 27 Indian colleges), the National Museum of the American Indian's "Fourth Museum" concept, NASA's network for the Cherokee and the Navaho, and NYSERnet's work in New York for the Onadago Tribe are all examples of how Native people are connecting to the information superhighway. How do American Indians and Alaskan Natives feel about these new telecommunication initiatives?

The Native Communication Survey commissioned by the National Indian Policy Center found that the majority of the respondents reported uncritical acceptance of these technologies and the communication technologies' ability to support the tribal communities' beliefs. The respondents' answers implied that the values expressed in the media are entirely in the control of the producers, independent of the technology that delivers the message. Media theory contradicts this rather naive world view. To quote the truism, "the medium is the message." Any technology has a tacit set of values embedded within it. Those who use the technology implicitly agree to those values. Broadcast technologies of the past have supported values related to hierarchical control, centralized power, and one message for millions of users regardless of their social diversity. This ideology is imbedded within the technology and, like television, may be destructive to community and tribal values.

Those of us who are members of listservs on the Internet, discussion groups on the FreeNets, community BBS systems, or commercial networks such as the WELL or America OnLine are all asking questions concerning the emerging norms and values of our "electronic communities." Native networkers are now asking the same questions, but in our case we are specifically concerned about tribal rights and sovereignty. We wish to reaffirm that the realm of cyberspace will be governed by a philosophy of government-to-government relations, including tribal control of information about ourselves and tribal control of the policies governing the telecommunication medium itself, especially on reservations.

Native communication professionals agree that in an increasingly unregulated telecommunication market in which text, video, and radio have merged, they must take action to protect their self interest. There is growing agreement that tribal autonomy and self-determination can only be served if Indian people own a share of the communication infrastructure and become active producers of information, especially when it is about and for themselves. For this to happen, Indian people must write and produce their own stories and films, and they must manage and control their own communication companies. In today's world of emerging network information systems, they must create and distribute information, and control the organizations that manage such information. This is the business of economic development in the age of information. Such development will produce careers for young Native people, many of whom have already demonstrated a remarkable ability to utilize computer technology within the context of the goals of their tribal communities.

The changes to society wrought by communication technologies are profound. It is imperative that tribal policy makers begin to develop a critical perspective for understanding network information systems, the proposed NII, and information and telecommunication policy so that we can possess our share of the technology and shape it to our own needs. LaDonna Harris, President and Founder of Americans for Indian Opportunity, recently spoke on behalf of native people at NTIA hearings in Albuquerque. She noted that 1) Indian America is a very special situation and should be treated very differently from other ethnic communities, 2) Tribal governments and Tribal peoples are totally excluded from current Information Highways, and 3) Indians active in information technology development are not given the opportunity to participate in national planning for telecommunications.

Indian leaders who attended the "First Tribal Telecommunications Forum" in Denver last November (hosted by Americans for Indian Opportunity with a grant from the National Science Foundation) and are familiar with the medium are concerned that its vast potential will not be harnessed to promote cultural and economic progress, but will instead perpetuate the historical subjugation of Indian people. We have been passive consumers of information about ourselves for too long. One of the first tasks in this process is for tribal developers, educators, and leaders to address the impact of this new technology by articulating values about the basic purpose and uses that communication networks can have for Indian people. To quote Randy Ross in the presentation of the Forum findings to the NSF, "We don't want to find ourselves the road kill on the Information Highway".

Acknowledgment

Parts of this chapter were written with support from NSF Grant SBE-9212935.

Notes

[1] Richard Brown, *Knowledge is Power: The Diffusion of Information in Early Knowledge, 1700–1865,* New York: Oxford University Press,, 1989, p. 280.

[2] Jim May, "Technological Needs in Indian American: Joining the Information Age," *Journal of Navajo Education,* Winter 1992, Vol. 9, No. 2.

[3] James Murphy and Sharon Murphy, *Let My People Know: American Indian Journalism, 1828–1978,* Norman, OK: University of Oklahoma Press, 1981.

[4] Ibid.

[5] George D. Baldwin, "Networking the Nations: The Emerging Indian Network Information Systems," *Journal of Navajo Education,* Winter 1992.

[6] Randy Ross, "Tribal Rights and Cultural Identity in Cyberspace," *Artpaper,* June 1993, Vol. XII, No. 10, p. 10.

[7] Candace S. Green, "The Teepee with Better Pictures," *Natural History,* October 1993, p. 71.

[8] Richard Schaefer, *Racial and Ethnic Groups,* Glenview, IL: Scott, Foresman, 1990.

[9] Marsha Kinder, *Playing with Power in Movies, Television, and Video Games: From Muppet Babies to Teenage Mutant Ninja Turtles,* Berkeley: University of California Press, 1991.

[10] Arlie Piltz and Paul Resta, Planning Document for the National Museum of the American Indian and the Use of Technology, NMAI, Smithsonian Institution, Washington, DC, 1991.

[11] American Indian Higher Education Consortium, *Campus telecommunications facilities and profiles: The current capability of AIHEC Colleges,* Interim Report #3, AIHEC Telecommunications Project, Washington, DC: November 30, 1992.

[12] Baldwin, "Networking the Nations."

[13] Ross, "Tribal Rights."

[14] Baldwin, "Networking the Nations."

References

Americans For Indian Opportunity. 1994. "The First Tribal Telecommunications Forum: Final Report to the National Science Foundation." Bernadillo, New Mexico.

Carey, John. 1969. "The Communication Revolution and the Professional Communicator", *Sociological Review Monograph,* vol. 13, January, pp. 23–38.

Lundstedt, Sven B. (ed.). 1990. *Telecommunications, Values, and the Public Interest.* Ablex Publishing Co.

Minow, Newton N. 1991. How Vast the Wasteland Now? Gannett Foundation Media Center. New York, NY.

McPhail, Thomas L. 1987. *Electronic Colonialism: The Future of International Broadcasting and Communication.* Sage Publications.

Mander, Jerry. 1991. *In The Absence of the Sacred: The Failure of Technology and the Survival of Indian Nations.* Sierra Books.

Mosco, Vincent. 1989. *The Pay-Per Society: Computers and Communication in the Information Age.* Ablex Publishing Co.

National Indian Policy Center. 1993. *Native Communications Survey.* The George Washington University. Summer.

Office of Technology Assessment. 1990. *Critical Connections: Communication for the Future.* Congress of the United States. U.S. Government Printing Office.

Traber, Michael. 1986. *The Myth of the Information Revolution: Social an Ethical Implications of Communication Technology.* Sage Publications.

The Role of Public Libraries in Providing Public Access to the Internet

Carol C. Henderson and Frederick D. King

The Internet is a fast-growing component of the evolving national information infrastructure. Yet gaining access to the Internet and locating the information resources available over the network requires equipment, telecommunications connections, and information-seeking skills that many Americans do not yet possess or cannot afford. The information superhighway has the potential to deepen the divisions between the information "haves" and "have-nots."

One community institution is well positioned to provide public access to the Internet and its information resources: the public library. These libraries are publicly supported in almost every community specifically to provide equitable access to diverse information sources and services. Using public libraries to access the Internet and its information resources would be a natural and logical extension of the public library mission.

"Public access" in this paper means providing public terminals at the library through which patrons could gain access to the Internet as well as allowing remote users to access the library via the Internet. Public libraries offer significant advantages in serving this public access role. They are ubiquitous institutions that the majority of Americans use regularly to find information in all formats, including electronic information. Much of the information on the Internet originates with government agencies, and the public already looks to libraries for access to public and governmental information. Public libraries are widely regarded as politically neutral sources of information and as significant community information resources.

The role of the librarian is also an asset. Librarians are sophisticated users of information technology and are trained to help users articulate their information needs and to assist them in retrieving the appropriate information. Librarians also have experience, from their work with information in other formats, in dealing with administrative and policy issues such as privacy, censorship, standards, and intellectual property that are becoming increasingly important in electronic networks.

However, public libraries also face barriers to taking on the role of providing public access to the Internet. Few public libraries are now connected to the Internet. Affordable access is still a barrier, as is the lack of user-friendliness. In addition, a commitment to this new role by any public library will involve a considerable expenditure of staff time and resources for training and support of both the library staff and the public.

Some of these barriers are being overcome. Lessons can be learned from the experience of the growing number of organizations who are brokering or directly providing Internet access, training, and support for libraries, as well as from experimentation with Internet services by the libraries themselves. This paper presents the advantages of and barriers to providing public access to the Internet through public libraries. It describes some of the progress that is being made on issues of access, training, and funding, and recommends additional actions that will be needed in order for libraries to fulfill their public access role.

Public Library Roles, Users, Services, and Support

A brief review of public library roles, users, services, and support demonstrates the potential of the institution as an access point for and information provider on computer networks.[1] With 15,482 main libraries and branches, the United States has the world's most extensive public library system. One survey found that some 74 percent of children and 53 percent of adults reported using the public library in the preceding year; 32 percent of adults had used it in the preceding month. Users are racially diverse; 42 percent of African Americans interviewed in a 1991 household survey by the National Center for Education Statistics said they had used a public library in the preceding year, as did 32 percent of Hispanics, 55 percent of whites, and 52 percent of all others.

Although a variety of library services are used by the public, borrowing a book is the most popular (91 percent of uses), followed by using reference materials (77 percent). In 1991, public librarians answered some 222 million reference questions. Public library users borrow more than 1.4 billion books, magazines, video and audio tapes, computer software, and other items each year. Public library circulation increased 5 percent in 1991, continuing a trend of steady increases over the past decade.

A 1992 Gallup Poll indicated that the general public sees several "very important" roles for their public libraries, including supporting research and education, providing access to community information, reference materials, and popular literature, and providing a center for community activities and a comfortable place to read, think or work. Many of these roles are already being accomplished at least partly through the use of electronic information services; Internet access would simply add another source of electronic resources. Computer-related services are available to the general public in the following percentages of public libraries serving populations of 100,000 or more:

- CD-ROM databases (79 percent)
- Remote database searching (71 percent)
- Microcomputers (62 percent)
- Microcomputer software (57 percent)
- On-line public access catalog (60 percent)
- Dial-up access to on-line catalog (29 percent)

Capabilities of Public Libraries

Given that public libraries are available almost everywhere, are heavily used public institutions, and are important to the public as sources of information in various aspects of their daily lives, the public library clearly has potential for providing public access to the Internet. Further, public libraries already have many of the capabilities that would allow them to become effective users and providers of Internet service. The most important of these include the capabilities to: provide equitable access to their services; provide unique network information resources; offer training and assistance for the public; open up the library as an electronic doorway to new sources of information and expertise; and provide an electronic reference desk.

Equitable Access Provider

The most compelling reason to offer access to the Internet through public libraries is that libraries provide equitable access to their services. Libraries could offer sites for access to the network, the equipment and software needed to access it, and the information resources available through it. Most households cannot connect to the Internet on their own; they lack the equipment (a computer and modem) as well as the training. The U.S. National Commission on Libraries and Information Science made this point in its summary of the results of a July 1992 open forum:

> The Library as a public place within a community is important for those potential network users who do not have personal or institutional computers or cannot gain access to the network. The social context of the library provides these citizens an information mediation specialist to help interpret network resources.[2]

As more commercial information services become available over the Internet, pricing mechanisms will vary. Based on library experience with current commercial electronic information services, it is likely that at least some of these services will be priced for the institutional or corporate subscriber, and not for individuals who may have only occasional need for access to only a small portion of an information source. In this environment, the public library would provide the electronic equivalent of one of its traditional functions—it would provide access to a wide variety of information sources and viewpoints regardless of a user's economic status or research skills.

Information Resource Site

Targeting public libraries as Internet access sites offers another advantage: libraries are information resource providers themselves, and connecting them to the Internet could make this information more widely available. Public libraries have developed a variety of databases that are not currently available elsewhere.[3] These include:

- Community-based information and referral files listing government services, social services, and human service resources
- Query files of answers to questions frequently asked by the public
- Genealogy files for specific local geographic areas
- Local newspaper indexes
- Codes of state and local laws and regulations
- Programming information and ideas for public performance
- Annotated reading lists
- Catalogs of holdings
- Tour and day-trip itineraries for local historical sites

Making these databases available online would make it possible to search them by specific terms and to broaden or narrow searches by using boolean searching techniques. Making them available over the Internet would give access to a wider audience.

Much of the information available via the Internet originates with government agencies. Public libraries provide access to public governmental information from the federal, state, and local levels of government. Libraries have long had special responsibilities under law and custom for partnering with governments to provide public access through the federal depository libraries and through state depository systems. In the Depository Library Program, for instance, the Government Printing Office distributes federal government information (print materials, microfiche, and electronic formats) at no cost to 1400 libraries located in every congressional district. These libraries agree to maintain and organize the materials, make them freely available to the public (including provision of any equipment needed to make use of the information), and provide assistance to those who need the information. Library users expect to find all sorts of government information, from tax forms to census data. The library as the local access point for electronic government information is a natural extension of its current role.

Library science as a field had much to offer in the organization of electronic information for easy use. Librarians have been collecting and organizing information for over 2500 years, and have developed classification and indexing systems that are badly needed throughout the Internet.

Training and Assistance for the Public

Public libraries are involved in many "freenets" or community networks. Unlike most sites for public access terminals (in government buildings and universities, shopping malls and laundromats), libraries have staff members who provide consultation and training in the use of their resources, including electronic information resources. Building on this advantage, libraries could provide training in the use of networks and networked information resources, give point-of-use consultation, guidance, and technical assistance, and develop on-line training and interpretive aids.

Library as Electronic Doorway

The Internet opens up a new kind of networking for the public library—linking it electronically to its users, to the full contents of library collections, and to new sources of information and expertise. Rare is the public library that attempts to meet its users' needs on its own. For the past 25 years, thousands of libraries of all types have used computer and communications technologies to share bibliographic information for cataloging and interlibrary loan. The Internet could link libraries further so that they could share full-text, graphic, and multimedia library resources. Libraries could link their personnel for new kinds of reference services. Libraries could have better access to non-library sources of information, such as government agencies and academic specialists. Finally, library users could have access to the local library from any location with a computer and modem. The New York State Library calls this vision of the library the "Electronic Doorway" concept.[4]

Electronic Reference Desk

The Internet offers libraries a chance to expand their role as providers of reference services. Early experiments with "electronic reference desks" have been popular. The Illinois Valley Library

System's use of the Heartland Freenet offers one example. The Heartland Freenet is a community network available to residents of the Peoria, Illinois, area. As with many freenets, its main menu is arranged like a community, with selections for different "buildings" such as the Administration Building, Community Center, Business Center, Senior Center, Teen Center, Home and Garden Center, and Library Center. As described by Bryn Geffert, the "Library Center" on the Heartland Freenet menu included "The Reference Desk," which allowed users to ask questions of a reference librarian who researched and posted lengthy answers and citations.[5] The service was trusted, successful, and popular. The Reference Desk was a volunteer effort, and use became so overwhelming that it was discontinued. Many users were vocal in their disappointment when it disappeared.

Another service that has built on the experience of the Heartland Freenet is "Reference Q & A," started in September 1993 by CapAccess, a freenet in Washington, DC. This service is a cooperative effort by public library systems in the Washington metropolitan area, which take turns answering incoming questions. Users send questions to a central CapAccess mailbox; the questions, answers, and source information are posted on a bulletin board available to all. This is a promising area of opportunity for libraries to leverage existing resources and infrastructure to provide easier access.

Barriers to Public Library Provision of Internet Access

While the potential for public libraries as public access points for the Internet is strong, the barriers are considerable. Few public libraries are currently connected to the Internet, although the number is growing rapidly. Access is still expensive. In addition, the Internet is not yet as user-friendly as a public information resource should be, so libraries must make a major commitment of staff time and resources in order to take on this new role.

Few Public Libraries on the Internet

The first major barrier to public libraries as public access points on the Internet is that so few are connected currently. Preliminary results from a 1994 survey conducted by the National Commission on Libraries and Information Science (NCLIS) indicate that 20.9 percent of public libraries are connected to the Internet in some way and 79.1 percent are not. Public libraries serving larger populations are more likely to be connected: 77 percent of those serving populations of over 1 million have Internet access, but only 13.3 percent of libraries serving populations under 5,000 are connected.[6]

McClure and his team found a need for raising awareness among public librarians of the importance and use of networked resources.[7] Most librarians already use computers linked to state or nationwide databases, but they need to be convinced that a new set of procedures and costs will be worth the investment of scarce time and money. Sometimes upper library management was seen as not conversant with the latest technologies. In other cases, librarians needed ammunition to convince local governments, which were themselves technologically out-of-date.[8]

Problem of Affordable Access

Options for dial-up access to the Internet have been expanding. Dial-up access is now available at prices ranging from $15 to $100 per month, and is convenient for the occasional Internet user, since it requires merely a telephone line and a modem to establish a connection to a host computer that is connected to the Internet. However, such entry-level connectivity to electronic mail and file transfer capabilities is only the beginning of the cost for libraries, many of which will also incur long-distance charges. In addition, dial-up access, which represents today's affordable access for a stand-alone library not affiliated with an institution, is not sufficient for serving public needs. Even today's fastest modems are too slow to provide acceptable performance for emerging Internet tools.

Becoming a full node on the Internet requires a full-time Internet connection and a computer dedicated to Internet functions. This type of connection enables a library to become a "server," or major information provider, as well as accessing remote information. For instance, as a full node, a library could link its terminals together in a local area network, make its online catalog and other library databases available over the network, and consider transmitting or receiving full-text, graphics, and multimedia resources. The expense of becoming a full node on the Internet is a formidable barrier for many public libraries. As Robert Bocher of the Wisconsin Division of Library Services noted on PUBLIB, an Internet discussion list for public libraries, it costs about $14,000 annually to be a full member of WiscNet, the state network providing Internet access. For an entire campus, that is not a major expense, but for many public libraries it is. Forty-five percent of U.S. public libraries have budgets under $50,000; in Wisconsin it is 54 percent, according to Bocher.[9] These costs do not include local staffing costs for technical support and user support.

The cost of access and scarcity of funding were also problems identified by Charles McClure in his 1991-92 study exploring key issues and possible roles for the public library in the evolving networked environment.[10] Public library participants in the McClure survey indicated that in a time of tight budgets for current activities it was difficult to allocate resources to support a new initiative. Funds may be reallocated, but not until libraries involved have a clear understanding of what costs are entailed and what benefits would be obtained.

User-Friendliness Lacking

The Internet, including supporting software tools evolved among computer engineers, research scientists, and hackers, for whom ease of use was not a priority. The Internet is still in its frontier stage; explorers must often trudge into uncharted territory. This environment is not geared to the pressured world of the average busy public library where learning on the spot about a new access tool or solving a technical glitch is an annoyance neither the overworked librarian nor the busy patron can tolerate very often.

Both the McClure study and the PUBLIB discussion group stressed that access to the network must be easy and straightforward. Public librarians identified the lack of user-friendly interfaces and tools, the lack of databases and resources geared to public use, and the "bottomless pit" of information on the Internet (not all of it useful to public libraries and their users) as problems. The standardized organization of knowledge achieved by libraries' bibliographic systems is missing. McClure found that public librarians recognized that the network user should have a range of skills and knowledge—especially in commands and systems protocols—which they did not have and were unlikely to get in the near future. . . . There also was the perception that the organization of information and resources on the network was a "mess." This was seen as a serious barrier in their effective use of the Internet.[11]

Training and Support Needed for Staff and Public

Libraries must obtain technical support and training for librarians and the public. This issue has come up on PUBLIB and in the McClure study, especially the need to train staff before offering Internet services for public access. Librarians want to know what's available, how to find it, what the technological problems may be, and how to solve them before using the Internet on behalf of users or providing direct public access.

Administrative and Policy Issues

As public libraries gain access to the Internet, develop staff familiarity with it, and finally provide direct public access, a host of administrative and policy issues must be addressed. In general, these are not unique to public libraries, and are not treated in detail in this paper. They include:

- Privacy and security issues
- Censorship; access by minors
- Intellectual property and fair use of copyrighted materials
- Public access to commercial information services
- Whether and how to impose limits on public use when demand outstrips resources

Libraries' experience may be instructive on many of these issues. Libraries have strong policies regarding the privacy of library circulation records, and many state laws further protect the confidentiality of such information. Public libraries are veterans of censorship battles in every form of information they have acquired for public use. Tools and policies developed by the library field and put to regular use in libraries provide a solid foundation that may give libraries an advantage over other institutions just coming to grips with these volatile problems.

The Copyright Act incorporates provisions that balance the rights granted to creators and owners of intellectual property with fair use provisions and library exemptions designed to foster uses of copyrighted works for research and criticism, news reporting, education, and related purposes that benefit society as a whole. Librarians are involved in discussions of how to make sure the concept of fair use is incorporated in the electronic networked environment. At the same time, librarians are also actively seeking to ensure that licensing and other institutional arrangements allow library users access to commercial electronic information services.

The ability of public libraries to meet users' needs has always been limited by available resources, whether space, hours of operation, available staff, or the acquisitions budget. Adding Internet access or any other electronic information resources adds equipment, software, phone lines or other telecommunications capacity, and the budget for these items to the complexity. In addition, Internet access raises new issues. Should libraries limit Internet access to the library-like function of information retrieval and forgo e-mail accounts for library patrons? How does one distinguish between e-mail that is "just chat" and e-mail for the purposes of obtaining needed information?

Progress on Access, Training, and Funding

Progress is steadily—but slowly—being made on Internet access for public libraries, as a growing number of public libraries gains access using funding from a variety of sources. In 1992, John Iliff, a moderator of the PUBLIB Internet discussion group, received only 20 responses to an informal survey over the Internet that asked public librarians with Internet accounts to identify themselves.[12] However, in April 1993 PUBLIB had more than 200 participants, by May 1994 PUBLIB and a related list, PUBLIB-NET, had almost 1800 subscribers, and in February 1995 the two lists had a total of over 3000. This number probably corresponded roughly to the number of public libraries actively using the Internet at that time, according to Jean Armour Polly, the co-moderator of PUBLIB,[13] although some of the subscribers were from outside the United States or were not directly connected to public libraries.

Increasingly, the providers or brokers of Internet connectivity include existing library or library-related networks—cooperative, not-for-profit regional or state-based library service organizations that broker national bibliographic network services and other technological services for groups of libraries. Training options for librarians are offered by many of these same brokers of Internet services for libraries, especially state library agencies and library networks. An example is the CAPCON CONNECT service offered since 1992 by CAPCON, a nonprofit library services organization located in Washington, D.C. CAPCON brokers bibliographic services, coordinates cooperative purchasing discounts for online and CD-ROM database subscriptions, runs a microcomputer assistance program for libraries, and offers a professional continuing education program.

In partnership with the NSF affiliate SURAnet, CAPCON in October 1992 established itself as a node on the Internet to provide dial-up Internet access for public, academic, and specialized libraries. More than 80 libraries signed up within the first six months, and after eighteen months the figure had risen to over 200. Librarians in these libraries use the Internet for a variety of purposes such as e-mail and discussion group access to expertise in other libraries and searching databases and other Internet information resources on behalf of library users. Apart from routine technical problems, the project has gone smoothly. CAPCON will be upgrading its equipment soon and plans to offer more advanced services.

CAPCON developed a menu-based interface, a user manual, and a training course for librarians. More than 400 people have attended CAPCON training sessions. The network recently hired an Internet training and support specialist and expects to see a sharp increase in training. Dennis Reynolds, CAPCON Library Network President, says the experience confirmed his notion that the Internet requires more than just plugging in and handing out passwords—training and ongoing support are also essential.[14]

Other networks are offering similar Internet connectivity and support services and training for libraries. NYSERNet is a not-for-profit organization whose mission is to advance education and research in New York State through the interchange of information via computer networks. In cooperation with the New York State Library, NYSERNet offers a "new connections" program that makes it convenient and affordable for libraries to try out network services.[15] In January 1993, NYSERNet used grant funds to begin Project GAIN (Global Access Information Network), an experiment to connect five rural New York State public libraries and one Indian nation school to the Internet. The project's objectives included connecting library sites to the Internet, providing necessary training and support, educating participants as to the resources available on the Internet, and integrating use of the Internet into the basic activities of the library. Libraries were given computers, modems, software, printers, Internet connectivity, and a subsidy to cover long-distance telecommunications costs to the nearest dial-up point.

Librarians with NYSERNet connections have used the Internet for their own professional development and to improve reference service to patrons. One librarian managed to locate a newspaper article held at the University of Virginia after two nearby universities had been unable to find it. In another library, a 51-year-old farmer learning how to read was put in touch with new readers throughout the country. Stories such as these, plus the enthusiastic support from participants, led NYSERNet's project evaluation report to call Project GAIN an "unqualified success." It found that the libraries were eager to continue their connections past the June 1994 cutoff date and had either allocated extra funds or were trying to raise funds to remain connected.[16]

Stimulus funds from the state or local level can be important in enabling public libraries to try new services. Federal library program funds under the Library Services and Construction Act (LSCA) have long been used for interlibrary cooperation and resource sharing. In the last few years, LSCA funds have begun to be used for Internet-related projects and connectivity for public libraries. LSCA funds are allocated through state library agencies, which have responsibility for library development throughout their states. An April 1993 survey showed that 25 states have used some LSCA funds for Internet connectivity and Internet training for librarians.[17]

North Carolina's state library agency provides an example of how LSCA funds can be used to seed public library connectivity. The North Carolina Information Network, created with LSCA and state support, uses public libraries as electronic access points for a variety of state government information and databases, particularly to reach citizens and small businesses in rural areas. Incentives for library participation have included allowing the smallest and poorest libraries to participate and be trained before having to obtain funding to use network services. State government information includes state job vacancies, state contracts and bids, state administrative codes and legislative information, state statistics, and connections to university and other library catalogs in the state. As noted in the McClure study, the provision of taxpayer-supported, state-produced information has been popular and an important factor in the growth and use of the network.[18]

An even more ambitious project is underway in Maryland, where LSCA funds have been used to develop Sailor, a statewide information system. Using Gopher, a menu-based document retrieval program, users can access state and local information, reference sources, and other information throughout the world. Maryland's Division of Library Development and Services (DLDS) is establishing a statewide telecommunications network to make Sailor available at no charge in libraries and by local dial access throughout the state. DLDS is also providing Sailor training to Maryland librarians. Although Sailor is not providing individual Internet accounts to the public, some Maryland libraries have begun to offer accounts for a fee.

Other states have found other ways to fund Internet connections:

• In Michigan, a pilot program funded by the Kellogg Foundation links the information resources of the University of Michigan libraries with more than 90 public libraries. Reference service is provided to the public libraries for any type of community development question. Full Internet service is in the works.[19]

• Access Colorado, a network administered by the state library agency, has established a telecommunications network based on the Colorado SuperNet infrastructure. The purpose is to link library and non-library databases, and—most important for small and rural libraries—provide toll-free dial-up access for all state residents so they can search the network from any location.[20]

• The Cleveland Public Library and associated institutions (CLEVNET) have been using the Internet to deliver information to patrons since 1989. Using Gopher, the library is providing access to information as diverse as the 1995 Proposed Federal Budget, the full text of literary classics, and material about the Grateful Dead.

• In July of 1993, the Seattle Public Library began offering Internet access through its online catalog system, which is available on 200 terminals in library branches and on 20 dial-in lines. The nine selections on the Internet menu include the Heartland Freenet, the Library of Congress gopher, and a source for White House news. Electronic mail and file transfer are not offered, although users may send and receive mail by becoming registered users of the Heartland Freenet. Statistics from August 1993 indicated that about one fifth of terminal use in branches and one fourth of dial-up connections included a use of the Internet. Staff have encountered few problems; although there was some concern about coping with the diversity of resources available on the Internet, Jim Taylor, Automated Services Coordinator, reported that "most of the public understands that the net is very diverse and uncontrolled and that we are providing a vehicle, but not much of a map."[21]

• CARL Systems, Inc., a library vendor based in Colorado, offers a system that provides network access for library catalogs as well as commercial and locally-produced databases. The system has been installed in dozens of public libraries in Massachusetts, Maryland, Connecticut, Colorado, Texas, and other states. CARL libraries are linked, enabling users in one library to search material in libraries all over the country, and the system is accessible by Internet.

Actions Needed

While steady progress is underway to address barriers of access and training, a more coordinated effort will be needed if the majority of the nation's public libraries, especially those serving small towns and rural areas, are to provide public access to the Internet. Other issues—such as ease of use, intellectual property, and how the Internet fits into the development of a universal information superhighway—may be even more difficult to resolve, and will require coordination by a larger number of players. These players must include federal, state, and local governments; state library agencies; library cooperatives, networks, and associations; libraries themselves; and the private sector.

Public libraries have the potential to serve many roles in providing public access to the Internet. But as McClure points out,

these roles must be created; visions for these roles are needed now; and immediate public library involvement in the design and structure of the Internet/NREN is needed to insure that the public library is a key player and stakeholder in the evolving national networked information society.[22]

President Clinton provided a hopeful sign in his 1994 State of the Union Address when he stated, "We must also work with the private sector to connect every classroom, every clinic, every library, every hospital in America into a national information superhighway by the year 2000." Although legislation is pending in Congress that could provide preferential telecommunications rates for libraries, all the administration has done so far is to add libraries to the list of entities that are eligible to compete for limited funding for pilot projects and new connections grants. For instance, the Telecommunications and Information Infrastructure Program (TIAAP), administered by the National Telecommunications and Information Administration provides matching grants for state and local governments and non-profit institutions to provide educational, cultural, health care, library and public information, public safety, or other services. NTIA received over 1070 applications totaling over $560 million for this program; competition for the grants was stiff. Library projects received 5 of the 92 grants awarded in 1994 for a total of $1,851,840 of the $24,362,928 awarded. Libraries also participated as partners in projects submitted by other applicants.

Given public libraries' advantages as public training and assistance sites, and thus as creators of demand for Vice President Gore's vision of an information superhighway, the administration should consider devoting a modest amount of new funding to the program that already exists to stimulate library use of new technology and to leverage other sources of funding. Even $20 million annually in added LSCA funds devoted exclusively to Internet connectivity and training for public libraries would send a powerful message. Such a strategy would involve state library administrative agencies as allies through their administration of the federal funds. The statewide developmental responsibilities of these agencies could be a major help to small and rural library connectivity and support. Funding through LSCA would also allow states the flexibility to begin with the libraries most ready and able to take on public Internet access. The example of the early libraries would then create demand by other libraries. A specific federal program would stimulate the vision, spur the needed coordination, and foster a new role for an essential community institution—the public library as the public's electronic doorway. The American Library Association and other library groups are developing a proposal to restructure LSCA to focus more specifically and more flexibly on access to information resources through NII technology.

Notes

[1] The information and data about public libraries in this section are taken from "America's Libraries: New Views in the '90s," a 4-page 1993 update to "America's Libraries: New Views," a special report published by the American Library Association, Chicago, 1988, which draws on several national sources of data about libraries.

[2] "Report to the Office of Science and Technology Policy on Library and Information Services' Roles in the National Research and Education Network," U.S. National Commission on Libraries and Information Science, Washington, D.C., November 13, 1992.

[3] Laura J. Isenstein, "Public Libraries and National Electronic Networks: The Time to Act Is Now!" *Electronic Networking*, Vol. 2, No. 2, Summer 1992, pp. 2–5.

[4] "Technology & Access: The Electronic Doorway Library," prepared by the Phase II Statewide Automation Committee, The University of the State of New York, The State Education Department, New York State Library, Division of Library Development, Albany, New York, 1989.

[5] Bryn Geffert, "Community Networks in Libraries: A Case Study of the Freenet P.A.T.H.," *Public Libraries*, March/April 1993, pp. 91–99.

[6] Jeanne H. Simon, NCLIS Chair, in testimony before the U.S. Senate Subcommittee on Education, Arts, and Humanities, April 19, 1994.

[7] Charles R. McClure, Joe Ryan, Diana Lauterback, and William E. Moen, *Public Libraries and the INTERNET/NREN: New Challenges, New Opportunities. Syracuse,* NY: Syracuse University, School of Information Studies, 1992.

[8] Isenstein, "Public Libraries and National Electronic Networks."

[9] Robert Bocher, Wisconsin Division for Library Services, message on PUBLIB, December 1992.

[10] McClure et al., *Public Libraries and the INTERNET.*

[11] Ibid.

[12] Geffert, "Community Networks."

[13] Conversation with Jean Armour Polly, April 12, 1993.

[14] E-mail message from Dennis Reynolds, May 4, 1994.

[15] Steve Cisler, "Apple Library of Tomorrow Announces 1993 Winners for Community Networks," Posted on PUBLIB and elsewhere on the Internet, March 1, 1993.

[16] Charles R. McClure et al., *The Project Gain Report: Connecting Rural Public Libraries to the Internet.* File retrieved from NYSERNet FTP archive, 1994.

[17] The American Library Association Washington's Office surveyed state library agencies in April 1993 on their use of LSCA funds for Internet-related projects. Field study project of University of Maryland graduate library science student Dawn Williams.

[18] McClure et al., *Public Libraries and the INTERNET.*

[19] Sue Davidsen, The M-Link Project, University of Michigan Library, message on PUBLIB, December 1992.

[20] "Access Colorado," *Public Libraries*, Vol. 32, No. 1, Jan/Feb 1993, p. 48. Item notes that the information was taken from a handout provided by the Colorado State Library.

[21] Jim Taylor, posting on PUBLIB (electronic discussion group), September 21, 1993.

[22] McClure et al., *Public Libraries and the INTERNET.*

Accommodating New Classes of Users

The Internet and the Poor

Richard Civille

Introduction

As the public Internet, the precursor to the National Information Infrastructure, becomes more valuable, it creates more opportunities for those with access. By July 1994 there were an estimated 20 million individuals using the Internet in some manner in the United States, with Internet growth almost doubling yearly over the past few years. If this trend continues, the total number of Americans using the Internet may begin to surpass the number of those below the poverty level—39.3 million in 1993—by the end of 1995. This indicator could define the emergence of a two-tiered society of information haves and have-nots, especially since home ownership of personal computers and individual use of networked information have been growing most rapidly within groups with higher incomes and educational levels. Such a condition may have serious implications for low-income groups, who tend to lack access to advanced information technology, and to states that may be left behind due to economic differentials affecting information infrastructure investment.

The Clinton Administration assigns a high priority to promoting the use of the National Information Infrastructure by all Americans. Yet there is little understanding of how and to what degree different classes of individuals are using networked information services from their homes. This paper examines a survey of home computer use conducted by the U.S. Bureau of the Census in

October 1993 as well as previously collected data from 1989. These surveys begin to provide some baseline and trend data on individual use of networked information services from home.

This paper proposes a universal service policy that could encourage a leveling effect between information haves and have-nots. Such a policy would flow from a federal framework or set of guidelines, and would provide states considerable flexibility, allowing decision making at the local level. Such a policy would combine market incentives and individual tax credits to increase computer ownership among low-income households, provide electronic mail services for children and job-seekers, promote development of public access network services, and fund network literacy programs through adult education programs, public libraries, and schools.

The Face of American Poverty in the Information Economy

As the information economy expands, individual earning power has declined for many, and opportunities to move ahead have grown more limited as well. By 1987, even the traditional earning power conferred by four years of college began to decline, while the cost of a college education continued to rise.

The past recession drove over 4 million people into poverty, and for many, the ongoing recovery will not result in the return of former jobs and benefits such as full health coverage. The poverty rate has grown steadily from a low of 12.8 percent of the population in 1989 to 14.8 percent in 1993 and to 15.1 percent—39.3 million individuals—in 1994, the highest rate in ten years. In 1993, 22.7 percent of all children lived below the poverty line, the highest level since 1964. While 1989 was a recession year, this most recent increase in the poverty rate took place during a robust economic expansion. Traditionally, poverty rates fall during the second year after a recession, and 1993 was such a year. Between 1989 and 1993, however, median household income in the U.S. fell by 7 percent in real terms, after rising by 10 percent between 1983 and 1989. While the recession officially ended in March 1991, median household income has not yet recovered to its pre-recessionary level of $33,585 in 1989.[1]

The minimum wage has not kept pace with inflation for well over a decade. Today, many working poor cannot escape poverty, even with full-time jobs. While only five percent of males in their prime earning years (between the ages of 35 and 54) had low annual earnings in 1974, this figure rose to 7.5 percent by 1989 and to 8.9 percent in 1990. Between 1990 and 1992 the wages of men who left full-time jobs and then found full-time employment dropped 20 percent, from $529 a week in their old job to $423 a week in their new job.[2]

The effect on young workers (of both genders) has been even more pronounced. During the great depression, real household income fell by 25 percent. By 1990, young male and female high-school graduates earned 26 percent and 15 percent less, respectively, than they did in 1979. For full-time workers between the ages of 18 and 34, the proportion of those with low earnings roughly doubled between 1979 and 1992. From 1981 to 1989, the number of homeowners between 25 and 29 years of age declined by 11 percent, while the number of renters rose by 16 percent.[3]

Impressive gains in manufacturing productivity, brought about through process efficiency improvements using information technologies, have not created equivalent employment opportunities. There will be no new jobs in warehouses where just-in-time inventory systems have eliminated the need for them. The same effect is about to roll through the reinvention of government, as automated service delivery systems eliminate hundreds of thousands of jobs across the country. Finally, if one assumes that the younger generations tend to be literate in the use of computers and information technologies, the dramatic loss of real income in this population group over the past ten years is particularly disturbing.

The Two-Tier Society

Currently, the number of Americans using the Internet and the number under the poverty level are both increasing. Unless trends reverse, data suggest that by late 1995 at least 39 million will be at or below the poverty line, and the number may be higher. By the end of 1995 there may also be over 40 million individuals using networked information services from home. If these projections are accurate, only 5.09 million of these network users (12.7 percent) would be living in households earning under $15,000. Proportional use of other media technologies such as telephones, radios, VCRs and television—both broadcast and cable—is far more balanced across income levels than the individual use of networked information.

There is some evidence to suggest that low-income Americans want greater access to certain types of information. A recent consumer survey indicated that the poorest Americans—those in households earning less than $15,000 a year—are the most interested in acquiring independent consumer product information on automobile and health insurance, eyeglasses, and prescription drugs. Upper income consumers are less concerned. Lower income individuals spend a higher proportion of their income on such needs than upper income individuals do and thus want better informed purchasing decisions.[4]

Should policy makers be concerned about a growing gap between information haves and have-nots in terms of individual access to and use of the emerging National Information Infrastructure? The Urban Institute has found that

Lifetime incomes are becoming more unequal. The bad jobs in our economy are now paying less in real terms than they did in the early 1970s and the people who hold them aren't moving out of them with any more frequency than before. We can expect their lifetime incomes to be lower than those of people who held these jobs in the past.[5]

The Economic Policy Institute noted a "historically large surge in income inequality" in the period 1979-1989. Along with rapid gains among upper income families, with "62.9 percent income growth of the top one percent," came "stagnant or falling incomes for the bottom 80 percent of families."[6] Indeed, the United States now has the largest low-income class, the smallest middle class, and the third largest high-income class of the eight major industrial democracies.

Internet Growth and Economic Opportunity

Measures of Internet Growth

Based on current data, is there a way to predict future growth in network usage? The October 1993 Current Population Survey indicated there were 29.9 million Americans using networked information services either at home or at work. There were 19.7 million using such services at work, and 14.7 million using such services, including the Internet, from household computers. According to Internet Society figures, there were 2.06 million host computers on the Internet in October 1993, with 1.23 million of them (63 percent) in the United States.[7] While opinions vary, a common convention is to assume that ten people use each host computer on the Internet. On this basis, perhaps 12.3 million Americans had some form of Internet access in October 1993. Another way of saying this would be that 41.13 percent of the individuals using networked information services were perhaps using the Internet in some manner, such for as electronic mail.

There is no effective way to know this number with precision, and it may be much higher. Many hosts have far more than ten users. Examples include commercial services such as America Online, which has over one million individual accounts, or community networks such as the Cleveland Free-Net with over 20,000 registered users or CapAccess in Washington, DC with over 10,000. Many corporate local or wide area networks have hundreds if not thousands of users connected to host computers linked to the Internet, and the same is true of many schools.

By October 1994 the number of Internet hosts had grown to 3.9 million worldwide, with 2.67 million (68 percent) in the United States. Assuming ten users per host, this suggests there were 26.7 million Internet users in the United States in October 1994. The Internet Society calculated an 81% growth rate of Internet hosts between July 1993 and July 1994; if this growth rate continues unchanged through October 1995, there could be 48.06 million individuals using the Internet either at work or at home in the United States.

Another way to project growth is to take the 81% annual growth rate of Internet hosts established by the Internet Society and apply it to the 1993 CPS data. This is particularly interesting for the 14.7 million who used networked information services from home computers. By October 1995 this figure would grow to 47.6 million residential users of networked information services—including the Internet, which is sure to become an increasingly larger component of individual use. Applying the Internet growth coefficient to the total figure of 29.9 million individuals who used networked information services either from work or at home is quite striking. An 81% growth rate over two years would result in 96.9 million users by October, 1995.

Such numbers may seem impossibly high. Yet the Internet is the precursor to the National Information Infrastructure. The data clearly show accelerating growth in both Internet hosts and individual use of networked information services from home. An increasing number of previously independent computer networks are interconnecting to the Internet. And, increasingly, media and communications industries are merging into this broader infrastructure as well. This suggests that, even if one disputes the figure of ten people connected per host and uses a smaller figure, a coefficient based on 1993 CPS data and annual growth of Internet hosts may indeed provide a stable predictor of growth for at least the next few years. (More frequently conducted surveys could also improve these estimates.) The price/performance gains of modems, the entry of the Internet into popular culture heralded by the July 1994 cover of Time Magazine, new services such as Mosaic, and the emergence of new private service providers around the country will all be contributing factors to continued rapid growth.

Internet Electronic Mail And Economic Advantage

Probably the most frequent individual use of the Internet is text-based electronic mail.[8] Internet-based electronic mail provides a means for a person to easily and efficiently broaden and maintain a network of personal acquaintances beyond the parochial boundaries of school, community and close friends. It is becoming significantly easier for those with Internet access to seek new opportunities by extending their personal networks more efficiently than those who lack access. If, as the evidence suggests, users already tend to come from upper income families with college educations, it can be expected that income gaps will continue to widen at an accelerating rate.

When seeking new opportunities, simply going through a "friend-of-a-friend" is often not sufficient, especially if it only leads to new acquaintances within a community boundary, such as a low-income neighborhood. The acquaintance must be novel. Electronic mail appears to significantly reduce the costs of acquiring and maintaining new acquaintances beyond community boundaries, an ability that those with discretionary time and money tend to take for granted.

The range and quality of personal acquaintance networks has been shown to affect individual success in the job market. "Our acquaintances ('weak ties') are less likely to be socially involved with one another than are our close friends ('strong ties')."[9] Networks of personal acquaintances serve as "bridges" between islands of other close groups of friends, workers, business associates, or research communities. Bridging these islands of personal relationships through acquaintances broadens one's knowledge of the world, expands horizons of opportunities, and helps in career advancement or changing jobs in a weak economy. Weak Tie theory argues that

Individuals with few weak ties are confined to the provincial news and views of their close friends. This will not only insulate them from the latest ideas and fashions, but also may put them in a disadvantaged position in the labor market, where advancement may depend on knowing about job openings at just the right time.[10]

For some, fear of losing Internet access as a result of a layoff may rank with the fear of losing health insurance.

The value of weak ties lies in any chain of acquaintance that connects two people who otherwise may not know each other. Such a set of weak ties actually provides a person a bridge to an entirely new community or set of ideas. The weak tie theory has been addressed in the literature consistently over the past ten years and supported in a number of studies.

This phenomena is taken for granted by Internet users. Indeed, it is the basis of hypertext systems such as the World Wide Web that provide the user an ability to spontaneously link to previously unknown information resources through a novel connection suggested in the material being browsed. These resource connections often lead one to new acquaintances and relationships associated with them.

Recent inquiries have begun to address the use of electronic mail in the maintenance of personal acquaintance networks. Internet mail has been found to be a highly efficient means of establishing and maintaining personal acquaintance networks. It is fairly clear to an Internet user that having access to "distributed lists in email systems greatly reduces the costs to the individual of discovering others with common interests."[11]

October 1993 Current Population Survey

The Clinton Administration established an interagency task force to promote development of the National Information Infrastructure. This process involved executive orders, wide dissemination of a vision document outlining a policy agenda, and establishment of a private sector advisory council and numerous working groups examining a wide array of issues ranging from intellectual property to advanced applications.[12] A key Administration principle calls for advancing access to an NII that can be "used by Americans, for example to create new jobs, provide new services and products, educate our children, and promote better health care."[13] A presidential executive order issued on September 15, 1993, created a United States Advisory Council on the National Information Infrastructure (NII) to advise on application development strategies including "electronic commerce, agile manufacturing, life-long learning, health care, government services and civic networking."

The President defined the NII as "the integration of hardware, software and skills that will make it easy and affordable to connect people with each other, with computers, and with a vast array of services and information resources. Data on how individual Americans are using networked information services—particularly from home—is particularly important to gather and analyze in order to measure the effects of Administration policy goals and activities concerning the National Information Infrastructure.

While the government has not implemented any particular survey strategy designed to measure how Americans are affected by the NII in their daily lives, Census data has been collected concerning home computer ownership and individual use. The U.S. Bureau of the Census contracts with federal agencies to provide monthly statistical samples through the Current Population Survey (CPS). For example, the Bureau of Labor Statistics prepares monthly unemployment figures through analyses of data collected by the CPS and paid for by BLS.

As a component of the October 1993 CPS, the Census Bureau conducted a survey of home computer ownership and use as part of an annual school enrollment survey contracted by the National Center for Education Statistics (NCES).[14] Previous school enrollment surveys for NCES that included home computer use supplements had been conducted in 1989 and 1984. The sample size for the October 1993 Current Population Survey is 143,646 individuals in 55,809 households, with 32,764 children under the age of 15 and 110,882 adults (persons age 15 or older). These data provide a good baseline for identifying trends on how Americans are being affected by the National Information Infrastructure and the new economy it represents.

The survey counts computers in households as well as peripheral devices such as CD-ROM drives and modems, and it asks a range of questions about how the computer is used by household members. Household members are asked how often a computer is used and the purposes for which it is used, which may range from word-processing to telemarketing to electronic mail. Each household member is also asked whether they use computers at school or at work and for what purpose.

There are limitations in the CPS survey instruments, which could be improved in the future. Use of networked information services must be inferred from the data. The CPS questionnaire has no single data point for networked information services, and certainly no data point for the Internet. To compensate for this, an output variable, "networked information services," was created by combining four data points concerning use of electronic mail, use of bulletin board systems, connecting to a computer at work, and using a computer for communication purposes. While respondents were queried about their use of personal computers for communications from either home or at work, no questions were asked about usage of electronic mail or other online services at school or in public libraries. General use questions were in some respects vague, for example asking respondents whether they used home computers for "analysis." It would also improve future surveys if questions were asked about why members of households with computers do not use networked information services, as these might yield information about barriers to use. Finally, because the CPS home computer use data has only been collected on a four year cycle, it is difficult to measure the rates of change in important trends of ownership and use.[15]

Because the data on computer and network use is collected along with labor and education statistics, it becomes possible to cross-tabulate important variables such as race, sex, household income, employment status, educational attainment, and general geographic location. The 1993 October CPS is thus by far the largest, richest, and most recent data set available that can help provide an understanding of how individuals and groups are being affected by the emerging National Information Infrastructure.

Home Computer Ownership and Use of Networked Information Services

Networked information refers to the vast electronic information resources that can be acquired through the Internet and to the commercial online services, library automated catalog services, and other resources available over the NII. Networked information services include electronic mailing lists, newsgroups, databases, and electronic card catalogs on topics ranging from high energy physics to gardening to antique automobiles to federal grants to local city council minutes.

Out of a total 98.6 million households in October 1993 there were 26.5 million — representing sixty-nine million Americans—with personal computers, up from 13.7 million in 1989 and 6.9 million in 1984. The percentage of households with personal computers was 26.9 percent in October 1993, up from 15 percent in 1989 and 8.2 percent in 1984. Of households with computers, 9.19 million (34.7 percent) had modems, up from 3.25 million (23 percent) in 1989.[16] (See Figure 1.)

From either their home or their workplace, 29.9 million individuals (11.4 percent of the population) had access to networked information services in October 1993. In 1989, only 8.6 million individuals (3.7 percent of the population) used networked information services from either home or at work.

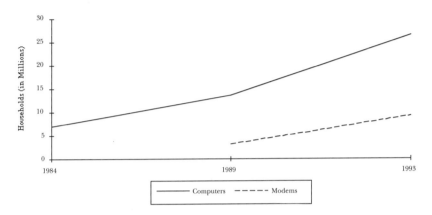

Figure 1   Households with Computers and Modems, 1984–1993.

Of all individuals using networked information services in 1993, there were 19.7 million (7.7 percent) using such services from work and 14.7 million (5.75 percent) from home. In 1989, there were 5.78 million individuals (2.5 percent) using such services from work and 3.9 million (1.7 percent) from home. (See Figure 2.)

Of those using network services at work in 1993, 5.5 million also did so at home (27.6 percent of all users). On average, about two thirds (65 percent) of the members of any household that has a computer are computer users, and 49 percent of households with personal computers have at least one member who uses network information services.

General Characteristics

The majority of individuals using networked information services are likely to have some form of access to the Internet (at least electronic mail), tend to live in middle to upper income households in metropolitan areas either in the northeast or western states, and are likely to have at least a four year college degree if they are not currently enrolled in school. The average age of individuals in households with a computer is 43.5. The average age of those living in a household without a computer is 50.5. The average income of a household with a computer is $52,036, whereas the average income of households without computers is $27,425.

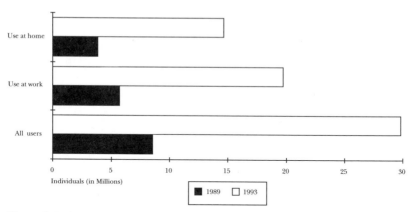

Figure 2 Individual Use of Networked Information Services, 1989–1993. Source: U.S. Bureau of the Census.

Using a computer at work or at school is a strong predictor of home computer ownership. Of all users of home computers, 71.7 percent also use them at work or at school. Computers are present in 38.6 percent of all households with a member at least 15 years of age enrolled in school, compared to only 20.5 percent of households without students. For children under 15, 29.8 percent have access to a home computer.

There were 34.7 million men (27.9 percent) living in households with personal computers and 33.9 million women (25.9 percent) in 1993, compared to 15.1 million men (17.6 percent) and 14.5 million women (15.3 percent) living in households with personal computers in 1989. In 1993 there were 14.7 million men using networked information services either at work or at home and 14.3 million women using such services. However, there were 10.9 million men who used networked information services from a personal computer at home, compared to only 2.8 million women. In 1989 there were 5.4 million men and 5.4 women using networked information either at home or work, with 3.3 million men and 1.5 million women using such services at home. These data show a dramatically accelerating gender gap in the individual use of networked information services at home, between 1989 and 1993. This gap suggests that women are far less likely than men to use networked information services for personal reasons. (See Figure 3.)

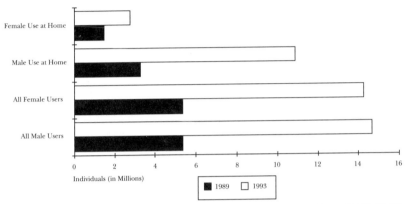

Figure 3 Gender and Use of Networked Information Services, 1989–1993. Source: U.S. Bureau of the Census.

With some interesting exceptions, education, income, geographic location, and ethnicity are predictors of use for home computers and networked information services. The following sections dicsuss these factors in detail.

Education Attainment Distribution

Trends show significantly different rates of individual network use at home across levels of education attainment. While gaps are significantly narrowing between college and high school graduates, individuals who have not graduated from high school are being left far behind. (See Figure 4.)

• There were 2.1 million high school dropout householders with personal computers in their homes in 1993, up from 1.37 million in 1989. There were 604,000 individuals in these households using networked information services from computers in their homes in 1993, up from 54,000 in 1989.

• There were 28.2 million high school graduate householders with personal computers in their homes in 1993, up from 8.6 million in 1989. There were 6.1 million individuals in these households using network services from computers in their homes in 1993, up from 554,000 in 1989.

• There were 27.5 million college graduate householders with personal computers in their homes in 1993, up from 19 million in

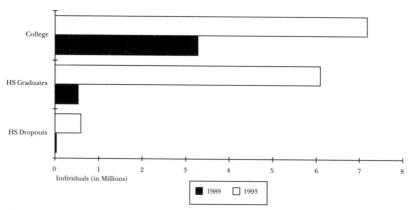

Figure 4 Education Attainment and Use of Networked Information Services, 1989–1993. Source: U.S. Bureau of the Census.

1989. There were 7.2 million individuals in these households using network services from computers in their homes in 1993, up from 3.3 million in 1989.

Income Distribution

Household income is a predictor of home computer ownership and use of networked information services. Individual use of networked information services from home increased at an accelerating rate within upper income groups but grew at a slower rate within lower income groups. In 1989 there were more individuals with household incomes greater than $50,000 using networked information services than any income group. In 1993, this had changed, with the number of individuals in households earning between $30,000 and $50,000 becoming the largest group of home users. (See Figure 5.)

• Of individuals living in households earning less than $15,000 a year, there were 4.7 million with personal computers in 1993, up from 2.5 million in 1989. There were 764,000 of these individuals using networked information services from computers in their homes in 1993, up from 264,000 in 1989.

• Of individuals living in households earning between $15,000 and $30,000, there were 9.2 million with personal computers in 1993, up from 7.2 million in 1989. There were 1.8 million individuals

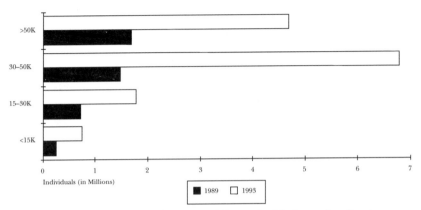

Figure 5 Household Income and Use of Networked Information Services, 1989–1993. Source: U.S. Bureau of the Census.

using networked information services from computers in their homes in 1993, an increase from 734,000 in 1989.

• Of individuals living in households earning between $30,000 and $50,000 a year, there were 15.7 million with personal computers in 1993, up from 9.7 million in 1989. There were 6.8 million people from this income group using networked information services from computers in their homes in 1993, an increase from 1.5 million in 1989.

• Of individuals living in households earning over $50,000, there were 24.4 million with personal computers in 1993, up from 8.2 million in 1989. There were 4.7 million from this income group using such services from computers in their homes, an increase from 1.7 million in 1989.

Racial and Ethnic Distribution

Income, education and location may be stronger driving forces in creating information haves and have-nots than race and ethnicity, but the use of computers and networks does vary somewhat between racial and ethnic groups. Asians have the highest percentage of home computer ownership of any racial or ethnic group. In households with computers, Native Americans, traditionally a low-income group, may use networked information services to a larger extent than any other ethnic group. These findings raise interesting questions about the extent to which race or ethnicity serve as predictors for computer ownership or use of networked information services.

Out of a total 7.3 million Asian individuals, there were 2.7 million living in households with computers in 1993, the highest percentage (37.3 percent) of any racial or ethnic group. There were 706,677 individuals (9.7 percent) from this group using networked information services in 1993 with 360,000 using such services in their homes.[17]

Out of a total of 212.6 million White individuals, there were 61.1 million (28.7 percent) in households with computers, an increase from 37.7 million in 1989. There were 26 million individuals (12 percent) from this group using networked information services in 1993, of whom 12.5 million used such services in their homes, an increase from 4 million in 1989.

Out of a total of 32.2 million Black individuals, there were 4.3 million (13.4 percent) living in households with computers in 1993, an increase from 1.6 million in 1989. There were two million individuals (6.7 percent) from this group using networked information services in 1993, of whom 746,000 used such services in their homes, an increase from 89,000 in 1989.

Out of a total of 1.56 million Native American individuals, there were 197,000 (12.6 percent) living in households with computers in 1993[18]. There were 120,000 individuals from this ethnic group using networked information services. There were 47,000 individuals from this group using such services in their homes.[19]

Out of a total of 23.3 million Hispanic individuals, there were 2.9 million (12.4 percent) living in households with computers in 1993, an increase from one million in 1989. There were 1.1 million individuals (4.8 percent) from this group using networked information services in 1993, of whom 495,000 used such services in their homes, an increase from 88,000 in 1989.

Geographic Distribution

Overall, the western United States has the highest percentage of home computer ownership (32.6 percent). There are three smaller subregions with high percentages of home computer ownership (greater than 30 percent): the New England Division (33.7 percent), with states such as Vermont and Massachusetts; the Mountain Division (32.8 percent), with states such as Colorado and New Mexico; and the Pacific Division (32.5 percent), with states such as California and Washington. The subregion with the lowest home computer ownership is the East South Central Division (16.3 percent), with such states as Mississippi and Tennessee—home of information highway advocate Vice President Gore. Use of networked information services follows a similar geographic trend, with the highest use in the Mountain Division (14.2 percent) and the lowest in the East South Central Division (7.1 percent).

Metro and Non-Metro

Changing demographics due to economic restructuring away from natural resource extraction characterize much of rural America, as does inadequate and costly telecommunications. In 1993 there were 197.6 million individuals living in metro areas and 55.6 million living in non-metro areas. There were 57.26 million in metro areas (29 percent) living with personal computers in their homes but only 10.7 million (19.3 percent) in non-metro areas. Of all individuals, there were 24.5 million (12.4 percent) using networked information services either at work or at home in metro areas and 4.24 million (7.6 percent) in rural areas. Of all individuals living in households with personal computers, there were 11.7 million (20.4 percent) using such services at home in metro areas and 1.9 million (17.2 percent) in rural areas.

It is notable that the overall percentages of individual use of networked information services at home in both metro and non-metro areas is nearly equivalent, regardless of the fact that costs tend to be higher in rural areas. "When information age technology is being used it is often to be used with even greater intensity in rural households than their urban counterparts—reflecting greater incidence of home-based business activity as well as greater need to overcome economic limitations associated with geographic space."[20] Another trend that should not be overlooked is a growing tendency for some white collar entrepreneurs to leave cities to seek a rural lifestyle. These individuals may be financial traders, writers, designers, software developers, or others with similar skills that are not geographically bound. According to the Center for the New West, these individuals require rural towns to provide a climate conducive to small business, access to the Internet and high speed data services, commercial world-wide courier services, same-day delivery of the major newspapers of record, proximity to a regional airport, and a local clerical and administrative labor pool. With these characteristics in place, a typical "lone eagle" can bring in an average of $150,000 a year in additional revenues to a local rural economy. (See Figure 6.)

Working Class and College Towns

A critical mass of skilled workers often fuels a local marketplace that caters to their expertise. Highly skilled mechanics and welders are attracted to industrial manufacturing cities, academics to college towns. Yet the local marketplaces for the information economy may not develop in traditional working class areas, creating future ghettos of have-nots. How do working class and college towns compare?

Predictably, Flint, Michigan—home to General Motors—and Ann Arbor, home to the University of Michigan, highlight dramatic differences in computer ownership and use of networked information services. In 1993 there were 452,712 people in Flint and 241,536 in Ann Arbor. (See Figure 7.) There were 24,120 individuals (14.4 percent) in Flint living in households with personal computers, while Ann Arbor had 51,955 individuals (55.6 percent) living in households with personal computers in 1993. There were 25,000 individuals using networked information services (5.4 percent) in Flint, while Ann Arbor had 64,000 using such services (26.6). There were 11,196 individuals using networked information services in homes with personal computers (17.1 percent) in Flint, while Ann Arbor had 38,087 using such services (34.7 percent).

Blue Collar Workers

The growth of the information economy often appears to come at the expense of traditional industrial manufacturing jobs. It appears likely traditional blue collar workers will become increasingly

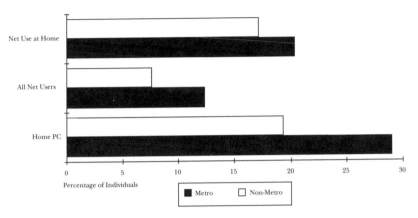

Figure 6 Individual Use of Networked Information Services from Metro and Non-Metro Areas. Source: U.S. Bureau of the Census.

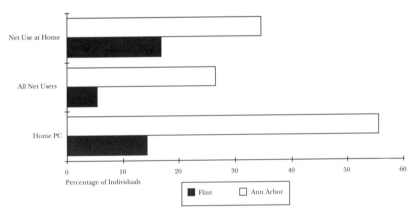

Figure 7 Individual Use of Networked Information Services in Flint and Ann Arbor, Michigan. Source: U.S. Bureau of the Census.

marginalized as information have-nots. One survey of likely voters observed that

blue collar men are surprisingly interested in this [information highway] issue. The blue collar workers who are particularly activated in this issue are, by and large, younger. They are partial to technology and worried about their own job skills and their children's education. They also are particularly supportive of a government role in education and of policies that make technologies more broadly available[21].

There were 51.8 million blue collar workers (26.8 percent) out of a total adult population of 197.6 million in October, 1993.[22] There were 10 million blue collar workers (19 percent) living in households with personal computers, compared to 26.9 percent in the overall population. There were 3.62 million (6.68 percent of all blue collar workers) using networked information services, compared to 11.4 percent in the population as a whole. There were 2.6 million using such services from a computer at home.

Universal Service and the Internet

It is likely that opportunities in the new economy will increasingly flow to those with access to the National Information Infrastructure—especially those who can strategically apply its resources, as in using electronic mail to enter labor markets. Access to networking could also encourage civic involvement. For example, a recent consumer survey suggested that voting in elections was a highly desired use of networked information services and that "60 percent of respondents expressed a moderate-to-strong interest in being part of public-opinion polls; 57 percent would like to participate in interactive, electronic town-hall meetings with political leaders and other citizens; and 46 percent want to send video or text e-mail to elected representatives."[23]

The Internet delivers social and economic value to those individuals using it effectively. Unlike the use of television, telephones, radios and VCRs, individual use of networked information services appears to be accelerating at higher income and education attainment levels; therefore, benefits are flowing at an accelerating rate to these groups as well. It is not at all surprising that this trend parallels a ten-year trend in widening income gaps as the information economy becomes more pervasive. Universal service policy needs to address these growing inequities.

A universal service policy that could encourage a leveling effect between information haves and have-nots should be developed for the National Information Infrastructure and specifically the public Internet. Such a policy would have a federal framework, that is, a minimum set of standards and expectations set by national legislation. However, this federal framework would need to provide state and local jurisdictions considerable flexibility and decision-making capacity. It would combine market incentives and individual tax credits to increase computer ownership among low-income households, promote development of public access network services, and fund network literacy programs through adult education programs, public libraries, and schools.

A Universal Service principle was articulated in the 1934 Communications Act "to make available, so far as possible, to all the people of the United States a . . . wire and radio communication service." Definitions of universal communications service continue to evolve with advances in technologies and changes in public expectations. Policy debates tend to swing between the notion of universal access—the equivalent of dialtone—and an evolving notion of universal service for the NII, which considers end user equipment, content development and usage skills. For example, telecommunications industries would tend to limit their role to a notion of universal access—providing connections to schools, libraries and civic institutions.[24] Providing support for training, end-user equipment and content development are often seen as roles for government and public private partnerships.

The issue of universal access should be considered separately from that of universal service, meaning that in an individual's ability to obtain access to network services is an issue separate from the provision of the services themselves.[25]

Universal Service does more than promote social equity and fair play. Before considering aspects of the proposed approach to Universal Service, it is helpful to first mention the law of the network externality, a characteristic of telephone economics that applies to the Internet and the NII. Basically stated, the value of a network depends upon the number of people who can be reached through that network. A corollary of the law holds that the value of an individual network connection is greater than the individual private value (which in some cases is less than the cost) because connection increases the value to others on the network.[26]

The law of the network externality provides an economic case for universal service policies. Because the Internet is a distributed network of networks, value is added not only to members of newly connected networks but to the entire set of previously connected networks. This is why commercial services such as CompuServe and Prodigy have reversed earlier positions and connected their subscribers to the growing public Internet rather than trying to control captive membership bases. Connecting their services to the Internet simply makes their subscriber services more valuable, thus attracting new customers or retaining existing ones.

Policy Should Provide for State and Local Flexibility

It is too early to understand what Universal Service for the NII should be, and a period of experimentation within the "laboratory of the states" should be encouraged, before establishing federal baselines. Therefore, any federal framework for Universal Service should provide flexibility for states to develop their own priorities and financing mechanisms, and empower local communities to establish their own criteria, programs and services. Wisconsin and Colorado are two states on the forefront of establishing universal service policies. The two types of state-based financing mechanisms described suggest important ways to support network literacy programs and public access network services at the community level.

In June 1994, Wisconsin passed a law deregulating the telecommunications industry in exchange for a mix of price caps, investment guarantees, worker retraining funding, and development of both a universal service fund and an advanced applications foundation. All telecommunication providers will contribute to the Wisconsin universal service fund. The fund will assist low-income and disabled customers in high-cost areas in accessing advanced services capabilities and will promote statewide affordable access to high-quality education, library, and health care information services. The Wisconsin Advanced Telecommunications Foundation will establish a 25-million-dollar endowment fund through a mix of state appropriations, service provider matches, and other contributions. The Fund will support telecommunication application projects and consumer education in advanced telecommunication services. A priority for the Fund will be local government, educational institutions, libraries, and school districts with below-average allowable revenues[27].

In Colorado, a Telecommunications Advisory Council report recommended the state assembly create a Colorado Network Users' Trust Fund in 1995. The proposed shared public investment pool would support public access and universal service priorities until they were met, and would then be dissolved. The Trust could be funded through a mix of subscriber fees similar to Lifeline and service provider contributions. The report points out that assessing a one-dollar-per-month fee on 3 million residential and business lines in Colorado would build a 180 million dollar fund in five years[28].

Offer Tax Incentives for Low-Income Home Computer Ownership

A combination of tax credits could make it possible for low-income households to better afford personal computers and access to networked information services.

Accelerating depreciation schedules for personal computers used in business could rapidly create a secondary market of quality used equipment that could flow to low-income households and poverty-level microenterprises. In order for a business to qualify for an accelerated depreciation, it could be required that the equipment be provided to a school, charity organization, or low-income individual, with the name of the recipient to be listed on the tax form.

Existing mechanisms such as the Earned Income Tax Credit could be used to create a one-time credit for the purchase of a new computer system for household use. The EITC would be useful because it is already designed to target low and moderate income working families with children. This mechanism could also be used to provide credits for the purchase of networked information services, software, and training that could be set to various levels depending upon family size and household income.

Provide Email to Low-Income Children and the Unemployed

Internet-based electronic mail may well be a public good, with implications concerning the types of basic services that should be bundled into any new consideration of Universal Service policies. Free, public access to Internet mailing lists can create new opportunities for displaced workers and low-income children to broaden their networks of personal acquaintances for employment and education prospects far outside their schools and neighborhoods.

Free access to Internet-based mailing lists could become a jumping-off point for a young student, enabling him or her to not only follow the current debate on a particular research topic but actually find out about and acquaint themselves with members of particular research communities. For example, CapAccess, a public access network service in Washington, DC, promotes Internet electronic mail in public schools. A middle school librarian involved with CapAccess worked with a parent's group called Citizens Advocating Science and Technology (CAST). Parents learned about a vast array of topic-based Internet mailing lists to which their children could subscribe to through free CapAccess accounts.

There are an increasing number of popular books on the Internet available in general bookstores, many of which catalog Internet mailing lists. Such books serve as references school librarians can use to help students identify interesting lists. Messages distributed through Internet-based mailing lists typically include electronic and postal addresses and even telephone numbers of the sender, providing a way for subscribers to become better acquainted with each other if they wish.

For job-seekers, weak ties facilitated over electronic mail can increase the potential for strong ties that can result in new working relationships. Internet-based mailing lists have significant potential for transforming weak ties of acquaintance into strong ties that can result in instrumental actions and productive gains. As Pickering and King note, "The maintenance of weak ties can play a crucial role for an individual when he or she is forced to change jobs. Such a situation is a classic case when current job ties are likely to be useless, but ties to individuals in other employment settings might be very valuable indeed"[29]. For disadvantaged groups, an increase in weak tie interactions "reduces inequality, thereby creating a more equitable distribution of employment across groups."[30]

By encouraging broad access to internet electronic mail, universal service policy can effectively reduce costs associated with meeting new people and maintaining relationships that can lead over time to new employment and education opportunities. Internet-based electronic mail introduces a new process efficiency in creating and maintaining novel relationships. Weak ties can be efficiently and cost-effectively maintained by continued subscription and occasional postings to newsgroups and mailing lists. This helps retain options for more serious communications leading to new strong ties in other social or work domains. Exchange of employment information over a network also facilitates a free labor market. Policy that encourages such broad individual use of the NII could have a social and economic leveling effect.

Expand the Concept of Universal Service from POTS to PANS

Universal service policy can level the playing field in some respects by supporting community-based public access network services. The driving characteristic of universal service over the past sixty years has been access to plain old telephone service (POTS). In the information age, access is a more complex proposition that requires support for users as well as information content. While no formal surveys have been conducted, there are good indications that there are perhaps 200,000 individuals using public access network services (PANS) provided by community-based organizations.

There is good evidence that policy directives through the Information Infrastructure Task Force have resulted in broad investments across a range of domestic assistance programs. Such policy directives should be formalized into Congressional findings in legislative proposals for telecommunications reform. These findings should accent the roles of public libraries and local non-profit organizations in supporting universal service goals.

As Moltz notes, "Civic network programming can provide access to Internet, job rosters, community listings, educational resources, health information and governmental databases"[31]. Many of these types of services have traditionally been provided by public libraries. The Library Services and Construction Act (LSCA) has been a basic program supporting public library infrastructure. There is a proposal to recast the program to become the Library Services and Communication Act, which would establish public libraries as community-based access centers to networked information resources[32].

Currently, 20.9 percent of public libraries have some type of Internet connection. Library connections to the Internet are most prevalent in the west, at 28.2 percent, and the northeast, at 25.9 percent, following trends of both home ownership of computers and individual use of networked information services. Only 5.7% of public libraries have network connections provided through local public access network services, although 12.8% of all public libraries are providing content information to such services in some form.

The federal government has taken a leadership role through the National Telecommunications and Information Administration (NTIA) of the Department of Commerce, which has awarded close to one hundred Telecommunications and Information Infrastructure Assistance Program grants in 1994. About thirty percent of the grants supported community information service activities. The 1995 appropriation could increase from 24 to 60 million and should be able to support more than three hundred local projects. With only modest scaling, these public access network services could easily be providing low-cost access to the National Information Infrastructure to millions of individuals within five years. Because they are matching grants, they leverage substantial local partnership participation and investment as well.

There are other examples of how existing federal assistance programs are supporting universal service as well. The National Science Foundation assisted in providing Internet connections to over 1,000 schools and libraries in 1994. The Tennessee Valley Authority is working with local government and business leaders to plan Telecommunications Rural Application Centers in the Elk

River region of south central Tennessee and Northern Alabama. The Americorp National Service initiative is deploying 20,000 volunteers to work on community projects around the country, including information services. The Rural Development Administration has invested 20 million dollars in technology grants to rural schools and health care providers. The Economic Development Administration supports a project promoting telecommunications planning among a number of rural Colorado communities. The Department of Housing and Urban Development has awarded a large number of enterprise community (EC) initiatives. An EC project in Burlington, Vermont includes support for a Community Technology Center that will link residents, businesses, and social services to a local civic network, statewide networks, and the National Information Infrastructure.

With time, funding, and continued promotion of universal service goals by the Administration, the number of community-based public access network services and connected libraries could rapidly increase. However, unless a certain level of literacy skills in the use of networked information have been attained by the general population, access will be of limited benefit.

Network Literacy and Acquiring High-Performance Work Skills

The Office of Technology Assessment (OTA), in a report on adult literacy, pointed out that no more than 15 percent of literacy providers use computers regularly, and adult literacy applications are not high priorities for most vendors and developers in the technology industry[33]. Yet without the necessary skills to use the National Information Infrastructure, access is meaningless and competition for jobs will leave the unskilled far behind. Developing innovative community-based job training programs for displaced workers and disadvantaged youth that focus on high-performance workplace competencies and network literacy should be a key component in the formulation of universal service policy.

The National Education Goals state that "by the year 2000, every adult will have the knowledge and skills necessary to compete in a global economy and exercise the rights and responsibilities of citizenship." The Economic Policy Institute has found that attainment of computer skills "tends to widen pay differences between educational groups moreso than in the past."[34] Yet simply acquiring computer skills has become insufficient in the age of the Internet. It has become important to be literate in the use of networked information, and any universal service policy must address this. This is necessary to close income gaps as well as to promote civic participation.

Network literacy has been described as a critical skill for citizens in the future, who must be able "to identify, access, and use electronic information from the network if they wish to be productive and effective in both their personal and professional lives"[35]. The necessary knowledge includes awareness of the range and use of globally networked information resources and how to apply such resources in everyday problem solving and improving individual quality of life. Particular skills would include an understanding of how to search for, browse, and retrieve desired materials and how to manipulate networked information with other resources to add value. These are general adult literacy skills needed to survive in an information economy[36].

In an information economy, good jobs require analytical research skills, not simply the ability to read and write and follow instructions. Many workers are becoming "symbolic analysts"[37]. For example, a farmer becomes a researcher when faced with sophisticated analytical demands of modern agriculture, where critical choices balancing integrated pest management, environmental regulations, weather, and cost must be factored into assessing commodity prices for global futures markets. In past times, workers needed a fundamental education that would enable them to read, write, comprehend instructions, follow direction faithfully, and show up for work promptly. Useful as such skills were in the industrial economy, they were perhaps insufficient for good citizenship, and quite insufficient for the modern workplace. In the emerging high-performance workplace, "virtually everyone acts as a decision maker, gathers and sifts information, sets up and troubleshoots systems, organizes workflow and team arrangements, manipulates data to solve problems, and, on occasion, provides direction to colleagues"[38].

Preparing students in schools for such a workplace—and retraining displaced adult workers—is going to require network literacy.

This is because the high-performance workplace will be increasingly laced with networked information systems, and workers need to learn how to use them, to solve problems and to work effectively in teams. Not only will developing such skills produce high-performance workers, it can produce high-performance citizens as well, because the same skills enrich individual use of networked information services from home, for personal use.

The Secretary of Labor's Commission on Acquiring Necessary Skills (SCANS) provides a vision of the high-performance worker. SCANS outlines a set of five competencies involving the use of resources, dealing with interpersonal relationships, working with information, working with systems, and working with technology. The SCANS report envisions a high-performance worker who can 1) allocate time, money, materials, space, staff; 2) work on teams, teach others, serve customers, lead, negotiate, and work well with people from culturally diverse backgrounds; 3) acquire and evaluate data, organize and maintain files, interpret and communicate, and use computers to process information; 4) understand social, organizational, and technological systems, and monitor and correct them; 5) select equipment and tools, apply technology to specific tasks, and maintain and troubleshoot technologies. It is clear that within this vision of the high-performance worker, more recent debates concerning network literacy and universal service become quite relevant.

The SCANS report goes on to point out that high-performance skills should also be taught "in federally funded training programs for disadvantaged youth and adults, including displaced workers, under the Job Training Partnership Act (JTPA) of the Department of Labor, and public assistance training under the JOBS program of the Department of Health and Human Services."[39] Some of these programs, such as JTPA Youth Fair Chance Program, seem uniquely well suited to provide network literacy training to low-income individuals. For example, the Youth Fair Chance program provides training and employment opportunities to young adults aged 14 through 30 in low-income communities. The program provides for substantial community-based participation in program design, and state direction is minimal, which creates opportunities for locally directed innovation. Communities can use a range of program designs including "non-residential learning centers; alternative

schools; combined activities including school to work, apprentice-
ship, or postsecondary education programs; teen parent programs;
youth centers" and others[40].

Conclusion

National Information Infrastructure policy that leverages private
investments to build the information highway through public/
private partnerships, government funded research, or tax incentives must also demonstrate positive effects on low and moderate
income families and a potential for lifting Americans out of poverty
rather than creating a two-tier society of information haves and
have-nots.

A better understanding of residential use of the Internet or how
individuals use networked information for consumer education or
civic participation purposes would be invaluable. The federal
government should directly conduct surveys that can lead to a
better understanding of social and economic effects of the National Information Infrastructure on individuals. While the Current Population Survey is a superb framework for doing this, a
survey of home computer use every four years is inadequate. The
questionnaire used in the October 1993 CPS for the data evaluated
in this paper should be carefully reviewed, and a plan should be
implemented for a yearly survey using the CPS that is focused more
particularly on the individual use of the National Information
Infrastructure as well as individual wants and needs.

It is clear from the CPS data and other surveys that the growth rate
of the Internet is exploding, and this trend follows the increased
use of networked information services both at home and at work.
Without intervention, it is also highly likely that a two-tier society of
information haves and have-nots will emerge. A universal service
policy would combine market incentives and individual tax credits
to increase computer ownership among low-income households,
provide electronic mail services for children and job-seekers, promote development of public access network services, and fund
network literacy programs through adult education programs,
public libraries, and schools.

Notes

[1] U.S. Bureau of the Census. "Income, Poverty, and Valuation of Noncash Benefits: 1993 (P60-188)." Washington, DC, 1994.

[2] U.S. Bureau of the Census. "Dynamics of Economic Well-Being: Labor Force and Income, 1990-1992 (P70-40)." Washington, DC, 1993.

[3] U.S. Department of Commerce. "Housing in America." Washington, DC, 1992

[4] Marcia Mogelonsky. "Poor and Unschooled, but a Smart Shopper." *American Demographics*. July 1994.

[5] Isabel V. Sawhill and Mark Condon. "Is U.S. Inequality Really Growing?" *Policy Bites* No. 13. Washington, DC: Urban Institute, June 1992.

[6] Lawrence Mishel and Jared Bernstein. *The State of Working America 1992-93*, p. 201. Washington, DC: Economic Policy Institute, 1993.

[7] Internet Society, "Internet Survey Reaches 3.8 Million Internet Host Level— 3rd Quarter 1994 Growth Is 21 Percent." Press Release, November 4, 1994.

[8] Hal Varian and Jeffrey K. MacKie-Mason. "Economic FAQs About the Internet." University of Michigan, May 1994.

[9] Mark Granovetter and Nan Lin, eds. *Social Structure and Network Analysis*, pp. 105-130. Beverly Hills, CA: Sage, 1982.

[10] Ibid.

[11] Jeanne M. Pickering and John Leslie King. "Hardwiring Weak Ties: Individual and Institutional Issues in Computer Mediated Communication." In *CSCW Proceedings*. Association for Computing Machinery, November 1992.

[12] Information Infrastructure Task Force. *The National Information Infrastructure: An Agenda for Action*. Department of Commerce. Washington, DC, 1993.

[13] Information Infrastructure Task Force. *The National Information Infrastructure: Progress Report, Sept. 1993–1994*. Department of Commerce. Washington, DC, 1994.

[14] As this paper goes into publication, the CPS was about to release data from an October 1994 survey, commissioned by the National Telecommunications and Information Administration (NTIA) of the U.S. Dept. of Commerce.

[15] See note 14. The instrument is assumed to be the same one employed in October 1993.

[16] The following analyis is based upon 1993 source data compiled through a collaboration with the Rand Corporation in Santa Monica, CA compared with U.S. Bureau of the Census, Current Population Reports, Series P-23, No. 171, *Computer Use in the United States: 1989*. U.S. Government Printing Office, Washington. DC, 1991. The data are subject to sampling variability and other sources of error.

[17] Source data for 1989 was not available for this analysis.

[18] Source data for 1989 was not available for this analysis.

[19] The total number of Native American households in the October 1993 CPS survey were 1,703 out of over 55,000. The significance of these numbers should be viewed with caution.

[20] Bruce Johnson and John Allen. "Involvement in the Information Age: A Profile of Nebraska Households." University of Nebraska, 1993.

[21] Mellman Lake. "What People Think about New Communications Technologies." Washington, DC: Benton Foundation, 1994.

[22] The blue collar category is based on occupation codes 403–469 and 503–889, i.e., without farm workers but including various "blue collar services." See the "Detailed Occupation Recodes" section in the CPS documentation.

[23] Charles Pillar. "Consumers Want More Than TV Overload from the Information Superhighway, but Will They Get It?" *MacWorld*. September 1994.

[24] Residential access to high-bandwidth information infrastructure is generally seen as a long range universal access goal, but unfeasible in the short term. Universal access to public buildings is seen as feasible.

[25] U.S. Council For International Business. *Private Sector Leadership: Policy Foundations for a National Information Infrastructure*, p. 4. July 1994.

[26] Gerald W. Brock. *Telecommunication Policy for the Information Age*, pp. 74–75. Cambridge, MA: Harvard University Press, 1994.

[27] Because this law had only recently been enacted, it is far too early to tell how these mechanisms will actually be implemented.

[28] Colorado Telecommunications Advisory Commission. "In the Public Interest: The Colorado Information Infrastructure." September 26, 1994.

[29] Ibid.

[30] James D. Montgomery. "Weak Ties, Employment, and Inequality: An Equilibrium Analysis," *American Journal of Sociology*, vol. 99, no. 5, pp. 1212–1236. March 1994.

[31] K. Moltz. "Civic Networks in the United States." Mimeograph. New York: Columbia University, Graduate Program in Public Policy and Administration, 1994.

[32] Charles McClure, John Carlo Bertot, and Douglas L. Zweizig. "Public Libraries and the Internet: Study Results, Policy Issues and Recommendations." Washington, DC: National Commission on Libraries and Information Science, June 1994.

[33] U. S. Congress. Office of Technology Assessment. *Adult Literacy and New Technologies: Tools for a Lifetime.* Washington, DC, 1993.

[34] Lawrence Mishel and Jared Bernstein. *The State of Working America 1992–93*, pp. 91–96. Washington, DC: Economic Policy Institute, 1993.

[35] Charles McClure. "Network Literacy in an Electronic Society: An Educational

Disconnect?" In *Annual Review of Institute for Information Studies, 1993–1994.* Aspen Institute.

[36] Ibid.

[37] Robert B. Reich. *The Work of Nations.* New York: Random House,1992.

[38] U.S. Department of Labor. "Learning a Living: A Blueprint for High Performance. A SCANS Report for America 2000. Part I." Washington, DC, April 1992.

[39] Ibid.

[40] Mary T. Moore and Zev Waldman. "Opportunities or Obstacles? A Map of Federal Legislation Related to the School-to-Work Initiative." In *School-to-Work: What Does the Research Say About It?*, U.S. Dept. of Education, Office of Educational Research and Improvement. Washington, DC, June 1994.

Meeting the Challenges of Business and End-User Communities on the Internet: What They Want, What They Need, What They're Doing

Daniel Dern

As the Internet grows in size and scope it has begun to embrace new communities of users. Two of these rapidly-growing Internet communities—the "public end users" and the commercial business users—bring a new set of challenges, in the form of needs, desires and service stress loads, that must be acknowledged and addressed by the providers of Internet access and transport service and user services. This article offers an overview of these challenges and itemizes some of the possible solutions.[1]

Sizing and Scoping out the New User Community Segments

The original ARPANET, CSNET, BITNET and Internet communities were, in the main, truly that. Users, as a rule, came on as a function of a specific organizational, departmental or discipline-related affiliation. As a consequence, I suspect that it was likely that for any given new user there was a relatively small and clearly defined set of mailing lists, USENET Newsgroups, Telnet/FTP sites and other resources, as well as a core group of "fellow users." This meant that the "resource discovery" question was relative straightforward; similarly, a new user was likely to find mentors to help identify these resources, and to instruct them in basic how-to, netiquette, and the like.

The new "public/consumer end-user" "community" represents what might be called "unaffiliated users"—users accessing and using the Internet as individuals, rather than based on affiliation with a given educational, research, government, or commercial

organization (although many of the users may have such affiliations or purposes and other accounts through these affiliations).
It's easy to also view these as the "home/consumer" population of
the Internet, although I don't want to encourage this view.

Arguably, these users do not constitute a "community" in the
original Internet sense of the word, just a bunch of users, some of
whom may now or later belong to one or more communities. More
to the point, a great many of these are "unpurposed" users—
they've hopped on the Internet out of curiosity, to be (or attempt
to be) "cool;" they've come as a by-product of joining other on-line
services, they've come to "surf the net". . . in other words, they have
not necessarily procured access for specific discussions, resources
or goals. As a result, their desires and activities can easily distort the
usage flows, arbitrarily saturating popular sites and services—most
of which, it's important to remember, are labor-of-love offerings
made available for free, but with no guarantee of availability, or
intended in some fuzzy fashion for "the Internet community." But
within the past few years, media attention has made the Internet
appear a vast, often free super-resource, as opposed to a large,
shared resource that users must replenish as well as consume.
Moreover, much of the "neat stuff" on the net is somewhere
between "proof of concept" and "neat hacks." There is no way these
can be readily available to teeming millions of new cybersurfers
within the current provisioning of user services and resources.

Who's There: Categorizing Users by Access

In my original article, I categorized user populations based on type
of access: shell account versus SLIP/PPP versus full-time, modem
bandwidth versus LAN connection, messaging only (mail and
USENET, e.g., UUCP/nixpub and BBS) versus ability to make real-
time connections. Although the boundaries are blurring, these
distinctions continue to be relevant. Messaging-only users cannot
browse the Web or Gopherspace in real time or participate in
global MUDs, IRC, etc. On the other hand, for e-mail and USENET
participation, which is the staple for many long-term users, messaging-only connectivity (UUCP or other batch connections) works
well enough. Bandwidth to the desktop has become the real
cutpoint. As Webspace becomes more laden with richtext, graphics

and other multimedia objects, a 14.4 or even 28.8 Kbps connection is no longer fast enough for a screenful of data to pop up near-instantly—and at 2400 bps, it's a lost cause. 2400 bps works well enough for ASCII-only, e.g., ASCII gopher clients, email, and USENET News read through a shell account. But if a user intends to view GIFs and JPEGs and other images, that modem connection just isn't fast enough.

The absolute size of the unaffiliated end-user community is hard to tell, but we know it's gotten much, much bigger. A few years ago, Software Tool & Die's World had less than 2,000 users; today it's well over 6,000. NetCom has, I believe, in excess of 30,000 users. Other providers have experienced similar growth—and the number of providers grows almost daily. This suggests that the top 25–50 public access sites represent as much as a quarter million users. Add in several hundred other Internet providers (estimates range from 400 to thousands) and we're probably at half a million users. Toss in the various other groups—the hundreds or thousands of BBSs adding Internet connectivity, dozens of FreeNets, hundreds of "nixpubs" and other UUCP sites—and we're perhaps up to a million users. Maybe more.

And even that number is low. During 1993 and 1994, the major on-line services—America On-line, CompuServe, and Prodigy—joined Delphi with increasing degrees of Internet and USENET access (GEnie won't be far behind). This adds, in theory, several million more people capable of accessing the USENET, WWW/Gopherspace, etc. It's hard to know whether it's time to consider users of the on-line services "members of the Internet community." They've been able to participate via e-mail—which includes interfaces to FTP, USENET, Gopher, WAIS and other services—for quite a while. Probably only a fraction of these users will ever check out the Internet; even so, in one fell swoop, the "random user" population has clearly been multiplied, and the total potential user population significantly added to.

The Young and the Clueless

Another way to categorize the Internet's end-user population is by degree of Internet and other on-line experience. Many end users have already been on the Internet through their academic or work experience. They know how to FTP, e-mail, and participate in USENET, and probably have a good sense of netiquette; their individual accounts are to replace or supplement other access. Many others have previously been "in cyberspace" but not on the Internet. They've had BBS experience, used CompuServe, etc. These users have to get acclimated to the Internet's very different architectural paradigms and cultural behaviors, but come with at least a partial understanding of the reality of virtual life: that time or bits may cost you money, that you are sharing resources with a global community, and that citizenship and skill are essential.

The third group are those completely new to the on-line experience, perhaps even to computers in general. I've run into many of these "pre-clued" at talks I've given; their expectations and assumptions reveal how little sense the general populace has of information and library science realities, of what is and is not on-line, and what you can and can't do easily. This group represents our biggest challenge: to find ways to let them educate themselves in the parking lots of cyberspace, rather than on the main roads where other users are trying to get work done. Fortunately, there are hundreds of commercial books (I've written one), courses, seminars, CD-ROMs and videotapes available to help new Internet users. Unfortunately, at present, there is no "driver's test certification" needed to hop on the Internet. And it only takes a percentage of a percentage of new, well-meaning but ill-directed users (not to mention the less-than-well-meaning) to disrupt the activities of thousands, even millions, of regular Internet users.

The Business Community

Just as we don't know how big the pseudo-community of individual users is, so no one knows how many "commercial users" or "businesses" are currently on the Internet. But we know it's more every day. By the end of 1994, thousands of businesses of all types and sizes had gained some access, whether shell account, single-person SLIP account, or LAN connection.

The definition of commercial users and businesses itself is still a moving target. One definition is exclusionary: that which does not fall within the NSFNET AUP, or the AUP of other R&E-only

networks. But with the dismantling of the NSFNET "backbone," the NSFNET AUP becomes largely moot. Commercial users are thus what the name implies: individuals and companies using the Internet on behalf of jobs, work, business.

In any case, the Internet "Chamber of Commerce and Mall" has a large membership who would never have been seen here two years ago. There are financial services organizations, bookstores, printing and copy shops, book publishers, professional organizations, software developers, consulting groups, journalists, neon sign artists, and many, many more. IBM is here, as are Microsoft, Digital, Apple and Novell. Even Disney World established a commercial presence in November 1994.

What Do Commercial Users Want?

Commercial users want from the Internet the same type of service they demand from all their communications and other utilities, notably:

• Highly reliable, highly available "dial tone"

• Clear pricing, preferably fixed-price for "no surprises" budgeting

• Accountability and clear problem-resolution paths

• A choice of providers and a way to compare/contrast service offerings based on price, performance and features

• Assurance of security against intrusion and eavesdropping

• Universal connectivity unrestrained artificially by AUPs, especially where AUP limits or transgressions cannot be predicted in advance or reliably controlled against

• User front ends that:

    • are intuitive and easy to use,

    • if possible, make it possible to mask or embed the act of obtaining an account,

    • hide or obviate the technical pain of installing, configuring and running TCP/IP and a serial protocol (SLIP, PPP, etc.),

    • provide authentication and security for credit card and other financial transactions,

- support high-speed multi-media browsing (GIFs, JPEGs, audio, etc.).

Of these, all have to some extent been met, except the last. The bit size of image, audio and video objects remains too large to be pushed in real-time through a dial-up modem or ISDN B-channel connection; the LAN-class speeds of fiber (cable, CDDI, etc.) are needed.

- Value-added services: stock quotes and other financial information, airline schedules, searchable news (media) feeds, etc.

This last item has become a reality: the OAG can be reached as Oag.Com, Quote.Com and others offer access to stock market data, and other business information resources are emerging steadily.

These are all highly reasonable desires; without them, no business will voluntarily put the Internet to work for business-critical applications—nor should they. Some of the answers are here; others are mysteriously absent to date. For example, I am unaware of any independent analyst or consultant who can offer comparative analyses of Internet Service Providers, even anecdotally. Doing such a job represents a non-trivial amount of work to define metrics, collect data, and establish a market for it. (I'm not volunteering.) How well, for example, is frame relay working out? Who offers ISDN access to the Internet? How much bandwidth does a company need to link sites for Novell NetWare or Lotus Notes? What is the range of delay found at various sets of endpoints; what applications can—and cannot—tolerate these delays? How does Internet service compare against a private SNA network or other private/public options?

In the same vein, what is the incidence—and skill-level—of "crackers" on the Internet? How reliable are the current security mechanisms such as Privacy-Enhanced Mail or ANS's InterLock—and what, if any, liability insurance is available? How much does it cost to have a knowledgeable security consultant evaluate and secure an Internet connection? Do we have security test suites?

And equally, what are the provable benefits of Internet connectivity? The easiest starting point is reduced cost for access to business consumer databases like Dialogue and Dow Jones, and access via Internet tools to information such as the U.S. Federal

Register and Commerce Business Daily, UPI and Reuters news feeds, etc. Those of us who have been "on the net" know its intangible value—but network and MIS managers need to make a business case, showing avoided/reduced costs, revenue opportunities, or competitive advantages. We're seeing the first of these analyses—but again, clear-cut numbers are slow to emerge.

What do business users want to do? Communicating with trading partners—customers, suppliers and peers—plus access to specific on-line services seem to dominate at present. Companies unfamiliar with the Internet have great reluctance, in fact, to joining the Internet as a community; aside from the perceived threat to security, they see unbridled e-mail and USENET connectivity as a drain on productivity, and as another aspect of user computing they cannot control.

Commercial users also want the ability to establish "storefront presence"—to make their marketing, sales and support information available, and perhaps even permit on-line ordering and—for digitizeable products such as documents and software—on-line delivery. "Presence" has become a commodity service (although, like connectivity, clear metrics have yet to be established or providers rated). The WorldWide Web, in particular, has become the platform of choice for information-mounting.

Business users also want their trading partners—customers and suppliers—to be "on the net." This is closer to a reality; during 1994, the Internet crossed that mysterious threshold of critical mass of companies and individual users and established the gut sense that "it's worthwhile to be on the net."

In terms of Internet resources, business users appear to be consuming mostly bandwidth. Given that they are paying—quite probably at the higher rates—this means more self-funded "lanes on the Internet highway," which in turn may help Internet Service Providers migrate to faster, more cost-effective links and roll out more local POPs (Points of Presence). My opinion is that few businesses, other than smaller, Internet-experienced technical users, are placing a heavy demand on the Internet's user services infrastructure (whois servers, anonymous-FTP, free-for-user Gopher servers, etc.). Most businesses have their own accounts and hosts.

What this means is that the continuing stream of business users into the Internet should help build up the transport infrastructure, providing a growing set of permanent and on-demand alternatives to the current transit solutions (e.g., the CIX and ANS CO+RE). Over time, we can also look to the business community as a major source of demand for pay-for-use information services such as real-time and reference databases (e.g., financial data, schedules, professional and technical texts and publications). How much demand the business community will generate for "user services" is hard to predict. Another source of revenue for the Internet infrastructure providers will come from those businesses who enter the supply side, paying organizations like MSEN, Bunyip, the InterNIC and others to house their information and putting up their own Gopher and WAIS servers.

What Do Individual Users Want?

What do individual end-users want? Judging from the types of queries posted to USENET Newsgroups such as alt.internet.access. wanted and alt.bbs.internet, the answer depends on whether the user has previously had access to the Internet through their school or employer or has used other BBSs and on-line consumer services but is new to the Internet.

Experienced Internet users typically want to "stay on the net" and continue what they have been doing, predominantly exchanging e-mail and participating in USENET Newsgroups—activities that can be done from "nixpubs" and other USENET/UUCP sites without requiring real-time IP access. Some of these users will also want anonymous-FTP access, which can be done via e-mail or UUCP, although it is certainly easier with an IP connection and real-time Internet access. Another segment of users will want real-time Internet activities and services, from cruising the WorldWide Web, "Gopherspace" and WAIS servers to participating in multi-user activities such as MUD and role-playing games, the Internet Relay Chat (IRC), Go games and tournaments, etc.

Many experienced Internet users who have not previously paid for the privilege of using the Internet include "free" in their shopping list of criteria: free accounts, free telnet ports so they can access distant accounts, even ports with free out-dialing modems, fax gateways and transfer points to dump hardcopy into postal systems. Other users are prepared to pay for access, especially as near-unlimited shell and SLIP accounts become available in some metropolitan areas for $15-$40/month.

People coming to the Internet from BBSs and on-line services are more likely to be used to paying for access and services. Internet access through their current BBS or on-line service may represent no price difference; those getting "Internet accounts" happily find that Internet access may be far cheaper and less restrictive.

In the 1993 version of this article, I predicted that the next wave of commercial services for Internet users would include access to a wider range of dictionaries, encyclopedias and other reference materials, which would then become available to these sites' users as part of their standard hourly or monthly fees. This has yet to materialize, but I stand by my prediction. Meanwhile, what users with previous non-Internet on-line experience expect is the same kind of service that they currently receive from their BBSs and on-line consumer services, corporate LANs, windowing GUI-based personal computers and video games. For example:

• Easy-to-use user interfaces offering mouse and menuing point-and-click operation, built-in help, color, windowing, scrolling, etc. (e.g., Mosaic, Cello, NetScape, "Internet in a Box/Bag/Can"). The incorporation of Internet applications and protocols into the next generation of systems from Apple, Digital, IBM (OS/2) Microsoft (Windows 95, NT), Novell, Sun and others will make this an even greater reality.

• Relatively clear, comprehensive user services, e.g., "a directory of Internet users," lists of available Internet mailing lists, resources categorized by topic (e.g., "Microsoft Windows," "Viruses," "computer animation"). (I am still hopeful these will emerge, but progress has remained depressingly—though understandably—slow.)

Basic user aids like these are exactly what the Internet lacks. New users rarely understand why; they just know that their new "toy" is cryptically hard to use, doesn't seem to have what they expect, and makes it remarkably hard to find anything anyway.[2]

Some of the difficulties experienced by new users can legitimately be ascribed to shortcomings of the Internet in its new role: the lack of user services, poor front-ends, etc. Equal blame can be placed, however, on the paradigm shift from a single on-line service to a heterogeneous, multi-network system. The most obvious area here is appropriate usage—what is permissible where? Many Internet users harbor notions that date back to the ARPANET era, when there was a single network and one either had a connection or did not. Those who do not understand the notion of the NSFNET, non-NSFNET transit, and the Internet's composite nature either draw the line for other users too strictly, or cross over. The new educational battle line is over "commercial use and advertising"—trying to herd advertising away from inappropriate USENET and mail forums and over into Web and Gopher sites.

In addition to the problems experienced by new Internet users, there are the problems *created* by these new users. The resources and services available to Internet users have historically been made available using surplus resources, with the implicit understanding that the community would self-police its use and not generate excessive demands. But many new Internet users have yet to be taught this attitude. With public-access Internet sites, anyone with a personal computer and modem can become an Internet user. This is the equivalent of being able to buy an automobile and go driving without having to take a driver's education course, pass a test or become licensed. When an organization such as DELPHI, Portal or WELL makes Internet service available, it creates the reality of tens of thousands of users set loose on the "Internet on-ramp" and raring to go. These users don't necessarily do any harm, but they can place enormous, unanticipated loads on Internet services.

DELPHI, for example, began offering primarily telnet and FTP (plus e-mail); users seeking USENET, Gopher, WAIS, Internet Relay Chat, MUDs, etc. had to find public-access clients available by telnet. (I don't mean to single DELPHI out; they are simply a good example—and they rapidly brought the appropriate feeds, clients and servers up locally.) More recently, we've seen AOL give their users USENET access but hobble them with non-standard, essential-feature-deficient software, creating numerous problems; even more recently, CompuServe and Prodigy added USENET access—with somewhat more forethought and planning, although still problematic if only by virtue of the sheer number of new users involved.

In terms of Internet resources, I see the community of individual users as putting greater demand on the Internet's user services infrastructure—and stressing these services—versus primarily consuming bandwidth like the business community. The demand and revenues created by individual users may help sites to upgrade their links, e.g., from on-demand to permanent or from 56 Kbps to fractional, full and multiple T1. Of greater concern are the cultural stresses caused by "new-to-the-Internet" users. Aside from saturating popular public-access clients, they often add a disproportionate load to USENET Newsgroups and e-mail lists in the form of questions readily answered by FAQs, misdirected "subscribe/unsubscribe" messages, inadvertent replies to the entire list or group, quoting entire messages in follow-ups, etc. (You can see a lot of this on discussions that have BITNET or FidoNet gateways, where the conventions are different.) It feels like more and more of the groups I follow are spending more time on administrativia. One answer is the creation of more focused newsgroups; another, for better or worse, is the move to digest and moderated formats.[3]

The Good News: What Individual Users and Businesses Mean for the Internet

In a word, money for growth and for more nifty stuff. New users represent revenues to fatten the access and backbone transport infrastructure, fund the information infrastructure of whois++ and other directory services, and provide more archie and Veronica servers and mirror archive sites. They represent a market that can support development of commercial Internet user software—general front-ends like Spyglass Mosaic and NetScape and The Internet Adapter, specialties like SlipKnot, single-apps like Eudora, HTML/SGML editors, and more, as the market explosion of 1994 makes clear. They represent a marketplace for value-added information services, which also means more money going back into the infrastructure. They help make more of the Internet self-funding without relying on revenue from government, research or education users.

Business and unaffiliated users also bring validation. The Internet community has been saying since its beginning that it has viable technologies and methods; now there are people who believe this enough to pay money for it and to choose the Internet over other options (sometimes). And they bring a sense of perspective. The needs and desires of businesses and individuals are often different from those of the academic, research and government communities—but the filling of these new needs will benefit the original communities, whose own new users will also want ease of use and comprehensive suites of services.

What will help us get there? Here is my list as of late 1994:

• Better user services (e.g., searchable indexes of what's on line, user white pages, "Yellow pages").

• Better new-user software for on-line and off-line users on desktop and portable platforms like DOS, Windows, Macintosh and Amiga. These are becoming more available, but we still need truly easy to use, bulletproof-install products.

• Better "profiles" for new users, simple menuing systems, "start-here" Gopher menus

• Widely-available "Internet 101" education and training. Some of this is available, though of uncertain quality, and more is needed in any case.

• More pay-for-use (and paid-by-provider) services. Some progress has been made, but we still need more, as well as the facilities to enable them.

• Rationalization and removal of AUPs. The NSFNET AUP is no longer a problem, but we need new guidelines and user contracts in its place.

• Proactive PR by leading Internet players to dispel persistent Internet myths and misinformation, a continuing problem.

• Better backbone bandwidth provisioning/management to reflect ever-growing traffic levels, and bandwidth/QoS-intensive services like real-time video and audio (e.g., MBONE)

• Authentication that doesn't send passwords over local or wide-area connections in cleartext; e.g., non-reusable/one-time password systems (S/KEY, SecureID, etc.)

• Content authentication/privacy (e.g., PEM, PGP), including solutions that interoperate with MIME

Heading toward the Millennium

During 1994 it has seemed that we are always on the threshold of the next big growth spurt for Internet communities. Every month, something newer and weirder happens, and the Internet seems to be substantially different every three months.

Exciting new developments like Microsoft and IBM built-in browsers, Bunyip's Info-Tree, off-line e-mail and Newsreaders, and graphic front-ends will lower many of the traditional barriers. For better or worse, AT&T, MCI, Sprint and other IXCs and IECs have finally "woken up" to "the Internet market."

The public awareness of the Internet is there; the Internet community is (slowly) becoming better about articulating the benefits of being "on the net" for businesses. Many in the education community are seeing that major benefits of Internet participation can be obtained even with low-cost and "obsolete" technology such as Apple IIs, 8088 and 286-class PCs, below-9600 BPS modems and dial-up connections, migrating up as funding permits. The desires of the business and end user communities, and the money they are ready to spend both on Internet service and on Internet-enabled goods and services, will help create the products, services and infrastructure relevant to all Internet communities. Everyone will benefit.

The Internet remains one of the few places where individuals have and continue to make seminal differences and can become valued contributors. People like Scott Yanoff and Gleason Sackman have become "Internet heroes" by providing information lists; individual efforts like YAHOO and WebCrawler are helping tame the info-explosion. Tools like CU-SeeMe, Maven and SlipKnot keep the Internet frontier expanding.

Many worry that "big business"—providers or users—will destroy the Internet. I'm not worried; I believe there's always room for research, educational, hobbyist and hacker communities. And frankly, the essential technology is readily available to anyone who wants to buy it, as the growth of shoestring providers demonstrates; if the Internet no longer provided an adequate home, I would expect that a core of network users could and would create Internet II within 48 hours. Indeed, that's what a lot of what we have today is: a virtual network within the Internet owned and operated by the Internet community. Much of what businesses are doing today leverages these efforts, making the Internet in some ways a trickle-up enterprise.

Finally, as the services and populations available on the Internet expand, the use of the Internet's original core communities—R&E, government agencies, vendors, computer users—is also expanding. They, too, want to use business-type services, provide information to new communities, publish via WorldWide Web and Gopher and FTP. They, too, want what individual users and businesses want; the capabilities that individuals and businesses get serve the "old Internet communities" as well. So everyone wins. The challenge will be, can the Internet survive success?

Notes

[1] This article was originally written in early 1993; as I update/rewrite/revise this article, it is late 1994. To say the least, much about the Internet public-access and business landscape has changed dramatically since that time (indeed, even in the past two months!). I have attempted to strike a balance between preserving the original intent of the article with making it relevant to the realities of the Internet today, and hopefully for the coming year or so.

[2] The simple menuing and pseudo-menuing systems being provided do help; for example, one DELPHI user likes the fact that the DELPHI menu includes several anonymous-FTP archive sites in the choices. (So do many Gopher menus, e.g. for Macintosh, DOS, Windows and UNIX archives.)

[3] Please don't take this to mean I am against individual users or Internet beginners. I am an individual user, happily paying for my account, and most grateful for the changes that have made this possible. But unclued new users may hasten yet another "death of the net" before we're ready for it, technically or emotionally. We're speeding up inevitable changes, that's all.

Models for the Internet Local Loop

Miles Fidelman

Public access to the Internet is not about free or low-cost access to Internet-connected community bulletin boards, nor is it about public access terminals in libraries and other public spaces. Rather, public access is about building a broad-based utility service, where "Internet wall plugs" are as ubiquitous as telephone jacks, and public terminals are as common as public telephones. Public access is about integrating information networking into the fabric of day-to-day commercial and civic life as thoroughly as the telephone and fax machine are today.

For large academic and corporate sites, this level of service is already available, at costs comparable to basic telephone service. For small sites—homes, schools, municipal offices, small businesses and other organizations—neither service nor price are yet remotely comparable to those at larger sites.

The local loop—the "last mile" connection between an end user and the nearest Internet "point of presence" (POP)—is a critical component of delivering Internet service to small users. Large sites can purchase Internet service in bulk via a single high-bandwidth connection ("fat pipe"), with significant economies of scale. They can also use their internal facilities to bring service to end users. By contrast, small users must rely on local telephone and cable company offerings to reach the nearest Internet POP, and gain no benefit from internal economies of scale. Currently, most local loop service offerings are considerably more expensive than the internal cost-per-user associated with a large site's internal data network; thus small users are at a significant cost disadvantage vis-a-vis large users in accessing the Internet.

In order to achieve universal Internet service, on a level playing field for all users, two key steps can be taken: Local exchange tariffs can be adjusted to bring pricing of existing local loop services into line with the costs of large site internal networks, and data-oriented local loop services, with improved economies of scale, can be deployed by local exchange carriers.

The next section discusses the key role of the Internet as a "national enterprise network" that provides a national vehicle for electronic commerce. Following that is a discussion of the issues associated with extending current Internet services to smaller users, and several models for reducing current costs. The final section offers technical, policy, and regulatory recommendations for advancing toward ubiquitous Internet service.

The Internet as a National Enterprise Network

Much of the press for the National Information Infrastructure (NII) focuses on "500 channels of video" and other entertainment-oriented applications, and implies that the NII will be built from scratch by the nation's telephone and cable companies. It is more appropriate, however, to view the NII as a "national enterprise network" central to national economic competitiveness—and the Internet is well on the way to becoming just that. To some, the NII is no more than a vague concept espoused by the Federal Government (Vice President Gore's "information superhighway"), complemented by telephone and cable company pronouncements about vaguely defined services to be offered sometime in the future. To others, this author included, a National (in fact Global) Information Infrastructure already exists—in the form of the more than 23,000 inter-linked government, academic, and corporate data networks comprised by the Internet, which already serves over 20 million individuals worldwide as a key tool in the conduct of day-to-day work life.

Over the past two decades, most major corporations have implemented "enterprise networks"—data networks linking all computers within an organization—with the resultant streamlining of information distribution leading to considerable gains in productivity and competitiveness. Personal computers and inexpensive local area networks have made similar networks common within smaller organizations. In some industries, networking has extended industry-wide, and has become central to the conduct of business. Financial and securities transactions routinely move through "electronic clearinghouses." Reservations keyed into a travel agent's terminal automatically flow to airline, car rental, and hotel computer systems—leading to a waiting airline seat, the proper amount of fuel loaded into the airplane, possibly a special meal waiting, a car waiting, and a room waiting, all with minimal paperwork or human labor. In the research community, the Internet has become a critical vehicle for linking research teams and for disseminating research results to both academic and corporate audiences.

The NII promises to take corporate and industry-wide networking the next logical step: to ubiquitous networking that reaches every office and home in the nation. As our economy moves toward increasing interorganization cooperation—joint ventures, virtual corporations, just-in-time inventory, etc.—the need for interorganization enterprise networking is becoming acute. A key role of the NII must be to provide this service. Creating a data networking environment as ubiquitous and seamless as the telephone network is a critical first step to achieving the promised benefits of the NII: electronic exchange of manufacturing data, streamlined delivery of government services, improved education and job training, simplified health care administration, new markets for information services and technology, telecommuting, etc.

The Internet is the first evolutionary stage of the NII. Twenty years and billions of public and private dollars have been invested in building the Internet into the beginning of a ubiquitous, worldwide, interorganization enterprise network. It is now a worldwide collection of over 23,000 institutional networks in corporations, in government agencies, and in academia, woven into a vast and seamless "data superhighway." The Internet provides more than 20 million people worldwide with endless opportunities to share resources and collaborate, and it is increasingly used by federal and state governments for internal communications and to efficiently disseminate information to the public. Thirty percent of Internet networks are now commercial. A multi-billion dollar telecommunications equipment industry has grown up based on Internet technology and serving the Internet market. And the Internet is growing at over 5% per month in terms of networks, connected computers, and users.[1]

Extending the Internet to Smaller Users

The critical issue facing us now is how to extend Internet access to small users—how to extend the Internet beyond its traditional institutional user community, into small offices and homes.

Today's Internet vendors primarily serve larger organizations that have their own internal networks. In essence, the Internet market resembles the telephone bypass market, where service is delivered in bulk over high-bandwidth "fat pipes" and then distributed to end-users over customers' internal networks. Unlike the phone system, in which local telephone companies provide service to smaller customers as a universally available basic utility, small-user Internet service is available only haphazardly. Yet small businesses account for over 50% of the economy and well over 50% of new jobs and products (while larger firms are downsizing and outsourcing). They are disproportionately dependent on communications, both among a business's several small sites and with outside organizations. Most schools, libraries, and municipal offices have needs similar to those of smaller businesses.

Residential service is as important as small business service. Home-based businesses are one of the fastest-growing segments of the economy. Home service is also required to support telecommuting, which is becoming increasingly popular and in some cases mandatory to meet automobile trip reduction requirements now being imposed by the Environmental Protection Agency. Homes are also likely sites for use of distance learning services that can help maintain and upgrade both basic and professional skills.

Defining the Basic Service

As a fundamental goal, the basic, universal, small-user Internet service should be the same service that larger institutional users already receive: A 24-hour, high-speed, IP (Internet Protocol) "wall plug" at a flat price under $100 per month.

In an academic or corporate environment, access typically consists of a "network wall plug" that shares a faceplate with a telephone jack. This gives a desktop workstation or PC 24-hour, high speed, interactive access to machines connected both to the organization's internal computer facilities and to Internet facilities. Electronic mail simply "shows up." File transfers occur directly to and from a user's desktop machine. A user can access file servers and other facilities in a transparent manner, and can "publish" information to the network on a continuous basis. A user (and software acting on a user's behalf) can engage in multiple, simultaneous sessions across the network. The typical cost per desktop for such service in a 1000-user organization is under $50 per month, and includes local network service, Internet access, training and support, and shared central services (such as a news spooler and directory server).

Current Offerings for Small Users[2]

For a site with a single user, service comparable to that at a corporate or university site costs more than $500 per month. This much higher price is a result of two factors. First, most Internet vendors are in effect wholesalers: they are organized to deliver large quantities of service to large sites, and give substantial discounts to such customers. In contrast, providing service to single users is a retail business requiring different business models. Second, local loops are expensive. For example, in New England, a 19.2Kb port on NEARnet costs approximately $550/month plus an average leased line charge of $200/month, for a total of $750/month. Alternatively, a dedicated SLIP or PPP[3] port costs $200/month; 24-hour service in areas with unmeasured business calling adds $44 (total of $244), while in areas with measured calling (such as most of eastern Massachusetts) local access costs are around $670/month, for a total of $870/month. In short, heavy users, such as a small user wishing to offer 24-hour services via the Internet (to "hang a shingle on the Internet"), are priced out of the market.

Low-cost small-user services now available are not comparable to large site service in either service levels or pricing, making small users second-class citizens of the Internet. These services generally provide dial-up access to a time-sharing system that is in turn connected to the Internet. Electronic mail must be actively retrieved, like picking up mail at the post office rather than having it delivered to one's door. File transfer is a multi-stage process: a file must first be pulled across the network to the time-shared machine, and then downloaded to one's desktop, with one or more file translation steps required along the way. A dial-up user can typically pursue only one activity at a time. In addition, the available point-and-click interfaces that simplify Internet access cannot be used in this environment. Prices for dial-up services ranges from $1 per hour to over $10 per hour, not including local telephone charges. For a casual user, these prices are affordable, but for a user who wants 24-hour service or even business-hour service, charges add up quickly.

Models for the Internet Local Loop

This section outlines some approaches to providing institutional-quality Internet services to homes and small businesses. First, I outline how a university or business provides services to its end-users; identify a target price for single users; and estimate the costs of running an organization that could deliver such services. Then I evaluate a number of possible ways to create a low-cost local loop to connect each site to the network.

Core Services and Organization

At a typical large site, a central staff obtains Internet service via a "fat pipe" and distributes it to internal users via campus network facilities. In addition to managing internal network facilities, this staff is usually responsible for managing the addresses and network configuration of campus machines, running central service machines (e.g., for mail, news, printing), providing user support, etc. These same functions will be required to support small Internet users, and analogous centralized organizations will be needed to provide these functions. Economies of scale suggest that such organizations naturally fit at the community level for large communities, and at the telephone exchange level for rural areas containing smaller communities.

At a minimum, such an organization would maintain an Internet connection, 24-hour staffing by an average of two people, sufficient computer equipment to provide reliable 24-hour server capabilities, and various basic information services (e.g., a network news feed). A rough estimate for these costs is $85,000 per month, or $17 per user at a level of 5000 users; this includes all the basic costs of operating a business.[4] Targeting a somewhat arbitrary end-user price of $75 per month and 30% gross margin ($22.50 per user per month) leaves $35.50 per user per month to cover local loop access. I use this figure below as a baseline for evaluating the cost of different local loop approaches.

The following sections evaluate how well several models of local loop would provide the desired service, and what issues are associated with doing so for the target cost. I will focus on the toughest challenge—sites with a single user, and thus no economies of scale.

Access Based on Standard Telephone Company Services

There are two models for providing Internet access over standard telephone facilities: leased lines and dial-up connections. To serve a single end user, SLIP or PPP termination equipment is appropriate, regardless of whether a leased line or a dial-up circuit is used. Unfortunately, service comparable to campus network service is only partially achievable over such connections.

At a typical large site with a 1000-user 10Mbps ethernet, users are afforded average bandwidth of 10Kbps. This is easily achieved by a standard V.32bis/V.42bis analog modem serving a single user site. However, achievable peak speed is much slower. A campus network affords a peak speed of full ethernet bandwidth (10Mbps) in the local area, and somewhat less across the Internet. By contrast, an analog modem can at best achieve less than one percent of that speed. Since most interactive applications are "bursty" in nature, with large bursts of data intermixed with long periods of silence, peak speed is usually more important to users than average speed. For example, an application that displays images generated at a remote site will perform excruciatingly slowly over a dial-up connection. Note that even a shift to higher speed digital lines, such as dial-up ISDN lines operating at 64Kbps, will improve this situation only marginally.

For both the dial-up and leased line cases, an Internet service provider must buy two components: termination equipment (e.g., a terminal server) and local loop cable service (this does not include the cost of a user's computer, software, or modem/data service unit). The capital cost of termination equipment is estimated at $500 per port, or $14 per month amortized over 3 years. Out of the $33.50 figure calculated above, this leaves $19.50 per user for local loop costs.

Under current New England Telephone tariffs in Massachusetts, and assuming that all users are within the same LATA as the central Internet connection, the average cost of a leased line connection is about $200 per month, well over the target cost. A dial-up connection left connected for one month will cost a residential user approximately $34, a business user with unlimited local calling $62, and a business user with measured service $666.[5]

Sixty-two dollars per month, the cost where unlimited business service is available, represents a reasonable starting point for discussion. This cost could be reduced in several ways:

a. Central site connection costs can be reduced by purchasing bulk connections to the local central office over T1 or T3 facilities. Conservatively, this could save 30% of central port costs ($5.40/port).

b. Central site equipment could be collocated in the telephone company's central office, which would halve the number of central office connections. While there are space rental fees for collocation, the $62 per month could be reduced by perhaps 40%, to $37.20 per month.

c. Under current tariffs, collocation typically involves connection to the telephone company's switching equipment—even though all that is really needed is direct access to the local loop wiring going to end-user locations. A number of telecommunications players (e.g., cellular service providers) are pushing legislation that would "unbundle" access to telephone company equipment—for example, allowing a third party to purchase access to local loop wiring without paying for access to switching equipment. If such tariffs are approved, costs for local loop services would be reduced further.

Thus, reducing the cost of local loop service to the $21.50 per month calculated above appears achievable, through central office collocation and direct connection to local loop wiring. If such a local loop connection is used for 64Kbps digital access and compression is used on the data stream, it should be possible to offer barely acceptable performance characteristics for most users.

The Shortcomings of ISDN

Despite the widespread publicity surrounding ISDN[6], it is inappropriate for Internet local loop service for several reasons:

• ISDN circuit service, which provides switched 64Kbps connections, is unnecessary when an end user is only connecting to a single destination (i.e., it provides no more services than a simple dedicated wire). In addition, telephone switches are designed for the relatively short duration of voice calls. When a connection is kept open for long periods (e.g., when used for a 24-hour connection to an Internet provider), particularly heavy loading is placed on the switching equipment.

• ISDN packet service, if provided by the central office switch, is typically limited to 19.2Kbps service and an aggregate rate of 200 packets per second (128-byte packets) for current-generation switches. Both the low speed and the low total capacity are completely inadequate for Internet access; for example, the switch can only handle 11 users simultaneously engaged in file transfers.

• ISDN 64Kbps packet service, typically provided by an external packet switch, can provide the required speeds and capacity, but ties up a circuit connection[7] through the central office switch and is therefore expensive.

In all three cases, the ISDN switch provides no benefit over a direct connection between the local loop and a more standard Internet termination device such as a SLIP server or a router.

However, the use of ISDN digital termination units (the equivalent of a modem) across the local loop wiring appears to be a viable method for achieving higher speeds than achievable using analog modems over the same copper wiring.

Access via Emerging Local Loop Services

Several other services offer the promise of increased performance and lower prices for the Internet local loop:

• Frame Relay, ATM, and other metropolitan area networking services are becoming available from local telephone carriers. These services offer functionality and performance levels appropriate for Internet access. However, costs for these services currently approximate the cost of leased line service.

• Ethernet over cable television wiring has proven effective for private networks and for some municipal governments' internal networks. The functionality and performance of this technology is ideal for Internet connection. However, most cable operators have not deployed the bi-directional amplifiers required for providing this service. In March 1994 Continental Cablevision and Performance Systems International released the first commercial service offering of this type in Cambridge, Massachusetts. At this writing, the price of this service is $125/month for 24-hour, high-speed connection to the Internet for a single personal computer.

• Wireless data communication over the new PCS[8] service has the potential to deliver Internet local loop service, though no such services have yet been deployed. The capital cost of PCS deployment is considerably lower than wire or fiber-based transmission facilities, so lower costs are likely.

Recommendations

In closing, I offer several recommendations.

First, it is important to establish the concept of the NII as a national enterprise network and of building on the existing Internet. The goal of ubiquitous, affordable Internet service should guide policymaking and rulemaking for the NII at the national, state, and local levels.

Second, we need to develop an appropriate model for local Internet service organizations. If these service organizations are to provide affordable service, they probably require a customer base of around 5000 users to support basic staffing and facilities. To allow an organization to reach this size, and to provide investors with sufficient safety to justify investment, some form of market entry limitation is probably necessary—and some form of regulation or other mechanism will be needed to balance the granting of such a monopoly. An examination of current regulatory regimes, such as that governing CATV, and an examination of non-regulatory approaches (such as public ownership, public investment, public-private partnerships, or granting a single vendor distribution rights to municipal data in return for concessions) should be initiated immediately.

Finally, local loop tariffing must be reexamined with the goal of providing low-cost, 24-hour connectivity to the Internet. Development of a collocation tariff appropriate to Internet services should be a high priority for state telecommunications regulators. Carriers' proposals for new services and local loop upgrades should be scrutinized in this light.

Notes

[1] John S. Quarterman, Gretchen Phillips, and Smoot Carl-Mitchell, "Internet Services and Access." Presented at workshop on "Public Access to the Internet," May 26–27, 1993.

[2] See Miles R. Fidelman, "The Internet in Massachusetts." Paper presented at "Getting from Here to There: Building Information Infrastructure in Massachusetts," John F. Kennedy School of Government, March 1993.

[3] Serial Line Internet Protocol (SLIP) and the Point to Point Protocol (PPP) allow a dial-up PC or workstation to access all Internet services (e.g., direct file transfer, client-server transactions, use of point-and-click interfaces, multiple simultaneous activities). However, the cost of local loop access generally makes a leased line more cost-effective for users wishing 24-hour service.

[4] Internet feed: $100,000/year; 8 staff members at $100,000/year each (fully loaded); space, power, miscellaneous: $2000/month; computer equipment: $100,000 amortized over 36 months; information services at $5000/month.

[5] Basis of estimate for leased line: oral conversation with NEARnet. Basis of estimate for dial-up services: $18/month for phone line at central site + $16/month for unlimited residential service or $44/month for unlimited business service (only available in some parts of western Massachusetts) or $18/month plus .015/minute for measured business service.

[6] ISDN (Integrated System Digital Network) is a new generation of telephone technology that promises to provide voice, data, and eventually video services over an integrated telephone network. Telephone carriers have promoted ISDN very heavily as a solution to both voice and data needs. However, as currently deployed, ISDN data services are minimal. In particular, packet service (which is particularly oriented for data applications), while specified as available at 64kbps, typically is available only at slower speeds.

[7] Typically, high speed ISDN packet service is implemented with a separate switch external to the primary ISDN circuit switch. A user of packet service makes a connection through the circuit switch to reach the packet switch, thus tying up resources in both switches.

[8] PCS (Personal Communication Service) is a new set of wireless services that will support both voice and data. The FCC plans to auction spectrum for PCS near the end of 1994.

Internet Architectural and Policy Implications for Migration from High-End User to the "New User"

Terrence P. McGarty and Carole Haywood

Introduction

Recently a cable television company, Continental Cable, and a commercial Internet carrier, PSI, offered full-time access to the Internet for about $100 per month to any of the CATV company's customers in Cambridge, MA. The response was overwhelming, and customers are now connecting to the Internet via this service. In the same time frame, AT&T started a consumer test in New Jersey to give residential users access to the Internet for a free trial period to determine what uses they may put it to. One of the users is a group of antique appraisers who have found that the Internet allows them to share information, compare appraisals, and communicate with professionals on the provenance of certain rare items. Business users have also found that the Internet allows them access to Eastern Europe and the Far East much more effectively than does FAX or Telex. For example, a Polish company has been developing a telecommunications infrastructure with the help of U.S. engineers and business people via Internet messaging.

These events provide insight to the possible growth and development of the New Internet community. The New Internet user (called the "New User" in this paper) includes the consumer user, the casual user, the local library user, or the secondary or primary school user. The Internet initially is ancillary to the New User's general needs, but it frequently becomes an integral part of what they do. The New User is that latent user who may in the long run become the mainstay of the Internet community.

In this paper we analyze the New User community and look at the basic structures and paradigms of the current Internet. We attempt to project the needs of this New User community and assess what challenges these needs present to the existing Internet structure. Finally, we address the policy implications that this New User community places on Internet growth.

In the first section we focus on the existing architecture of the Internet. It is essential to determine the underlying assumptions and paradigms with which the Internet operates. This paper defines these in some detail, using the historical evolution as a prelude to future development. Specifically, we ask, *What are the current architectural constraints of the Internet and how may these be modified to ensure a full and complete development for the New User community?*

We then focus on the needs and opportunities for this group of New Users. The New User community is analyzed and contrasted with the current Internet community. We then discuss the ways New Users' applications may make use of the Internet. The user community is a growing and expanding base, and any discussion we make here will most likely be modified dramatically as New Users enter the community. The trend, however, is projectable: namely, that the Internet community will expand in new and innovative ways to new and nontraditional groups of users. The key question we address is, *Who will the New Users be and what demands will they place on the Internet, from both a technical and an applications perspective?*

The evolution of the Internet into the broad New User community will require changes to the current architecture in three areas: multimedia communications, access expansion and host migration. These three technological and architectural changes are discussed in detail. Multimedia communications is in its infancy. We present several of the key challenges that the Internet would face if it were to provide these capabilities to the New User. Access is the second but, in the short term, the most driving issue. Access is an issue of cost combined with flexibility; it addresses the means the means by which the New User obtains real-time communications access to the Internet. The last issue is host migration. It raises the question of whether a Personal Digital Assistant, in its broadest sense, is or may become a host on the Internet. This then leads us to focus on the issue, *What technologies can drive increased access to and applications of the resources available to the New User community, and what can the current Internet community do to facilitate these?*

We conclude the paper with a discussion of the policy issues that are brought out in developing the overall evolutionary alternatives for the New User migration. The authors believe that the migration is feasible and can be readily achieved in the context of the current design and design methodology. The policy challenge is to answer the questions of Internet evolution, namely, *Is the Internet a scaleable economic entity that can create value that will be accessible to the widest possible collection of users while retaining the value already provided to the high-end user community?*

Current Architectural Elements

The current architectural structure of the Internet has been described elsewhere at length. We review it briefly here to establish a basis for a detailed description of the system. Before doing so, it is important to view the evolution of the Internet concept in the context of several phases:

The Simple Internet (1968–1974): Beginning as an experiment in networking ("the ultimate petri dish"), in this period the Internet's predecessor, the ARPANET, was a simple network consisting of 56 Kbps (or less) circuits interconnected by Interface Message Processors, or IMPs. The user community was a collection of large-scale computer processing facilities, with end users who were uniquely identified with their host computers. The concept of time sharing in an operational context was not present. The original aim of the Internet was to provide remote access to complex computer resources. A typical example was access to the ILIAC IV supercomputer at the University of Illinois by a user at U. C. Berkeley. The concept was one of a human user having access to one of a variety of host machines at large remote computer facilities. There was no concept of user-to-user communications in the first stage.

The Internet Goes Global (1973–1981): In this period the TCP/IP protocol was developed and layered on top of the existing datagram network. Although originally aimed at remote login and file transfer (FTP), the afterthought, email, became 95% or more of the total network traffic. Email users could now expand their relationships: they now had access not only to remote host computers but also to many other individual users, thus creating a community of interest. This allowed Internet to become a distributed conversational medium, not just a remote processing vehicle. This was a seminal change in the paradigm.

Also during this period, the Internet went international with satellite connections to Goonhilly in the United Kingdom. COMSAT was used as an access node to the European community. Initially the international use was justified by the need to transfer seismic data needs and the requirement to backhaul large volumes of traffic. Ultimately, however, email dominated in all areas.

Military and Nonmilitary Split (1982–1986): During this phase the nonmilitary Internet evolved. DoD separated its network and the residual was spun off into a larger user community. Part of the reason for the split was that unauthorized accesses had been found and user scares from hacking had been observed. The nonmilitary user community expanded, allowing access to new user communities. The backbone also grew to T1 rate (1.544 Mbps).

The Mitotic Period (1986–1992): "Cell division" of the network occurred. DS3 (45 Mbps) circuits were added, and local and regional networks were adopted. Access closer to the end-user spread, personal computers proliferated, and the number of hosts grew explosively. The number of networks seen by the Internet grew from about 100 in 1988 to over 5,000 in 1992. The user's identity was still with the host. The dominant traffic was still email and its derivatives, and the first network virus, a self replicating "worm," ran amok for several days in 1988.

"New User" Access Era (1993–present): This era is the era of New User access and the proliferation of commercial user hosts and networks. The user community is expanding from the computer literate and comfortable to the infrequent user community and those whose expertise is frequently exceeded by their enthusiasm and expectations.

The Distributed Open Network (1996–): The network moves into a gigabit-per-second backbone, allowing for the first time real-time access to such applications as multimedia processing, video, and supercomputer networking. The protocols for access allow expansive addressing and accessibility. End-user access costs are reduced by access cost enablement/control policies and the introduction of 64 Kbps end-user transport access to all terminals. Host identity is now made consistent with user identity. Specifically, in this phase, the end user may have sufficient processing power and memory capability, as well as communications access capabilities, to be a host. In addition, we anticipate that there will be a further migration to the point where there are multiple hosts per end user, rather than the prior paradigm of multiple users per host. This challenge will dramatically stress the Internet in directions not seen previously.

The current Internet is structured in four layers, as shown in Figure 1. The four layers are the Backbone, Regional, and Campus networks and the Hosts.

The key to Internet facilitation and accessibility is the set of protocols accepted by the community to allow access by a wide variety of hosts in a complex and fully distributed fashion. These protocols are the software and system agreements that allow disparate machines and software to talk across equally disparate networks. The current protocols focus on data transactions, with some innovations allowing images and limited multimedia, namely voice and video. The future challenge will be the development of new and innovative protocols to allow New User access to grow while enriching the capability of the information transferred.

The current Internet architecture thus has two main elements. The first is the semi-hierarchical structure of Backbone, Regional, Campus and Host, and the second is the agreement on a single protocol to talk across the Internet, currently embodied in the TCP/IP suite. These elements reflect a great deal about how the Internet is managed and its growth potential. Several observations can be made about the Internet in its current embodiment:

- **The Internet has a strong host orientation.** The Internet is host computer–oriented. It is focused around the host as the entity through which all users access the network and communicate. The user may be limited by the limitations of their host. For example, the host may not permit use of certain functions in the areas of file transfer and processing. Software packages such as the Eudora

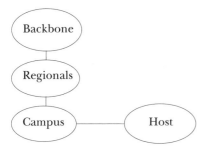

Figure 1 The Internet Architecture.

Internet access system requires a POP host and networks such as Delphi lack that capability. Thus a user of Internet on Delphi's host may not have the same access as a user on an MIT host. New users will have powerful devices that can themselves act as hosts. The only limitation, currently, is communications access, namely its availability and cost. If low-cost, high-speed access becomes available, then the number of hosts may expand. A host per user, or even many hosts per user, is possible. The concept of a host may then have to be expanded to include the new and wider variety of electronic entities, including both physical and virtual devices. In addition, wireless access devices, Personal Digital Assistants, and distributed processing devices must be integrated into the Internet design, since they will allow hosts to be portable and move from location to location. One must be able to "find" the host, since it will roam around the network.

• **The Internet has low intra-network intelligence.** Limitations of processing in the network have been due to the simplicity of the routers and reliance on the "intelligence" of the host. New network elements are highly intelligent, and even PDAs and wireless devices contain dramatically greater intelligence to perform processing. The ability of the network to drive more processing and intelligence to the periphery, and to the new fully distributed host environment, will enable the Internet to add new degrees of access and services flexibility. For example, if the Internet can provide a very-high-speed, almost error-free transmission path, and if the end-user hosts are extremely intelligent, then the ability to do very sophisticated multimedia communications can be effected by the end users directly, allowing rapid migration of capabilities in the network. If the Internet has this enhanced communications capability, then one can develop high speed protocols that are shared among users, using the Internet as a high speed computer "backplane" and not just as a datagram network.

• **The Internet uses the telephone network and expects poor transmission link performance.** The underlying structure of the Internet protocols and their processing was designed to deal with a poor quality transmission path of copper twisted pairs in the old telephone network. In contrast, the new fiber optic networks are almost error free. In fact, with the processing at higher protocol layers, one may now assume error-free transmission. This means that latency—the delay incurred by the need to retransmit data when errors occur—which was prevalent when using the old analog telephone lines, may be totally eliminated. This is a critical factor for multimedia transactions. Designers will be able to assume error-free transmission and will be able to send large blocks of data, such as video, in mega-packets. The delay in the network will be minimized, and multimedia conferencing will become a reality.

On the other hand, the new wireless communications services may not have higher data rates until their designers better understand how to deal with multipath from many buildings and other radio propagation factors that cause errors and reduce transmission rates. Thus the network must handle error-free fiber combined with error-prone wireless.

• **The Internet is based on telephone links with moderate data transport speeds.** The layered structure of the TCP/IP protocol suite allows for flexibility in low- to moderate-speed networks. At higher speeds the protocol suites begin to breakdown. Fiber networks will soon allow gigabit-per-second transmission, and high resolution images and video will be integrated into complex multimedia objects. This will require a significant rethinking of what the object control must look like and the development of new and innovative protocols.

• **The Internet transmits with a high disaggregation of data.** The network assumes a high degree of disaggregation of the data as they are sent from one location to another. Specifically, it packetizes data extensively, assuming that it can do so because communications are between computers, which are capable of processing the packets. The current assumptions are that data from one location are independent of data from other locations. In a multimedia environment, this will no longer be the case. Data will be virtually aggregated into a compound multimedia object, thus creating a virtual multimedia object whose elements may be from a disparate set of users on the Internet. For instance, my mouse movement at one location will be related to my voice at another and a third party's video at a third. The concatenation and orchestration of these disparate entities will be viewed as a single totality.

• **The Internet provides single-medium messaging from host to host.** The TCP layer focuses on getting a single stream of data through. Modifications can be made for voice or even video streaming, but a full multimedia network is not achievable. An enhanced multimedia TCP/IP-type system will need to be constructed that allows the entire suite of users access to multimedia sessioning, with high data rates and access via fully distributed high-end processing devices, at dramatically lower costs.

• **The Internet was intended as a data communications tool across the academic community.** No intelligence was built into the network to guarantee arrival of messages, nor to mitigate congestion. Issues of security and virus protection are management options left to the discretion of the host configuration.

We see from the above set of observations and trends that the old architectural assumptions are being challenged by both the high-end users and the New Users. The Internet backbone is being upgraded to 45 Mbps DS 3 circuits and the campus networks to 100 Mbps. The Regional Bell Operating Companies (RBOCs, such as NYNEX) are mainly providing data access only at 1.5 Mbps DS 1 rates, but fiber migration by Competitive Access Providers (CAPs), CATV migration of fiber to the home, and even the new Personal Communications Services (PCS) wireless communications network will change this limitation on local access imposed by the local RBOCs by introducing new competitors in the Local Exchange market who will provide high-speed data access at lower prices. Multimedia communications and wide area portable/mobile access for New Users will also emphasize the need for more intelligence within the network and not just layered onto the existing protocol suites.

Users and Uses

There are currently five user communities that can be considered
New Users. Each of these user communities has different needs and
different requirements from the Internet, and sees the Internet
offering access to a different variety of services and applications.
They are summarized as follows:

1. Commercial casual users. The casual user is the user who has
recognized that the Internet provides a community of interest and
access to information in its broadest base. The commercial casual
user is the one in a corporate environment whose initial desire is to
use the Internet for email and other such limited applications. If
one recalls the ARPANET in the mid-1970s, the dominant use was
email, which accounted for over 95% of all use. Now email is below
30% and dropping as other uses are discovered. The email functionality is an entry point into the Internet. It is the service that will
capture the casual commercial user, say an R&D Manager or
Executive, whose staff of researchers are already high volume users
of the Internet.

2. The K-12 user community. K-12 is an explosive area. There are
many examples of schools at all levels encouraging students to use
the Internet as both an educational tool as well as a cultural
learning device. The Internet, as a global network, allows students
to communicate with others around the world. The classic story is
the student who wrote an 'A' graded paper on Aborigines by
communicating with Australia directly over the Internet. There are
two countervailing factors, however, that are pressing at this opportunity. One is the growth of the multimedia curriculum exemplified by in class video education that is real time. The other is the fact
that over 98% of classrooms have no telephone access. In most if
not all cases of education through new electronic media, it is easier
to get the satellite dish, the VCR, the television, and the computer,
than to get the RJ-11 telephone jack! We will argue in this paper that
CATV and wireless will make a dramatic change in this area.[1]

3. The health care user community. The Internet is a data backbone
network that is in essence the basis of a multimedia transaction
based infrastructure. The Internet will eventually allow the transport of images and voice communications. It already encourages

spatially and temporally displaced conversationality. Furthermore, the Internet is a transaction network, transacting everything from data transport to email. Health Care is an industry in search of productivity improvements. It has been shown elsewhere, that over 35% of the expenses in Health Care are due to the handling of paper for patient billing and non critical record management.[2] Also, quality of care, as contrasted to cost of care, is improved with increased flow of information and displaced conversationality between not only the specialties but also the total Health Care Team. It is argued that the Internet can be the catalyst that enables the internetting of Health Care for both productivity improvements and quality of care improvements.

4. The higher education user community. Not all universities have access to the Internet, nor do all students have either the required proficiency or knowledge of what the Internet can do for them. In many ways it has been the "techie's toy" that is now expanding its way into other areas. This can be seen in the number of user groups exploding in many non-technical academic areas, as well as in the explosive growth of electronic publishing. The latter is the first true example of the growth of an electronic industry with the enabling capability of an electronic marketing and distribution channel, namely the Internet.

5. Residential casual users. The residential user is becoming one of the largest growing segments. The residential user has had access over the years to such networks as CompuServe and Prodigy, the erstwhile videotext attempt by Sears and IBM that has never been profitable. Ironically, CompuServe, a text driven system, is successful because it meets the consumer's needs. The CompuServe user is migrating to the Internet since the Internet is a broader community of users and also because university students can communicate home via the Internet. Thus access to the Internet via CompuServe or direct access via gateways such as General Videotex are opening doors for the residential user.

Architectural Evolution

The New User community has a different set of requirements for both the use of and access to Internet facilities. The emerging demand for multimedia services and the potential mobility of the New User present several challenges to the Internet architecture that may change its elements in an evolutionary sense. In this section we develop some of the key new dimensions in the expansion of the Internet architecture. These dimensions reflect not only the needs of the New User but also those of the remaining established user base. The main catalyst is the New User, however, because the expansion of applications, the reduction in costs of access, and the redefinition and commodification of the host concept are fundamentally driven by the expanded nature of the New User applications.[3] The two major dimensions along the Internet change axes are lowered costs and higher capabilities of communications and processing. The new paradigm against which the new architecture will be measured is multiple hosts per user, rather than multiple users per host.

The first major issue is that of access to communications. In this dimension dramatic changes are occurring. Local exchange access, also known as the "last mile" problem, is one key issue. ISDN was and still is an option, yet it always has been too little and too late. Alternative access mechanisms such as wireless PCS and CATV may lead to the elimination of ISDN. ATM (Asynchronous Transfer Mode, or packetized high speed networks integrating voice and data) switching is another technology change element that has a great deal of potential for expanding local access as well as long distance access.

A future communications and processing issue that will define the architecture is whether dark fiber—the provision of access from a host to fiber with no telephone company intermediary switching—will become a viable commercial option. Dark fiber could allow intelligent hosts to control the communications processing in a highly distributed fashion using intelligent high-layer protocols. This exemplifies the concept of intelligence at the periphery of the network, namely at the host. This concept states that communications should be minimalist in form: that is, communications providers should do nothing that limits the creativity of the processing hosts' intelligence and capabilities. Intelligence in the network results frequently in what has been termed the hierarchical network paradigm, a design that has been at the heart of telecommunications for over 100 years. Intelligence at the periphery is a paradigm that enables distributed processing and enables the end user maximum flexibility in design and in the provision of services. Until dark fiber becomes an available commodity, switching will remain a centrally provided host service. Host processing capability or intelligence, and not the communications network intelligence, will in any case be the driver that will enable and promote new and innovative services to the New User community.

We believe that there are three main technological changes which will impact New User migration as well as the existing base. These are:

• **Multimedia Communications.** Multimedia communications is generally the least understood and most discussed area in both computers and communications. The challenge of multimedia communications is to create what we have called "displaced conversationality." This means the provision of all sensory inputs and outputs to any human user, at any time and place, required for the transmission of information in order to transact a series of events that lead ultimately to an agreed consensus among the parties involved. Simply put, it means that I can talk in simple terms with anybody else, using whatever displays, video, data, voice or other annotations I desire, either simultaneously or at a delayed period of time. This will place significant new demands on the Internet. It raises the question of whether the Internet must now consider raising the level of protocols it supports above just TCP (the transport control protocol) into what we have called the session control protocol, SCP. Does the Internet evolve into a SCP/TCP/IP network?[4]

• **Access Expansion.** Access implies any and all physical communications means that a user may have to access the Internet, through a Campus system, a Regional, or even the Backbone. Today, we expect the access to be achieved via a telephone line or possibly a LAN. In this paper we extend the means of access in two dimensions: CATV and wireless. CATV access means broadband access, even with the systems in place today. This means 50 to 100 Mbps access in wide areas of coverage, and complement the advances in multimedia communications. The second access innovation is wireless access. This access scheme will enable extensive host migration to PDAs (Personal Digital Assistants) and the migration of network identity from host to person, increasing demands put upon the network to "Find Me!"

• **Host Migration.** Historically, an Internet user was identified with a host. The user had access via the host and the user was merely an extension of this host. This made sense when the user required access to the host for the host's shared resources. With the increased power, capabilities, and ubiquity of personal computers, migration of identity from the host to the user is more likely. The development of PDAs, which are now user-resident hosts rather than host-resident users, is a technology driven change that will cause significant architectural change in the Internet. The user can now be in possession of the Host and the host can be connected to the Internet in a wireless fashion; thus the need for "Find Me!" functions in the Internet fabric.

The issue we now consider is not what these changes are, but what the implications of these changes are for the Internet and the New User community. Will these changes be feasible within the evolving Internet? Will they be more likely to occur in other networks? And if they are Internet compatible, how can they be implemented? We will attempt to place these issues in perspective. However, it cannot be denied that the New User community, as well as the established user base, will demand the capabilities that are being discussed, and that the confluence of market demand and technological innovation will make this a reality.

Multimedia Communications

Multimedia communications is simply displaced conversationality. From the New User perspective it represents a truly transparent medium of talking, of sharing ideas and conversations with others in a simple fashion, blending seamlessly all elements of communications that typically are in any normal human conversation. Multimedia communications is not merely the devices and displays, it is not merely advanced CD players with enhanced sound. It is a conversation with others, using all of the available senses, combining meaning and content between a group of individuals displaced in time and space. The key architectural and technical question is whether the Internet can and will support the types of multimedia communications that are envisioned. It is the opinion of the authors that the elements to do so are available and, further, that the New User community is anticipating that such service will be available.[5]

When we introduce the multimedia communications concept, we anticipate a context in which multiple users will share in the use of multimedia objects. Thus multimedia communications requires that multiple human users have sensory interfaces to multiple versions of complex objects stored on multiple storage media. In contrast to data communications in the computer domain, where humans are a secondary afterthought and optimization is made in accordance with the machine-to-machine connection, multimedia communications is a human-to-many-other-humans communications process that must fully integrate the end user into the environment. Multimedia communications thus generates a sense of conversationality, is sustainable over longer periods, and has an extreme fluidity of interaction. The current Internet already affords a sense of conversationality; it is the expanding of that conversationality to a wider array of multimedia objects that is the challenge.

We concentrate on three issues in the area of multimedia communications: the data objects, the conversationality of the interaction, and the overall communications architecture. It is the concept of conversationality, of displaced sharing of information and creating transactions of the mind, that makes the definition of multimedia communications more expansive than traditional data communications and represents a challenge for integration into the Internet fabric. Displaced conversationality demands interaction, and such *transparent interaction* will become the most important capability and functionality of the Internet, especially as it addresses the New User.

The major observation that we make is that the standard approach to communications system design, starting from the physical layer and working up, is the wrong way to proceed for multimedia. Specifically, in a multimedia environment, one must, in order to gain user acceptance, design the system from the top layers down.

We briefly review two of the key elements of multimedia communications that relate to Internet expansion: multimedia data objects and multimedia communications protocols.[6] Multimedia Objects relate to the *"what"* of the communications process, and Multimedia Communications Protocols are the *"how."*

Multimedia data objects

In a traditional computer communications environment, the data objects have significant structure, and they are frequently integrated into a system-wide database management system that ensures the overall integrity of the data structures. In a multimedia environment, the data elements are more complex, taking the form of video, voice, text, and images; they may be real time in nature or gathered from a stored environment. More importantly, the users may create new objects by concatenating several simpler objects into a complex whole. For example, we can conceive of a set of three objects composed of an image, a voice annotation, and a pointer motion such as a mouse movement. The combination of all three of these can also be viewed as a single identifiable multimedia object.

Multimedia communications protocols

The protocols in communications systems are designed to facilitate the interaction between users. The development of new communications systems protocols will be driven by the implementation of new and innovative protocol concepts and the needs of the end users. The protocols must be interactively processed by all active elements in the network and by the host environments.

Protocols occur at different layers in the communications process. One standard way of classifying protocols is the seven-layer Open Systems Interconnection model.[7] Those familiar with the Internet are aware of the TCP/IP protocols: TCP deals with the transport layer, also known as layer four, while IP is a datagram protocol at layers two and three. Layer one typically deals with physical interfaces such as that of the telephone jack or the modem. Layer five is called the session layer; it was developed to deal with the possibility of having "conversations" among users, but had seen little use until the last few years. This is the layer that is most useful for enabling multimedia communications.

The services provided by the session layer fall into four categories:

- **Dialog Management:** This function provides users with the ability to control, on a local as well as global basis, the overall interaction in the session. Specifically, dialog management determines the protocol of who talks when and how this control of talking is passed from one user to another.

- **Activity Management:** An *activity* can be defined as a sequence of events either within a session or encompassing several sessions. The activity management function ensures that all steps in an activity are taken and reported on. For example, in a medical application, we can define an activity called "diagnosis" that may consist of a set of multiple sessions between several consulting physicians. We define the activity as beginning when the patient arrives for the first visit and ending when the primary physician writes the diagnosis. The session service helps ensure that all patients have a complete diagnosis and are provided treatment consistent with that diagnosis. It does this by creating a set of events that constitute the diagnosis activity and tracking all of these events to ensure that each step is taken. Thus activity management for medical diagnosis means that all tests are taken, evaluated, and reported to the doctor and patient, and that a course of treatment is undertaken. In this case activity management could mean no need for malpractice!

- **Synchronization**: At the heart of a multimedia system is the multimedia data object. Each object has its own synchronization or timing requirements; a compound object has an orchestration problem. Synchronization is like the timing kept by a good violinist. If we combine many multimedia objects, we create the need for orchestration—the synchronization of many synchronized objects. Orchestration is then analogous conducting a symphony. The session service of synchronization must ensure that the end-to-end timing between users and objects is maintained throughout. We can readily see that its usefulness is a combination of how well each object is synchronized and, more importantly, how well the overall conversation is orchestrated!

- **Event Management:** The monitoring of performance, isolation of problems, and restoration of service that constitute event management are a key element of the session service.

Providing these levels of protocols in the Internet environment is realizable if there is an expansion of the protocol layers currently in use. It would require an agreement among the host community to incorporate and expand the existing TCP/IP set and generate a Session Control Protocol set, thus providing a SCP/TCP/IP protocol set.

Let us consider two examples of where multimedia communications may be of help for the Internet New User community.

Example 1: (Health Care).[8] A physician desires to consult with several other physicians on a specific patient problem. The patient is in a rural area, has had a echocardiogram, and has been tested in his regional hospital in a nuclear scan using Technetium 90. The results are in two different places, and the patient's physician is in a third. The concern is about the patient's mitral valve and whether it needs surgery. A consultation between the physician in Berlin, NH, the regional hospital in Manchester, NH, and the chief cardiologist at Mass General in Boston can be performed using the Internet. The images can be shared, voice annotation and text annotation supplied, movements of the images made, and shared commentary presented. The entire process may then also be made part of the patient's record for future review.

Example 2: (K-12 Education). An instructor has developed a botany project for the analysis of complex plant structures. The instructor is in Boston, and she has a collaborator in the suburbs of Canberra, Australia. The students are in various locations throughout the United States. The instructor can demonstrate the principles with graphics, which are interactive between the students, while the researcher in Canberra can show field samples of the botanical specimens in their local habitat, including surrounding vegetation. The students can interactively create a field sample by capturing the sample in differing views. The instructor can then grade the student's work.

Access Expansion

Access is defined here as the physical connection between a local host or network entity and the body of the Internet. It is the last mile or the last 1,000 feet connection to the Internet. It also is generally the most costly. It may be provided by the local telephone company and a dedicated access line, or it may be the campus local area network.

We shall focus on the New User exclusively, and shall consider access as a full-time and real-time connection to the Internet from a single New User location. As a point of reference, PSI may charge a user almost $1,000 per month for such a connection, the costs being dominated by payments to the local telephone company. Such charges are the primary barrier to entry to the New User. Access fees must be changed if the New User is to be more than a sporadic user of the service. This section discusses two alternatives that are currently being developed—CATV and wireless access—and their architectural implications. These represent two of the most dramatic areas of change.

CATV[9]

The existing CATV entities have argued that their infrastructure is highly suitable to use for local and broadband access. It has been demonstrated that use of this technology is viable in many areas, but severe drawbacks have also been revealed.[10] The recently contemplated mergers between cable and telephone companies, namely Bell Atlantic and TCI, Cox and Southwestern Bell, and Time Warner and US West, are clear indicators that there is some perceived joint interest. The argument has been that cable can provide data and interactive services to the home more cost-effectively than telephone. The argument has not been operationally proven, however.[11] To demonstrate the potential of cable for local access, we review some of the cable architectures and directions.

The current CATV systems have a tree and branch architecture that is one-way, as shown in Figure 2. CATV systems have two major plant elements: the residential cable that services all homes and the

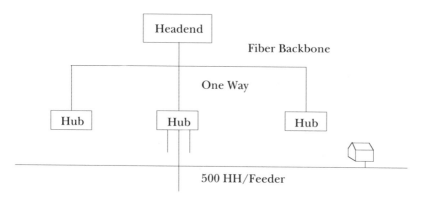

Figure 2 CATV Architecture.

institutional cable or loop, which was required for the cable franchises but never put to use. The institutional loop presents significant access alternatives. The institutional loop passes many homes and commercial locations and is designed for two-way high-speed data as well as video. Thus institutional cable is not a typical one-way video distribution system. It can be used for data applications and as an element in Internet access. CATV companies have also been adding additional backbone elements and have been using these as CAPs (Competitive Access Providers) in commercial areas.

CATV was initially two-way capable, and some systems such as the Warner QUBE systems were two-way activated. However, this requires the use of two-way repeaters, which are inactive in almost all plants. There is 50 MHz of bandwidth available in all CATV systems for residential use and 150 MHz for all institutional use. The question is how to take a one-way system and make it two-way.

One solution is shown in Figure 3. Two-way capability is achieved by creating a 50 Mbps or even 100 Mbps bus, comparable to that provided in FDDI.[12] This is achieved by looping the local feeder cables back to a bus fiber via a bridge. Thus the system looks like a broadband system and can provide any home or location with up to 100 Mbps service with minimal capital change in the CATV plant.[13] The question then is, what are the user requirements for such a system? For simplicity, we can assume that a single user accessing the system transfers 4 Mbit of files per hour. This is

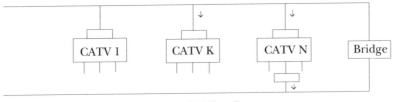

50 Mbps Bus

Figure 3 CATV Two-Way Plant.

approximately 1 Kbps, and if on average there are 8,000 users, we need about 24 Mbps to handle all of them.[14] Thus a cable system can theoretically handle a reasonable community of users.

There are several reasons for lack of CATV two-way broadband digital infrastructure at the present time. Specifically they are:[15]

1. **Interconnect:** In a reasonable radius from any large metropolitan area there are between one and several dozen CATV entities. The issue of interface and interconnect has never been adequately addressed, and there are no standards that allow for this. In addition, CATV switch access uses the same dated architecture as does cellular telephone, and thus is highly reliant upon the existing Local Exchange Carrier (LEC). This will merely drive up the cost of goods for the carrier.

2. **Availability.** CATV systems have a system availability—the percent of the time that the system works for all users—that is less than 90%, whereas communications networks have availability numbers in excess of 99.5%—that is, outages occur less than 0.5% of the time. The inherent structure, operations, and management of the two networks are currently incompatible. Specifically, CATV as currently operated cannot provide toll-grade quality service.

3. **Bandwidth.** Bandwidth in a CATV system is limited, except on institutional loops. Local bandwidth is structured for video, and the two-way systems have a limited return path. When we begin the multimedia applications, the bandwidth need will be even greater.[16]

4. **Performance.** Data transmission performance on coaxial or fiber/coax has been shown to be significantly impaired by the excessively noisy environment resulting from many open cable

access terminations in homes of current or prior subscribers. Admittedly this may be ameliorated by real-time noise suppression systems or interactive devices in the homes, but it will require significant rebuilds as well as management and administration of the subscriber loop.

5. **Inactivated Two-Way Returns.** Two-way cable almost ceased to exist as an operating entity with the demise of the famous QUBE system.[17] Currently less than 0.1% of the CATV systems have active and operational cable return paths and supported bi-directional amplifiers.[18] For the CATV system to function, this must be addressed.

However, we argue that these limitations can be eliminated from the current designs and thus allow significant Internet access. Specifically:

1. **Interconnect.** CATV companies are being pressured to establish interconnection among themselves at the head ends as well as to enter into the CAP, or Competitive Access Provider, business. This will ensure system-to-system access. Internet access can be achieved directly via a CAP point of presence, or PoP.

2. **Availability.** Trunk CATV transport is being upgraded to fiber, which is much more reliable. By establishing a bus network on top of that, alternative routing is possible and system availability improved.

3. **Bandwidth.** Using institutional loops 150 MHz is available, and with high signal-to-noise and controlled interference it is possible to achieve 300 Mbps on such loops. Thus a bus of 300 Mbps or more is achievable in today's architecture.

4. **Performance.** This is a major problem area generally due to open taps on the cable. This may require better maintenance and control, which is a methods and procedures problem for the CATV operators.

5. **Two-way.** This is achieved via the bus proposal.

Thus, CATV provides the Internet with a viable and current option for expansion into high data rates and multimedia capability.

Wireless

Wireless communications services introduce new sets of technologies that will create a new local loop access paradigm. The current view of the local loop is that of a bundled set of services that possess significant economies of scale and thus justify permitting the Local Exchange Carriers (LECs) to have a total monopoly in the local exchange. The new technologies allow dramatically lower capital costs per subscriber and also eliminate the scale and scope economies in local access.

Technology has changed dramatically in the past five years. The two current ways of providing voice service are wireline twisted pair telephone service and cellular voice service. New technological innovations have allowed the wireless PCS services to be provided by another form of technology. This technology takes advantage of a distributed telecommunications architecture and places as much "silicon" in the field as possible. It also performs as much processing as possible so as to minimize the functions required by the LEC interconnect.

One of the key questions is, what capacity can the wireless link have? Let us digress a bit to develop that answer. The following is a simple case:

- Assume that the wireless channel has 20 MHz of bandwidth.

- Assume that a modulation method is used that allows 1 bit per second per Hz of bandwidth.[19]

- Assume, therefore, that a 20 Mbps data channel is available.

Now assume that we want to take this 20 Mbps and share it among many users. How can this be achieved? First, one could break the bandwidth into many smaller bands and create a cellular system. In cellular, one takes the 20 MHz and breaks it into seven parts. Thus the cell, one of the parts, has only about 3 MHz of bandwidth and thus a 3 Mbps data rate. Second, one could use some form of signal spreading, thus retaining the data rate but reducing the overall capacity of the maximum rate.[20] Let us assume the latter.

Using either of these schemes we have a system of peak rate of 20 Mbps. How many instantaneous users may there be? That depends on how much each user uses the system. Let us take the medical example as a case in point. Let us assume a user transmits an X ray, which requires 2,000 by 2,000 pixels, at 16 bits per pixel. This is 4 million pixels, or 64 million bits! At 20 Mbps that is about three seconds. Clearly, in an Internet environment having a wireless termination and using a DS3 backbone or higher, such a connection is possible. Indeed, if one uses no more than one X ray per five minutes, many other users on the local wireless network will have access. Thus wireless access is an attractive access mechanism for the Internet, and especially Internet with multimedia.

What does wireless do for the Internet? There are several things that it does immediately:

Access expansion. Providing access to places not readily served. This would include, for example, school classrooms and other locations not now served by wire-based telephone.

Expanded bandwidth. Using wireless, it may be possible to take 20 to 40 MHz of bandwidth and create a 40 to 80 Mbps bus to allow PDA users access to a wide variety of services, including multimedia.

Terminal identification. Wireless has an infrastructure that will enable the "Find Me!" paradigm to be effected. It has more than the cellular roaming capabilities that we have seen evolve in the older analog cellular architecture.

Host Migration

Host migration means the identification of user with host and vice versa. The changes occurring in host performance and characterization that force consideration of host migration and the implications of this change are as follows:

- **Higher performance single processors**. The development of higher-speed and higher-performance workstations has dramatically changed the capabilities of the local host. The individual's workstation will have full host capability and interconnectivity, and the identification of the host will migrate down to the lowest common denominator, which will now consist of machines that have significant power.

- **Personal digital assistants**. PDAs will create a dramatic change on the Internet. The PDA is a wireless device that identifies with the individual. It is as powerful as many other host-like processors, but it dramatically changes the paradigm. It associates itself with a person at all times, and not with a location. The difference is comparable to that between the existing telephone network and the new PCS telecommunications network. The PDA will challenge the Internet to recognize the user qua user rather than the user qua host.

- **Wireless host access.** Wireless access presents challenges of expansion, connectivity, interconnectivity, and addressability. In 1975 and 1976, the senior author was responsible, with others, for establishing the first wireless access to the ARPANET via Intelsat. The challenge at that time was connecting the earth stations in West Virginia to that at Goonhilly in the UK. Earlier Kahn and Abramson had developed the Packet Radio approach, but had limited ARPANET access. The challenge in both of these cases was the need to develop new data protocols, namely TCP/IP, because of the unique capabilities of the channel. We shall see the same challenge here, but now we must expand the protocol sets to include SCP/TCP/IP.

- **Multiple hosts per user.** The user will have the identity and may be connected to multiple hosts. Moreover there may be a set of many-to-many connections. The issue of "Find Me!" will be expanded to connect to and communicate with the user "Now!"

- **Enhanced Host Access Software.** The end users currently access the Internet via UNIX-like calls and commands. A few simplified front-end devices are available but are limited. The expansion of New User host access capabilities, such as through a Windows-type environment in a multitasking mode, will dramatically increase the demand for host access software. In addition, a CATV or wireless packet access mode, rather than a twisted pair local loop, tariffed on a per-packet or even fixed-rate basis, will dramatically expand host migration and increase demands on host software.

Policy Implications

There are several areas that the New User impacts upon in terms of policy decisions:

Access

The issue of access should be seen as an issue of flexibility and ubiquity as opposed to an issue of regulation and revenue assignment. The concern is that while multiple means of access to the Internet are becoming available for the New User (and the high-end user as well), the access fees that are currently charged by the LECs reflect a worldview that is of a pre-divestiture nature and represent an attempt to continue to support the local user at the expense of the long-distance user. With the Internet being the long-distance company, in effect a pseudo IEC, and the local access being separate from the LEC, should the user be required to continue to reimburse the LEC for access at the other end, independent of who placed the call? The answer should be "No." The issue is, however, not that simple. The argument is changed significantly when the alternative access schemes are introduced. If one uses a wireless scheme or a cable scheme, access fees should be eliminated and access should be subject to competitive market pricing and not monopolistic LEC pricing.[21]

Security and Privacy

The Internet is a global network and it is projected that there will be a one-to-one mapping of host and user, although the user may be identified with many such hosts. This begins to raise the question of security in this environment. If users can now be accessed at any time and place, via a wireless capability and into a PDA, and can thus be networked to the users' other hosts, what security access controls should there be in the network? As the SCP or session capabilities place more intelligence in the network, including the backbone, what safeguards must be developed to ensure integrity and privacy? It is argued that these new movements into multimedia, access, and host migration engender new and different concerns about security and privacy.

Carriage Issues

The carriage issues involve several questions. The first is, what type of carriage is provided by the Internet? Is the Internet ultimately a common carrier? If it is, what does that imply about access and access control and discipline? We argue that the Internet is truly a common carrier as stated in common law. As a common carrier, the Internet has the responsibility of being an open network with open interfaces. This is readily achieved by the workings of the Internet Society, which sets the standards and establishes the overall architectural evolution for the Internet. The Internet is unique in its ability to deal with users in a fully distributed format.[22]

Authorized Use and Users

Authorized users and uses are coupled issues. As the Internet is opened up, as users are directly connected through host migration, and as access is commonly accepted as a real-time and ongoing process, the question is raised as to who is a user and what are the appropriate uses. Is there to be a distinction between New Users and commercial users? Should there be a pricing differential between such user groups? At what point is a fixed access fee appropriate, and when is it required to change?

Conclusions

This paper is a first attempt to lay out and describe the options for expanding the Internet into the New User community. We address the issues of architectural change and stress our concern about protocol "creep" in the network to the higher layers. To handle the New User community it will be necessary to deal with higher layers in the Internet, layers that have not been focused on in prior generations. This paper also addresses the issue of changing technologies and how they may affect the paradigms that make the Internet what it is today and what it may become tomorrow. The issues raised are those concerning the change in host definition driven by increased processing and improved communications. The processing dimension relates to the question, how much more power and control are we to place in the end users' hands? The area of multimedia communications is a typical area where this issue will play significantly. The communications dimension relates to the changing nature of local access and the changing position of the RBOCs as Local Exchange Carriers. The FCC on July 15, 1994 issued its Fifth Report and Order on PCS. By the end of 1995 there will be three to six new Local Exchange Carriers in almost all major U.S. markets. This change will tower above any of the changes that we may have seen in the breakup of AT&T and competition in the inter-exchange market. It will be one of the dominant drivers in expanding Internet use and enabling the multiple-hosts-per-user world described in this paper.

Acknowledgments

The authors would like to thank several individuals who helped in discussions leading to this paper. Vint Cerf, formerly of CNRI and the Internet Society and now with MCI, has provided many insights into the Internet, both history and evolution. Rich Mandlebaum of the CATT Center at Polytechnic University has provided the perspective of the network and Regional player as well as insight on the user community. Gad Selig, formerly of ANS, has added the perspectives of ANS and their implications as the Internet migrates to a more commercial segment. Richard Solomon of MIT has provided insight into pricing methodologies and mechanisms. Brian Kahin and James Keller of the Kennedy School at Harvard continued to provided the insight into many of the policy areas. David Tennenhouse, of LCS at MIT, has provided a sense of direction of the TCP/IP migration to handle the challenges of multimedia. Carolyn Gideon has provided superb editorial advice and has helped improve the clarity of many of the arguments made herein.

Notes

[1] In fact, the Burnaby South Secondary School, which opened in British Columbia in February 1993, has built its visionary "village of learners" campus around a communications infrastructure of coaxial cable in every room to take advantage of multimedia learning aids. It refers to its embedded network capabilities as its "information highway."

[2] McGarty, *Health Care Policy Alternatives*, Telmarc Group Report, 93-004, May 1993.

[3] The Host is defined here as the computer and communications complex that provides the end user with access to the Internet or to another end user. The redefinition and commodification of the host is based two factors described earlier, increased end-user processing capability and reduced high speed communications access. The host is being redefined by the trend toward identifying multiple hosts per user rather than multiple users per host, as well as by the concept of a portable or mobile host. At the same time, the host is commodified by the dramatically lowered costs for both computer power and communications, which allows multiple hosts per user.

[4] McGarty [11]. The Session Control Protocol, SCP, suite is described in this paper. It uses the OSI seven-layer model that has been the basis of many of the communications system protocols. TCP is a layer four protocol and SCP is a layer five protocol. SCP is used to handle complex multimedia objects that are generated by many dispersed users at different times. It enables the concept called displaced conversationality in a multimedia environment.

[5] The details of what it will take to achieve true multimedia functionality in the Internet are significant. Detailing such issues as what is needed, what barriers are there in the current Internet design that must be overcome, who will do the changes, and what are the risks would need an lengthy exposition. Suffice it to say that there are no fundamental barriers to introducing multimedia into the Internet environment. In fact, there are small efforts already underway that show how to do this. The Internet Users Society will be one vehicle, but more importantly, it will be the innovativeness and creativity of the end users, as usual, that will make it a reality.

[6] See McGarty [11], which describes the full architecture of a multimedia system. See also McGarty [10], which refers to many current systems for the delivery of these services.

[7] Tanenbaum, p. 440. The author describes the session layer here and elsewhere in the book provides full details on the seven-layer model.

[8] See McGarty [8], [9] for examples of this case. The actual networks were built and the applications developed. Use of an Internet backbone was contemplated at the time this was developed (1989–1991).

[9] The authors wish to note that when this paper was first published, May 5, 1993, there were no CATV access alternatives. In August of 1993, Continental Cable of Boston and PSI of Reston, Virginia signed a joint agreement to allow Internet access to the Continental Cambridge customer base at a proposed rate of $100 per month, a factor of 10 less than the telephone rates. As of this writing of this version of the paper there were no known customers on the proposed network.

[10] See the paper by McGarty and McGarty [4] describing the consumer trials with the QUBE system. The senior author was the first to develop and deliver a full motion video-on-demand system to customers over a cable and telco integrated system. In 1983 the senior author had a joint venture with Warner, GTE, Bank of America, Bell of Pennsylvania and DEC. This was a data-over-voice telco network integrated with the cable system in Pittsburgh. The system used a bank of 100 video disk players and was the predecessor of the current Warner 500 channel system in New York and Florida. The system used a space division multiple access (SDMA) scheme, splitting video packets on the head-end–hub–sub-hub networks.

[11] The classic case is the example of Manhattan Cable, now Time Warner cable, in New York City. It was the first such entity to deliver 56 Kbps service. It was out-marketed by Teleport and by MFS. It had an early strategic position, but due to its lack of understanding of the telephone business and, more fundamentally,

the fact that cable is not a telecommunications system but an entertainment distribution system, its availability and reliability was too low for commercial applications. It has since been reduced to a non-player in the market.

[12] Cable systems are generally split with a 50 MHz band on the return path (the path from the home to the headend). All of the other bandwidth is from the headend to the home. See McGarty and McGarty [4] .

[13] In fact, it can be argued that the CATV plant is left unchanged. A third party may find it appropriate to build the backward-flowing bus, and thus require no capital change to the CATV operator's plant. This may be a good way to proceed, given the new regulation imposed on cable companies.

[14] See McGarty, "Access Policy," Telecommunications Policy Research Conference, October 1993, Solomon's Island.

[15] McGarty, T.P., and R. Veith, "Hybrid Cable and Telephone Networks," IEEE Comp Con, 1983; also McGarty, T.P., and S.J. McGarty, "Impacts of Consumer Demands on CATV Local Loop Communications," IEEE ICC, 1983.

[16] McGarty and Clancy [5]. The authors develop the model for integrated video, voice, text and data on an integrated cable-telco system. This paper, although for proprietary reasons not describing the full motion video on demand system, does present the detailed technical analysis.

[17] McGarty, T.P., and G.J. Clancy, "Cable Based Metro Area Networks," *IEEE Jour on Sel. Areas in Comm.*, Vol. 1, No 5, pp. 816–831, Nov. 1983; also McGarty, T.P., "Local Area Wideband Data Communications Networks," EASCON, 1982.

[18] For example, the author has been told by Continental that Cambridge was the only system with two-way activated feed in their entire network.

[19] The modulation efficiency, namely the number of bits per second per Hz, is often overlooked by those who try to size bandwidth capability. It should be remembered that it is not just the bandwidth, it is also the modulation that matters.

[20] "Spreading" is also called spread spectrum or CDMA (code division multiple access). This is discussed in McGarty [15], [16] and in the references contained therein. Simply stated, suppose we begin with a signal that may be 50 Kbps and could occupy 50 KHz. Spread spectrum takes that signal and multiplies it by a unique signal, its code, that is a higher-rate signal, typically 1,000 times greater, and thus spreads the original signal over 50 MHz. Each user has a unique code, and through a sophisticated means of signal processing, each user's signal can be recovered.

[21] McGarty [17]. The author has argued that access for new carriers to the local exchange market can be viewed in three ways.

Access as Externality: This is the long-standing concept of access that is the basis of the current access fee structures. The RBOC contends that it has certain economic externalities of value that it provides any new entrant to the local exchange market and that the new entrant brings nothing of value to the table in the process of interconnecting. The RBOC, which has the responsibility of universal service, permits the new entrant access to the RBOC's customers, which brings significant value to the new entrant. In fact, RBOCs argue that a new entrant would have no business if the RBOC did not allow it access to "its" customer base. This school of access is the "unilateral" school. Federal Communications Commissioner Barrett has stated publicly on several occasions that any new entrant should reimburse the RBOC for the value the RBOC brings to the table. The RBOCs, especially Bell South, are strong supporters of this view.

Access as Bilateralism: This is the view currently espoused by the Commission in some of its more recent filings. It is also the view of the New York Public Service Commission in the tariff allowing Rochester Telephone and Time Warner Communications to interoperate. It also is the view of Ameritech in its proposed disaggregation approach. Simply stated, Bilateralism says that there are two or more LECs in a market. LEC A will pay LEC B for access or interconnect and LEC B will pay LEC A. It raises the questions of what the basis will be for reimbursement, what rate base concept, if any, will be used, and what process will be applied to ensure equity. This is akin to reinventing the settlements process of pre-divestiture days. It is also know as the "Brer Rabbit" approach, saying not to throw us into the stick thicket of bilateral payments, but knowing that that is where the RBOCs were born and raised. Bilateralism is rife with expensive legal reviews and administrative delays. It clearly plays into the hand of the established monopolist. Suffice it to say that U.S. West owns a significant share of Time Warner, and that one would suspect that their presence is felt in this bilateralism approach.

Access as Competitive Leverage: This concept of access assumes that there is a public policy of free and open competition and that the goal is to provide the consumer with the best service at the lowest possible price. It argues that no matter how one attempts to deal with access in the bilateral approach, abuses will be rampant. Thus the only solution from the consumer welfare perspective is to totally eliminate access fees. The competitive access school says that the price the consumer pays for service should reflect only the costs associated with the consumer's provider and not those of the service provider of the person that the individual wants to talk to. For example, my local telephone rate does not change if I desire to talk to someone in Mongolia, even if their rates are much higher due to local inefficiencies. The competitive access school says that externalities are public goods, created by the publicly granted monopoly status of the past one hundred years. It states further that bilateralism is nothing more that an encumbrance that allows the entrenched monopolist to control the growth of new entrants and is quite simply an artifact of pre-divestiture AT&T operations. The only choice for the competitive access school is no access fees at all and price at cost.

The author has argued in this context that the only way to view access is as a competitive tool., and that the only competitive access agreement is the total elimination of access fees.

[22] In the Internet, the organization that manages the network reflects the form of the network. The organization is an open distributed form, unlike the hierarchical form of management of the RBOCs, which in turn have a hierarchical network.

References

1. Cerf, V., *Internetworking and the Internet,* CNRI, 1993.

2. Kahin, B., *Building Information Infrastructure,* McGraw Hill (New York), 1992.

3. McGarty, T. P., "Local Area Wideband Data Communications Networks," EASCON, 1982.

4. McGarty, T. P., S. J. McGarty, "Impacts of Consumer Demands on CATV-Local Loop Communications," *IEEE ICC,* 1983.

5. McGarty, T. P., G. J. Clancy, "Cable Based Metro Area Networks," *IEEE Journal on Selected Areas in Communications (JSAC),* Vol. 1, No 5, pp. 816–831, November 1983.

6. McGarty, T. P., "Alternative Networking Architectures: Pricing, Policy and Competition," Information Infrastructures for the 1990s, Harvard University, J. F. Kennedy School of Government, November 1990.

7. McGarty, T. P., "Image Processing in Full Multimedia Communications," *Advanced Imaging,* pp. 28–33, November 1990.

8. McGarty, T. P., "Applications of Multimedia Communications Systems for Health Care Transaction Management," HIMMS Conference, San Francisco, CA, January, 1991.

9. McGarty, T. P., "Multimedia Communications Technology in Diagnostic Imaging," *Investigative Radiology,* Vol. 26, No 4, pp. 377–381, April 1991.

10. McGarty, T. P., S. J. McGarty, "Information Architectures and Infrastructures: Value Creation and Transfer," 19th Annual Telecommunications Policy Research Conference, Solomon's Island, MD, September 1991.

11. McGarty, T. P., "Multimedia Communications: Architectural Alternatives," SPIE Conference, Boston, MA, September 1991.

12. McGarty, T. P., "Communications Network Morphological and Taxonomical Policy Implications," 20th Annual Telecommunications Policy Research Conference, Solomon's Island, MD, September 1992.

13. McGarty, T. P., "Multimedia Communications in Medicine," *IEEE JSAC,* November 1992.

14. McGarty, T. P., S. J. McGarty, "Architectures et Structures de L'Information," *Reseaux,* No. 56, pp. 119–156, December 1992.

15. McGarty, T. P., "Access to the Local Loop," Kennedy School of Government, Harvard University, Infrastructures in Massachusetts, March 1993.

16. McGarty, T. P., "Wireless Access to the Local Loop," MIT Universal Personal Communications Symposium, March, 1993.

17. McGarty, T. P., "A Précis on PCS Economics and Access Fees Structures, Markets and Competition," NPC SC Seminar on "Wireless Technology and Policy Implications" at MIT Lincoln Laboratory, Lexington, MA, May 18, 1994.

18. Tanenbaum, A. S. *Computer Networks,* Prentice Hall (Englewood Cliffs), 1989.

19. Weinhaus, C. L., A. G. Oettinger., *Behind the Telephone Debates,* Ablex (Norwood, NJ), 1988.

20. Winograd, T., F. Flores, *Understanding Computers and Cognition,* Addison Wesley (Reading, MA), 1987.

Pricing and Service Models

Pricing the Internet

Jeffrey K. MacKie-Mason and Hal R. Varian

On December 23, 1992 the National Science Foundation (NSF) announced that it will cease funding the ANS T3 Internet backbone in the near future. This is a major step in the transition from a government-funded to a commercial Internet. This movement has been welcomed by private providers of telecommunication services and businesses seeking access to the Internet.

No one is quite sure about how this privatization will work; in particular, it is far from clear how use of the privatized Internet will be priced. Currently, the several Internet backbone networks are public goods with exclusion: usage is essentially free to all authorized users. Most users are connected to a backbone through a "pipe" for which a fixed access fee is charged, but the user's organization nearly always covers the access fee as overhead without any direct charge to the user.[1] None of the backbones charge fees that depend at the margin on the volume of data transmitted. The result is that the Internet is characterized by "the problem of the commons," and without instituting new mechanisms for congestion control it is likely to soon suffer from server "overgrazing." We shall propose an efficient pricing structure to manage congestion, encourage network growth, and guide resources to their most valuable uses.

We first describe the Internet's technology and cost structure, since a feasible and efficient pricing scheme must reflect both technology and costs. We then describe congestion problems in the network, and some past proposals to control them. We turn to pricing by first describing in general terms the advantages and disadvantages of using pricing to control congestion and then detailing our proposed pricing structure. We devote particular attention to a novel feature of our proposal: the use of a "smart market" to price congestion in real time.

Internet Technology and Costs

The Internet is a network of networks. We shall focus on backbone networks, although most of our pricing ideas apply equally well to mid-level and local area networks. There are essentially four competing backbones for the Internet: ANSnet, PSInet, Alternet, and SprintLINK.[2] ANS is a non-profit that was formed in 1990 to manage the publicly-funded NSFNET for research and educational users. ANSnet now provides the backbone service for NSFNET, as well as backbone service for commercial users through its subsidiary, ANS CO+RE, Inc. PSInet and Alternet are independent commercial providers of backbone Internet services to commercial and non-commercial users. Sprint is a major telecommunications provider as well as a provider of Internet transport services.

The Internet networks use packet-switching communications technology based on the TCP/IP protocols. While much of the traffic moves across lines leased from telephone common carriers, packet-switching technology is quite different from the circuit switching used for voice telephony. When a telephone user dials a number, a dedicated path is set up between the caller and the called number. This path, with a fixed amount of network resources, is held open; no other caller can use those resources until the call is terminated.[3] A packet-switching network, by contrast, uses "statistical multiplexing": each circuit is shared by many users, and no open connection is maintained for a particular communications session. A data stream is broken up into small chunks called "packets." When a packet is ready, the computer sends it onto the network. When one computer is not sending a packet, the network line is available for packets from other computers. The TCP (Transmission Control Protocol) specifies how to break up a datastream into packets and reassemble it; the IP (Internet Protocol) provides the necessary information for various computers on the Internet (the routers) to move each packet to the next link on the way to its final destination. The data in a packet may be 1500 bytes or so. Recently the average packet on NSFNET carried about 200 bytes of data (packet size has been steadily increasing). On top of these 200 bytes the TCP/IP headers add about 40; thus about 17% of the traffic carried on the Internet is simply header information.

Packetization allows for the efficient use of expensive communications lines. Consider a typical interactive terminal session to a remote computer: most of the time the user is thinking. The network is needed only after a key is struck or when a reply is returned.[4] Holding an open connection would waste most of the capacity of the network link. Instead, the computer waits until after a key is struck, at which point it puts the keystroke information in a packet which is sent across the network. The rest of the time the network links are free to be used for transporting packets from other users.

The other distinguishing feature of Internet technology is that it is "connectionless."[5] This means that there is no end-to-end setup for a session; each packet is independently routed to its destination. When a packet is ready, the host computer sends it on to another computer, known as a router (or switch). The router examines the destination address in the header and passes the packet along to another router, chosen by a route-finding algorithm. A packet may go through 30 or more routers in its travels from one host computer to another. Because routing is dynamically calculated, it is entirely possible for different packets from a single session to take different routes to the destination.[6]

The postal service is a good metaphor for the technology of the Internet (Krol, 1992). A sender puts a message into an envelope (packet), and that envelope is routed through a series of postal stations, each determining where to send the envelope on its next hop. No dedicated pipeline is opened end-to-end, and thus there is no guarantee that envelopes will arrive in the sequence they were sent, or follow exactly the same route.

The TCP protocol enables packets to be identified and reassembled in the correct order. TCP prefaces the data in a packet with a header containing the source and destination ports, the sequence number of the packet, an acknowledgment flag, and so on.

The header takes up 20 or more bytes. TCP sends the packet to a router, a computer that is in charge of forwarding packets to their next destination. At the routers, IP adds another header (another 20 or more bytes) containing source and destination addresses and other information needed for routing the packet. The router then calculates the best next link for the packet to traverse, and sends it on. The best link may change minute by minute, as the network configuration changes.[7] Routes can be recalculated immediately from the routing table if a route fails. The routing table in a switch is updated nearly continuously.

Over the past five years, the speed of the NSFNET backbone has increased from 56 Kbps to 45 Mbps ("T3" service).[8] The newer backbones have also upgraded to 45 Mbps. These lines can move about 1,400 pages of text per second; a 20-volume encyclopedia can be sent across the Internet in half a minute. Many regional networks still provide T1 (1.5 Mbps) service, but these too are being upgraded.

The transmission speed of the Internet is remarkably high. We recently tested the transmission delay at various times of day and night for sending a packet to Norway from Ann Arbor, Michigan. Each packet traversed 16 links: the IP header was read and modified 16 times, and 16 different routers calculated the best next link. Despite the many hops and substantial packetization and routing, the longest delay on one representative weekday was only 0.333 seconds (at 1:10 PM EST); the shortest delay was 0.174 seconds (at 5:13 PM EST).[9]

Current Backbone Network Costs

The postal service is a good metaphor for packet-switching technology, but not for the cost structure of Internet services. Most of the costs of providing the Internet are more or less independent of the level of usage of the network; i.e., most of the costs are fixed costs. If the network is not saturated the incremental cost of sending additional packets is essentially zero.[10]

The NSF in 1993 spent about $11.5 million to operate the NSFNET and provided $7 million per year in grants to help operate the regional networks.[11] NSF grants also help colleges and universities connect to the NSFNET. Using the conservative estimate of 2 million hosts and 20 million users, this implies that the 1993 NSF Internet subsidy was less than \$10 per year per host, or less than \$1 per user.[12]

Total salaries and wages for NSFNET have increased by a little more than one-half (about 68% nominal) over 1988-1991, a time when the number of packets delivered has increased by a factor of 128.[13] It is hard to calculate total costs because of large in-kind contributions by IBM and MCI during the initial years of the NSFNET project, but it appears that total costs for the 128-fold increase in packets have increased by a factor of about 3.2.

Two components account for most of the costs of providing a backbone network: communications lines and routers. Lease payments for lines and routers accounted for nearly 80% of the 1992 NSFNET costs. The only other significant cost is for the Network Operations Center (NOC), which accounts for roughly 7% of total cost.[14] Thus we focus on the costs of lines and routers.

We have estimated costs for the network backbone as of 1992-93.[15] A T3 (45 Mbps) trunk line running 300 miles between two metropolitan central stations could be leased for about \$32,000 per month. The cost to purchase a router capable of managing a T3 line was approximately \$100,000. Assuming another \$100,000 for service and operation costs, and 50-month amortization at a nominal 10% rate yields a rental cost of about \$4900 per month for the router.

The costs of both lines and switching have been dropping rapidly for over three decades. In the 1960s, digital computer switching was more expensive (per packet) than lines (Roberts, 1974), but switching has since become substantially cheaper. In Table 1 we show estimated 1992 costs for transporting 1 million bits of data through the NSFNET backbone and compare these to estimates for earlier years. As can be seen, in 1992 lines cost about eight times as much as routers.

The structure of the NSFNET backbone directly reflects its costs: lots of cheap routers manage a limited number of expensive lines. We illustrate a portion of the network in Figure 1. Each numbered square is an RS6000 router; the numbers listed beside a router are links to regional networks. In general, each packet moves through

MacKie-Mason and Varian

Table 1 Communications and Router Costs (nominal $ per million bits)*

Year	Lines	Routers	Transmission Speed
1960	1.00		2.4 Kbps
1962	10.00		
1963	0.42		40.8 Kbps
1964	0.34		50.0 Kbps
1967	0.33		50.0 Kbps
1970	0.168		
1971	0.102		
1974	0.11	0.026	56.0 Kbps
1992	0.00094	0.00007	45 Mbps

* Costs are based on sending one million bits of data approximately 1200 miles on a path that traverses five routers.

Sources: 1960–74 from (Roberts, 1974). 1992 calculated by the authors using data provided by Merit Network, Inc.

two separate routers at the entry and exit nodes. For example, if we send a message from the University of Michigan to Bell Laboratories, it will traverse link 131 to Cleveland, where it passes through two routers (41 and 40). The packet goes to New York, where it moves through another two routers (32 and 33) before leaving the backbone on link 137 to the JVNCnet regional network to which Bell Labs. Two T3 lines are navigated using four routers.

Relation between Technology and Costs

Line and switching costs have been exponentially declining at about 30% per year (see the semi-log plot in Figure 2). But more interesting than the rapid decline is the change from expensive routers to expensive transmission links. Indeed, it was the crossover around 1970 (Figure 2) that created a role for packet-switching networks. When lines were cheap relative to switches it made sense to have many lines feed into relatively few switches, and to open an end-to-end circuit for each connection. In that way, each connection wastes transmission capacity (lines are held open whether data

Partial NSFNET T3 Backbone Map

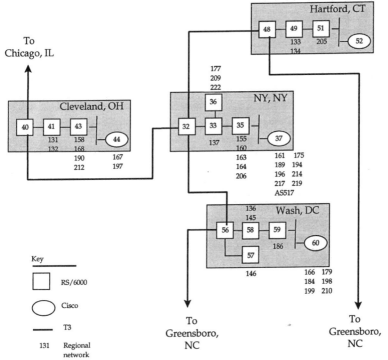

Figure 1 Network Map Fragment.

is flowing or not) but economizes on switching (one setup per connection).

When switches become cheaper than lines, the network is more efficient if data streams are broken into small packets and sent out piecemeal, allowing many users to share a single line. Each packet must be examined at each switch along the way to determine its type and destination, but this uses the relatively cheap switch capacity. The gain is that when one source is quiet, packets from other sources use the same (relatively expensive) lines.

Congestion Problems

The Internet is an extremely effective way to move information; for users, the Internet usually seems to work reliably and instantly.

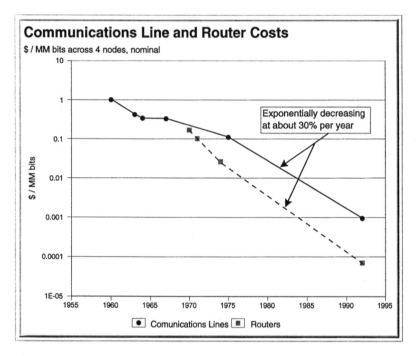

Figure 2 Trends in Costs for Communications Links and Routers.

Sometimes, however, the Internet becomes congested, and there is simply too much traffic for the routers and lines to handle. At present, the only two ways the Internet can deal with congestion are to drop packets, so that some information must be resent by the application, or to delay traffic. These solutions impose external social costs: Sally sends a packet that crowds out Elena's packet; Elena suffers delay, but Sally does not for the cost she imposes on Elena.

In essence, this is the classic problem of the commons. When villagers have shared, unlimited access to a common grazing field, each will graze his cows without recognizing the costs imposed on the others. Without some mechanism for congestion control, the commons will be overgrazed. Likewise, as long as users have access to unlimited Internet usage, they will tend to "overgraze," creating congestion that results in delays and dropped packets for other users. This section examines the extent of congestion, and explores some recent work on controlling congestion. Our proposal, which is based on charging per-packet prices that vary according to the degree of congestion, is explained later in the paper.

The Internet experienced severe congestion in 1987. Even now congestion problems are relatively common in parts of the Internet (although not yet on the T3 backbone). According to Kahin, "problems arise when prolonged or simultaneous high-end uses start degrading service for thousands of ordinary users. In fact, the growth of high-end use strains the inherent adaptability of the network as a common channel" (Kahin, 1992, p. 11). Some contemplated uses, such as real-time video and audio transmission, will lead to substantial increases in the demand for bandwidth, and congestion problems will only get worse unless there is substantial increase in bandwidth.[16] For example, Smarr and Catlett write:

If a single remote visualization process were to produce 100 Mbps bursts, it would take only a handful of users on the national network to generate over 1 Gbps load. As the remote visualization services move from three dimensions to [animation] the single-user bursts will increase to several hundred Mbps . . . Only for periods of tens of minutes to several hours over a 24-hour period are the high-end requirements seen on the network. With these applications, however, network load can jump from average to peak instantaneously. (Smarr and Catlett, 1992, p. 167)

This has happened. For example, during the weeks of November 9 and 16, 1992, some packet audio/visual broadcasts caused severe delay problems, especially at heavily-used gateways to the NSFNET backbone and in several mid-level networks. Today even ordinary use is causing significant delays in many of the regional networks around the world as demand grows faster than capacity. Of course, deliveries can be delayed for a number of other reasons. For example, if a router fails then packets must be resent by a different route. However, in a multiply-connected network, the speed of rerouting and delivery of failed packets measures one aspect of congestion, or the scarcity of the network's delivery bandwidth.

To characterize congestion on the Internet, we timed the delay in delivering packets to seven sites around the world. We ran our test hourly for 37 days during February and March 1993. Figure 3 and Figure 4 show results from four of our hourly probes. Median

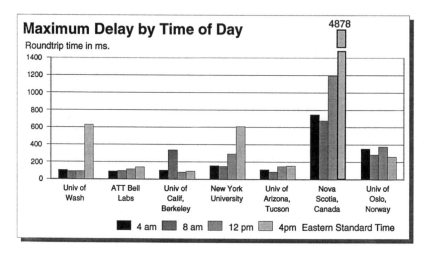

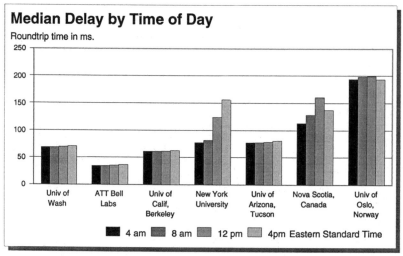

Figure 3 Maximum and Median Transmission Delays on the Internet.

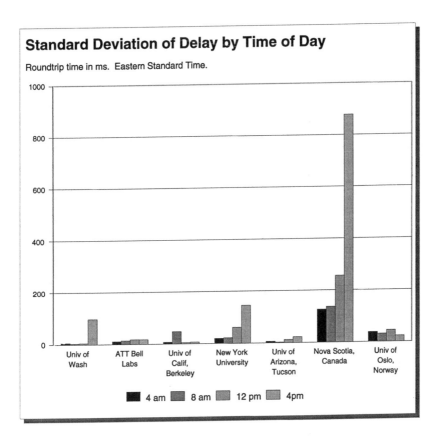

Figure 4 Variability in Internet Transmission Delays.

and maximum delivery delays are not always proportional to distance: the delay from Michigan to New York was generally longer than to Berkeley, and delays from Michigan to Nova Scotia, Canada, were often longer than to Oslo, Norway (Figure 3).

There is substantial variability in Internet delays. For example, the maximum and median delays vary greatly according to the time of day. There appears to be a large 4 PM peak problem on the east coast for packets to New York and Nova Scotia, but much less for AT&T Bell Labs (in New Jersey).[17] The time-of-day variation is also evident in Figure 5 (borrowed from Claffy, Polyzos, and Braun, 1992).[18]

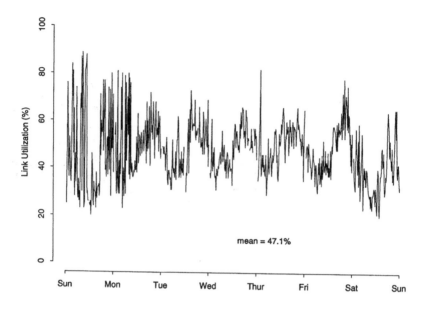

Figure 5 Utilization of Most Heavily Used Link in Each Fifteen Minute Interval (Claffy, 1992).

In Figure 4, we measure delay variation by the standard deviation of delays by time of day for each destination. Delays to Nova Scotia, Canada were extraordinarily variable, yet delays to Oslo were no more variable than in transmission to New Jersey (AT&T). Variability in delay fluctuates widely across times of day, as we would expect in a system with bursty traffic, but follows no obvious pattern.

How much delay is involved, and who is inconvenienced? As seen in Figure 3, during our experiment we never experienced delays of more than 1 second in round trip time except to the site in Nova Scotia. Is that too trivial a delay to be concerned about? Probably "yes" for e-mail. However, delays of that magnitude can be quite costly for some users and some applications.[19] For example, two-way voice communications must be limited to delays of 25 ms (500 ms with echo cancellers); likewise for interactive video.[20] Even a simple use like a terminal session can be very unpleasant if each character transmitted takes a second before echoing back to the screen. And, of course, without a better mechanism for congestion control, we expect delays to increase in frequency and duration.

Controlling Congestion

NSFNET usage has been growing at about 6% per month, or doubling every twelve months.[21] Although the cost of adding capacity is declining rapidly, we think it is very likely that congestion will continue to be a problem, especially as new very-high-bandwidth uses (such as real-time broadcast video) become common. It is becoming increasingly important to consider how congestion in networks such as the Internet should be controlled, and much work is needed. As Kleinrock (1992) writes, "One of the least understood aspects of today's networking technology is that of network control, which entails congestion control, routing control, and bandwidth access and allocation."

There is some literature on network congestion control; see Gerla (1988) for an overview. Most researchers have focused on schemes that offer different priorities and qualities of service depending on users' needs. For example, users could send e-mail with a low priority, allowing it to be delayed during congested periods so that more time-critical traffic could get through.

In fact, IP packets contain fields called "Precedence" and "Type of Service" (TOS), but most commercial routers do not currently use these fields.[22] To facilitate the use of the TOS field, its interpretation will probably be changed to the form described by Almquist (1992). Almquist proposes that the user be able to request that the network minimize delay, maximize total flow, maximize reliability, or minimize monetary cost. Prototype algorithms to provide such service are described by Prue (1988); a related proposal to ease congestion is in Bohn (1993). In this scheme a router looks up the destination address and examines the possible routes. Each route has a TOS number; the router looks for one that matches the TOS number of the packet.

To an economist, this is too inflexible. In particular, the TOS value "minimize monetary cost" seems strange. Of course senders would want to minimize monetary cost for a given quality of service: that is an objective, not a constraint. Also, it is unfortunate that TOS numbers do not allow for inequality relations. Normally, one would think of specifying the maximum amount that one would be willing to pay for delivery, with the assumption that less expensive service (other things being equal) would be better.

As Almquist (1992) explains, "There was considerable debate over what exactly this value [minimize monetary cost] should mean." However, he goes on to say:

It seems likely that in the future users may need some mechanism to express the maximum amount they are willing to pay to have a packet delivered. However, an IP option would be a more appropriate mechanism, since there are precedents for having IP options that all routers are required to honor, and an IP option could include parameters such as the maximum amount the user was willing to pay. Thus, the TOS value defined in this memo merely requests that the network "minimize monetary cost" (Almquist, 1992).

Almquist's remarks reflect the limited attention to pricing in most research to date, especially to control congestion. But without pricing it is hard to imagine how priority schemes could be implemented. What is to stop an e-mail user from setting the highest priority if it costs nothing? What political or organizational authority should be allowed to dictate the relative priority to give college student real-time multimedia rap sessions versus elementary school interactive classrooms?[23] Estrin (1992) and Shenker (1993) make the important point that if applications require different combinations of network characteristics (responsiveness, reliability, throughput, etc.), then some sort of pricing will be needed to sort out users' demands for these characteristics.

Faulhaber (1992) has considered some of the economic issues related to pricing access to the Internet. He suggests that "transactions among *institutions* are most efficiently based on *capacity per unit time.* We would expect the ANS to charge mid-level networks or institutions a monthly or annual fee that varied with the size of the electronic pipe provided to them. If the cost of providing the pipe to an institution were higher than to a mid-level network . . . the fee would be higher." Faulhaber's suggestion makes sense for recovering the cost of a dedicated line, one that connects an institution to the Internet backbone. But we don't think that it is appropriate for charging for backbone traffic itself because the bandwidth on the backbone is inherently a shared resource—many packets "compete" for the same bandwidth. There is an overall constraint on capacity, but there is no such thing as an individual's capacity on the backbone.

Although it is appropriate to charge a flat fee to cover the costs of a network connection, it is important to charge for network usage when the network is congested. During times of congestion bandwidth is a scarce resource. Conversely, when the network is not congested the marginal cost of transporting additional packets is essentially zero; it is therefore appropriate to charge users very little or nothing for packets when the system is not congested.

One problem with usage-sensitive pricing is the cost of accounting and billing. The cost would be astronomical if network providers were required to keep detailed accounts for every packet sent (comparable to call accounting by phone companies), because packets are very small units.[24] However, the accounting load could be greatly reduced. First, given the huge number of packets traversing backbones (currently over one billion per day on the NSFNET), charges based on a statistical *sample* of packets sent might be acceptable. Second, if usage is priced only during congested periods, most packets need no accounting. Third, traditional phone company accounting systems, which seem like the natural comparison, may not be a good model. They are centralized and off-line; we think that breakthroughs are likely in the area of in-line, distributed accounting, which will substantially lower costs.[25]

There has been some recent work to design mechanisms for usage accounting on the Internet. As a first attempt, ANS developed a usage sampling and reporting system, called COMBits, which collected aggregate measures of packets and bytes using a statistical sampling technique.[26] Unfortunately, COMBits collects data only down to the network-to-network level of source and destination; the resulting data can only be used to charge at the level of the subnetwork, and the local network administrator must split up the bill (Ruth, 1992).[27] In 1992, the a committee of the Internet standards body published a draft architecture for Internet usage reporting (IAWG, 1992). Braun and Claffy (1993) describe measurement of Internet traffic patterns by type of application and by international data flows, and discuss some of the accounting issues that must be solved. We are also undertaking research on methods for reducing accounting costs.

For the remainder of this paper, we assume that some amount of usage-level accounting will be economically feasible in the future, and focus on the problem of efficiently pricing network resources.

Should Prices Be Used?

Congestion is likely to be a serious problem in the future Internet, and past proposals to control it are unsatisfactory. We think an economic approach to allocating scarce Internet resources is warranted. Telecommunications lines, computer equipment, and labor are not free; if not employed by the Internet, they could be put to productive use in other activities. Bandwidth is also scarce: when the backbone is congested, one user's packet crowds out another's, resulting in dropped or delayed transmissions. Allocating scarce resources among competing uses is the central focus of economics.

In this section we discuss the benefits and costs of using economic methods to control congestion. Our objective is not to raise profits above a normal rate of return by pricing backbone usage. Rather, our goal is to find a pricing mechanism that will lead to the most efficient use of existing resources, and will guide investment decisions appropriately. Of course, a network need not be private to be priced; governments are perfectly capable of setting prices.[28]

Currently, the Internet uses a mix of two non-price resource allocation mechanisms: randomization and first-come, first-served (FIFO). With randomization, each packet has an equal chance of getting through (or being dropped). With FIFO, all packets are queued as they arrive; if the network is congested, every packet's delay is based on its arrival time in the queue. It is easy to see why these schemes are not efficient—delay is surely more costly for some packets than for others. For example, a real-time video transmission of a heart operation to a remote expert may be more valuable than a file transfer of a recreational game or picture. Economic efficiency is enhanced if the mechanism allocating scarce bandwidth gives higher priority to uses that are more socially valuable.

We do not feel that the service provider—government or otherwise—should decide which packets are more socially valuable; Soviet experience shows that allowing bureaucrats to decide whether work shoes or designer jeans are more valuable is a deeply flawed mechanism. A price mechanism works quite differently. The provider informs users of the cost of providing services; users decide for themselves whether their packets are more or less valuable than the cost of the packet transport service. When the backbone is congested, the cost of service will be high due to the cost of crowding out or delaying the packets of other users; if prices reflect costs, only those packets with high value will be sent until congestion diminishes.

Furthermore, if network congestion is properly priced, the revenues collected from the congestion surcharges can be used to fund further capacity expansion. Under certain conditions, the fees collected from the congestion charges turn out to be just the "right" amount to spend on expanding capacity.

One common concern about pricing the Internet is that "poor" users will be deprived of access. This is not a problem with pricing itself, but with the distribution of wealth; we could ensure that certain users have sufficient resources to purchase a base level of services by redistributing initial resources through vouchers or lump sum grants.[29] Indeed, total costs will be lower in an efficient network, so it will be less costly to meet distributional objectives than in an unpriced network.

Highways are often suggested as an analogy for the future of Internet. Many people argue that publicly provided interstate highways without tolls work well and should be the model. But this analogy is flawed. First, not all democratic governments agree that toll-free roads are the best allocation of social resources; most European countries have extensive toll systems, and even some U.S. interstates have tolls. More important, an interstate offers a single, undifferentiated service. Users who need different services pay for access to rail lines, canals, or airports. No one argues that use of *all* transportation networks should be free. The interstate highway system might be viewed as the one-size-fits-all universal access option (for those who can afford cars), with the option to pay for using a mode with a different combination of service characteristics. Likewise, a government might want to provide universal, free access to a baseline set of Internet transport services, and allow charges for usage of other services above a threshold. Appropriate free services might include plain-text e-mail (with lower priority when the network is congested) but not guaranteed, zero-delay multimedia broadcast.

Universal access and a base endowment of usage for all citizens could be provided through vouchers or other redistribution schemes. But for any given distribution of resources, how should backbone services be allocated? They are currently allocated (among paid-up subscribers) on the basis of randomization and first-come, first-served. In other words, users now pay the costs of congestion through delays and lost packets. A pricing mechanism will convert delay and queuing costs into dollar costs. If prices reflect the costs of providing the services, they will force the user to compare the value of her packets to the costs she is imposing on the system. Allocation will then be based on the value of the packets, and the total value of service provided by the backbones will be greater than under a non-price allocation scheme.[30]

In the rest of the paper we discuss how one might implement pricing that reflects the cost, including congestion costs, of providing backbone services. We begin with a review of some current pricing schemes and their relationship to costs.

Current Pricing Mechanisms

Most organizations do not connect directly to the NSFNET. For example, a university typically connects to its regional network; the regional connects to the NSFNET. The regional networks (and the private backbone networks) charge their customers for access, but not actual usage. Regionals, private backbones and users are not charged for connections to or usage of the NSFNET, which has been the primary backbone of the Internet. The full costs of NSFNET have been paid by NSF, IBM, MCI and the State of Michigan through 1994.

Table 2 summarizes the prices offered to large universities by ten major providers for T1 access (1.5 Mbps).[31] There are three major components: an annual access fee, an initial connection fee, and in some cases a separate charge for the equipment on the customer's premises (a router to serve as a gateway between the customer network and the Internet provider's network).[32] The current annual total cost per T1 connection is about $25,000 to $35,000.

Table 2 Representative Prices for T-1 Connection*

| Service Provider | Fee Components | | |
	Annual Fee	Initial Connection Cost	Customer Premises Equipment
ALTERnet	24,000	8,900	incl.
ANS	32,000	incl.	incl.
CERFnet	20,100	3,750	incl.
CICnet	10,000	15,000	incl.
JvNCnet	33,165	13,850	incl.
Michnet	24,000	14,250	incl.
MIDnet	6,000	15,000	incl.
NEARnet	30,000	13,500	incl.
PREPnet	3,720	1,900	not incl.
SURAnet	25,000	3,500	3,300

*Notes: Prices as reported by the vendors. These are prices for a large university. There are some variations in the bundle of services provided, so the prices are not strictly comparable.

Source: Compiled by Bill Yurcik, NASA/Goddard Space Flight Center, 11/13/92, with corrections by the authors.

All of the providers use the same type of pricing: an annual fee for unlimited access, based on the bandwidth of the connection. These pricing schemes provide no incentives to flatten peak demands, nor any mechanism for allocating network bandwidth during periods of congestion. It would be relatively simple for a provider to monitor a customer's usage and bill by the packet or byte. Monitoring requires that outgoing packets be counted at a single point: the customer's gateway router. However, pricing every packet would not necessarily increase efficiency, because the marginal cost of a packet is nearly zero. Since it is bandwidth that is scarce, efficient prices must reflect the current availability of bandwidth. Neither a flat price per packet nor time-of-day prices would closely approximate efficient pricing.

Matching Prices to Costs

As a general rule, users should face prices that reflect the resource costs that they generate so that they can make informed decisions about resource utilization. In this section we explain our approach to how users should pay for each resource. We consider:

- *The incremental costs of sending extra packets.* If the network is not congested, this is essentially zero.

- *The social costs of delaying other users' packets when the network is congested.* This is not directly a resource cost, but should be considered part of the social cost of a packet. Users bear this cost through delay and dropped packets, and would often be willing to pay to reduce congestion.

- *The fixed costs of providing the network infrastructure.* This is the rent for the line, the cost of the routers, and the salary for the support staff.

- *The incremental costs of connecting to the network.* Each new connection to the Internet involves costs for access lines and switching equipment.

- *The cost to expand network capacity.* This normally consists of adding new routers, new lines, and new staff.

We first consider how *ideal* prices would reflect these costs; then we consider how market-based prices might work.

The Incremental Costs of Sending Extra Packets

The price of sending a packet in an uncongested network should be close to zero; a higher price is socially inefficient since it does not reflect the true incremental costs. If the incremental cost is high enough to justify the cost of monitoring and billing, it should be charged as a per-packet cost. Much of the needed monitoring and billing system would be needed to implement our other pricing proposals.

The Social Costs of Delaying Other Users' Packets When the Network Is Congested

The price for sending a packet when the network is congested should be positive: if my packet precludes or delays another user's packet, then I should pay the cost I impose on the other user. If my packet is more valuable than hers, then it should be sent; if hers is more valuable than mine, then hers should be sent.

We can depict the logic of this argument graphically using demand and supply curves. Suppose the packet price were very high: only a few users would want to send packets. As the packet price decreases, more users would be willing to send packets.[33] We show this relationship between price and the demand for network access in Figure 6. If the network capacity is fixed at K, then the optimal price for admitting the packets is where the demand curve crosses the capacity supply. If demand is small relative to capacity, the efficient price is zero—all packets are admitted. If demand is high, users that are willing to pay at least the price of admission to the network are admitted; others are not.

This analysis applies to the extreme case where capacity is fixed. If an increase in packets from some users imposes delay on other users, but not outright exclusion, the analysis is slightly different. Suppose that we know how delay varies with the number of packets, and that we have some idea of the costs imposed on users by a given amount of delay. Then we can calculate a relationship between number of packets sent and delay costs. The relevant magnitude for determining the optimal number of users is the *marginal* cost of delay, the cost added by the next single packet (see Figure 7).

The efficient price is where the user's willingness to pay for an additional packet equals the marginal increase in delay costs generated by that packet. If a potential user faces this price, she can be able to compare her own benefit from sending a packet to the marginal delay costs she imposes on other users.

The Fixed Costs of Providing the Network Infrastructure

The initial investment in network infrastructure is a discrete decision: a certain amount of money can buy a usable network of minimal size. What criterion can be used to decide whether the initial investment is warranted? The natural principle to apply is that total benefits should exceed costs. The existence of an uncongested network is a public good that provides benefits for all users without exclusion; that is, Bob's use doesn't preclude Peter's use. Therefore we should add up how much all potential users

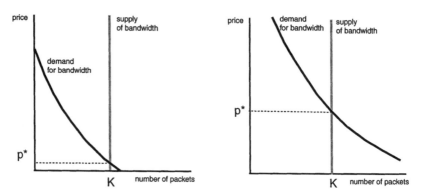

Figure 6 Demand for Network Access with Fixed Capacity. When demand is low, the packet price is low. When demand is high, the packet price is high.

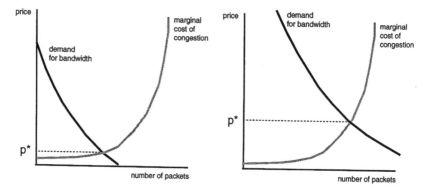

Figure 7 Demand for Network Access with a Marginal Cost of Delay. When demand is low, the packet price is low. When demand is high, and congestion is high, the packet price is high.

would be willing to pay for the network infrastructure, and see if this total "willingness-to-pay" exceeds the cost of provision.

In the case of a computer network like the Internet, it is natural to think of paying for the network infrastructure with a flat access fee. Each party who connects to the network pays a flat price for network access distinct from the usage-based fee described earlier. In general, these connection fees will vary, since different people and institutions value connection to the net differently. The infrastructure cost recovery will be efficient if each customer connects for a fee less than or equal to the amount she is willing to pay, because then no customers would be needlessly excluded. If the total amount that users are willing to pay exceeds the infrastructure cost, the fees could be assigned in a variety of ways, depending on market conditions and the network providers' objectives. For example, a public sector network might want to charge a higher proportion of the willingness-to-pay of large or commercial users, and a lower fraction of the willingness-to-pay of poor or residential customers. This scheme would resemble the cross-subsidization for universal access historically regulated in the Bell System's telephone service.

The Incremental Costs of Connecting to the Network

Each new user requires a connection to the network. In some cases, this connection may share an existing facility, for instance using a home phone to make a dial-up connection. Such a connection imposes no new costs and should be priced at zero. Other connections may require new cables, a router, and other investments. Each user should be charged the cost of installing a connection to the backbone as a single, one-time connection fee.

It may be that the public at large benefits from having more users connected, so that it would be efficient to provide a connection subsidy to ensure that some users who would not otherwise connect do so. This does not mean that when there are network externalities all connections should be free, but that it would be efficient to have some subsidy per connection that is related to the *public* gain from an additional connection. Theoretically, an even more efficient scheme would target those users who are most likely to abstain *without* a subsidy, but targeted subsidies are difficult to implement.

The Cost of Expanding Capacity of the Network

If network usage never reaches capacity, even at no cost for packets, then clearly there is no need to expand capacity. Usage prices that are based on congestion provide guidance about when to expand capacity. Consider the model with fixed capacity: Packet prices measure the marginal value of the last admitted packet. If the cost of expanding capacity to accommodate one more packet is less than the marginal value of that packet, then it makes economic sense to expand capacity. If expansion costs more, it is not economically worthwhile.

Hence optimal congestion pricing plays two roles—it efficiently rations access to the network in times of congestion, and it sends the correct signals about capacity expansion. In this framework, all the revenues generated by congestion prices should be used to expand capacity.

One advantage of this scheme is that only the users who want to use the network when it is at capacity pay for expansion. Users who are willing to wait do not pay anything toward expanding network capacity. We think that this point is important politically. The largest constituency on the Internet is apparently e-mail users;[34] a proposal to charge high prices for e-mail is likely to be politically infeasible. However, e-mail can usually tolerate moderate delays. Under congestion pricing of the sort we are describing, e-mail users could put a low or zero bid price on their traffic, and would continue to face a very low cost.

The situation is only slightly different in the case of delay costs. Here the price measures the marginal benefit of an additional packet, which is equal to the marginal cost of delay. If additional investment would reduce the marginal cost of delay by more than the amount users are willing to pay for reduced delay, then it should be undertaken, and otherwise not. (We examine the analytics of pricing a congested network in the Appendix.) If the packet price accurately reflects delay and congestion costs, it is the appropriate guidance to determine whether capacity should be expanded.

Pricing Summary

An efficient pricing mechanism would have the following structure: (1) a packet charge close to zero when the network is not congested; (2) a positive packet charge when the network is congested; (3) a fixed connection charge that differs from institution to institution. Current pricing is almost always limited to a fixed connection charge. The main difference in what we propose is the addition of a usage-sensitive charge when the network is congested.

Implementing Congestion Prices

We now describe one method to implement efficient congestion prices. The connection charges are simplest: the current method needs no alterations. Each customer pays a flat fee for connection; this fee often depends on the bandwidth of the connection. Presumably the bandwidth of the connection purchased by an organization is correlated to some degree with the organization's willingness to pay, so this should serve as a reasonable characteristic upon which to base connection charges.[35]

No charges for sending packets when the network is not congested is also easy to arrange—that's what we have now. The novel part of the pricing mechanism we propose is the per-packet charge when the network is congested. We have discussed how one might implement such a fee elsewhere (MacKie-Mason and Varian, 1993), and we briefly review that proposal here.

If congestion has a regular pattern with respect to time of day, or day of week, then prices could vary in a predictable way over time. However, this is relatively inflexible. We think that it would be better to use a "smart market": the price to send a packet would vary minute-by-minute to reflect the current degree of network congestion.

A smart market would not be terribly difficult to implement, at least conceptually. Each packet would have a "bid" field in its header to indicate how much its sender is willing to pay to send it. Users would typically set default bids for various applications, and override the defaults in special circumstances. For example, a user might assign a low bid to e-mail packets. Real-time audio or visual data might be assigned a high bid price. The network would admit all packets with bid prices that exceed the current cutoff amount, determined by the marginal congestion costs imposed by the next additional packet.

This mechanism guarantees only relative priority, and is not an absolute promise of service. A packet with a high bid gains access sooner than one with a low bid, but delivery time cannot be guaranteed.[36] Rejected packets could be bounced back to the users, or be routed to a slower network, possibly after being stored for a period in a buffer in case the congestion falls sufficiently a short time later.

A novel feature of such a smart market is that users do *not* pay the price they actually bid; rather, they pay the market-clearing price, which is always lower than the bids of all admitted packets. This is different from priority-pricing by say, the post office, where you pay for first-class mail even if there is enough excess capacity that second-class mail is moving at the same speed.

The smart market has many other desirable features. Its outcome is the classic supply-equals-demand level of service of which economists are so fond. The equilibrium price, at any one point, is the bid of the marginal user. Each infra-marginal user is charged this price, so each infra-marginal user gets a consumer surplus from the purchase. Further, as we show in the Appendix, the congestion revenues equal the optimal investment in capacity expansion.

The major differences from the textbook demand-and-supply story is that no iteration is needed to determine the market-clearing price—the market is cleared as soon as the users have submitted their bids for access.[37] Huberman (1992) describe some (generally positive) experiences in using this kind of "second-bid" auction to allocate network resources. However, they do not examine network access itself, as we are proposing here.[38]

We have assumed that the bid-price set by the users accurately reflects users' willingness to pay. Does our scheme provide the correct incentives for users to reveal this value—is there anything to be gained by trying to "fool" the smart market? Fortunately not; the dominant strategy in the second-bid auction is for users to bid their true values. By the nature of the auction, users are assured that they always get access when their value is higher than the current price, yet they will never be charged more than this amount, and normally less.

Other Concerns about the Smart Market Mechanism

Our smart market proposal is preliminary and tentative. It is only one theoretically appealing way to implement efficient congestion control. In this section we discuss a number of issues that must be studied and resolved before the smart market can be successfully implemented.

Who Sets the Bids?

We expect that bids would be set by three agents: the local administrator who controls access to the net, the user of the computer, and the computer software. Organizations with limited resources, for example, might choose low bid prices for all sorts of traffic. This would mean that they may not have access during peak times, but still would have access during off-peak periods.[39]

An organization might not pass usage-sensitive prices through to its users. If not, then all traffic types would normally be sent with the same, organization-wide priority bid. If organizations do provide price or other incentives to their users, then users can assign different bids to various data flows. Normally, users would set default values in their software for different services. For example, file transfers might have lower priority than e-mail, e-mail would be lower than telnet terminal sessions, telnet would be lower than audio, and so on. The user could override default values in special cases, for example when a particular e-mail message is especially urgent, if he is willing to pay an increased price during congested periods.

Off-Line Accounting

If the smart market system uses the sampling system suggested above, accounting overhead need not slow traffic much, since it can be done in parallel. All the router must do is compare the bid of a packet with the current value of the cutoff. The accounting information on every 1000th packet, say, would be sent to a dedicated accounting machine that determines the equilibrium access price and records the usage for later billing.[40] Such sampling would require changes in current router technology and might well prove expensive. For example, NSFNET modified routers to collect sampled usage data; they found that the cost of the monitoring system was significant.

Fluctuations in the Spot Market Price

Many colleagues are uncomfortable with the idea of fluctuating prices for bandwidth. Some feel that predictable prices, and hence budgets, are important to users. We have several responses. First, if prices and uses of the network turn out to be relatively predictable, expenditures would fluctuate very little. Enterprises have little difficulty now dealing with fluctuations in postage, electricity, and telephone bills from month to month; there is no reason to expect that network usage would be different.

Second, it is important to remember that in the smart market, prices only fluctuate *down*. The user sets the maximum he or she is willing to pay; the actual cost will never be higher. Furthermore, the user should have virtually instantaneous feedback about expenditures, so there should be little difficulty in budgetary control. As an extreme example, a user's employer might simply set a single bid price on all traffic: the unit price would only fluctuate down, and some cost would be borne in delay—when the market price was higher—rather than in expenditure jumps.

Finally, and most important, the price set by the smart market is a "wholesale" price, not necessarily a "retail" price. If a user does not wish to bear the risk of price fluctuations, he or she can always contract with another party who is willing to bear that risk; either the network service provider or a third party. The third party could offer different levels of service at different prices: "premium" service would send all packets immediately regardless of cost (to the third party); "economy" service would send packets only when the congestion price was below a certain level, and delay them when congestion was higher. The user would face an incentive to reduce traffic through a congested network because she would choose different priced fixed-budget plans.

For example, consider an extreme case where the network price has significant fluctuations: the price for an hour of teleconferencing at a particular time of day might be $200 or $50. A third party could offer to sell bandwidth to anyone who demands it at $100 an hour. If the price turned out to be $50, the bandwidth reseller would make a profit; if it turned out to be $200, the bandwidth reseller would take a loss. The purchaser would pay $100 no matter what.

If the price fluctuations are large, most retail customers might prefer to contract for bandwidth at a fixed price. But the existence of a spot market would be very important; it allows "wholesalers" to buy bandwidth on an "as available" basis, thereby encouraging efficient use of bandwidth.

In the end, cost fluctuations—either in the form of price or delay, or both—are unavoidable in a congestible network. In a well-functioning market users can choose to bear the mix of delay and price fluctuation directly, or they can pay a third party an "insurance premium" in exchange for a reduction in price or delay fluctuations.

Burstiness

Traffic on the network fluctuates quite significantly over periods as short as a few seconds; packet transfers are "bursty." Can the smart market keep up with such change?

We have two answers to this question. First, it is simple to buffer packets for short periods. During a burst of high-priority bids, packets with low-priority bids are buffered. After the high-priority packets are admitted, the low-priority packets move onto the network. In network engineering this is known as priority-based routing, and is reasonably well understood.

The second answer is a bit deeper. We conjecture that if usage were priced according to our scheme, network traffic would be much less bursty; the bursts exist because there is no charge for them. If bursts were costly to users there would be fewer. Users would have an incentive to use applications that smooth the network traffic flow. For example, in countries where electricity is priced by time of day, water heaters heat water in the middle of the night, when rates are low. If a refrigerator can be that smart, think what a workstation could do—if it faced the right prices.

Routing

As mentioned above, the Internet is a connectionless network. Each router knows the final destination of a packet, and uses its routing tables to determine the best way to get the packet from the current location to its next hop. These routing tables are updated continuously to indicate the current state of the network. They reflect failed links and new nodes, but not congestion on the links of the network. Indeed, there is no standard measurement for congestion available on current T3 networks.

Currently, all packets follow the same route at a given time; however, if each packet carried a bid price, this information could be used to facilitate routing. For example, packets with higher bids could take faster routes, while packets with lower bids could be routed through slower links. Obviously this description is very incomplete, but it seems likely that having packets bid for access will help to distribute traffic more efficiently.

Distributional Aspects

Charging prices for usage during congested times may be politically acceptable, because it would largely preserve the cost structure for the many current users who can live with some delay and unreliability. In a smart market, low-priority access to the Internet (such as e-mail) would continue to cost very little. Indeed, with relatively minor public subsidies to cover the marginal *resource* costs, it would be possible to have efficient pricing with a price of close *zero* most of the time, since the network is usually not congested.

If there are several competing carriers, the usual logic of competitive bidding suggests that the price for low-priority packets should approach the marginal cost—which, as we have argued, is essentially zero. In the plan that we have outlined the high-priority users would pay most of the costs of expanding the Internet.

Interruptible Service

Implementing the smart market mechanism for pricing congestion on the Internet would require adding new information to the TCP/IP headers, which will take considerable discussion and debate. However, there is an interim way to handle congestion pricing that requires very little change in existing protocols. Suppose that providers of Internet services offer two classes of service: full service and interruptible service. Users would pay a flat fee based on bandwidth of their connection and the type of service they prefer. Full service would cost more than interruptible service.

When the load on the routers used by the Internet provider reached a certain level, users who purchase interruptible service would be denied access until the congestion subsided. All that is needed to implement this rationing mechanism is a simple change to the routing algorithms.

The defect of interruptible service is that it is inflexible compared to the smart market solution: it applies to all participants in a single administrative billing unit and cannot be overridden by individual users. On the other hand it would be very simple to implement. See Wilson (1989) for a detailed study of the analytics of interruptible service.

The Roles of the Public and Private Sectors

The technical problems associated with a usage-pricing scheme, including our proposed smart market, are enormous. The current Internet has developed through a collaboration between the private sector and governments; we think the development of the future broadband Internet with mechanisms for accounting and usage-sensitive pricing will also require government involvement.

The NSF is moving the Internet backbone away from the "interstate" model toward the "turnpike" model, as evidenced by the emergence of private-sector backbone competitors. The "Interstate" approach is for the government to develop the "electronic superhighways of the future" as part of an investment in infrastructure. The "turnpike" approach relies on the private sector to develop the network infrastructure for Internet-like operations, with the government providing subsidies to offset the cost of access to the private networks.

We believe an intermediate solution is necessary. The private sector is probably more flexible and responsive than a government bureaucracy; however, competing network standards could lead to an electronic Tower of Babel. A publicly imposed standard is important—turnpikes have the same traffic regulations as Interstates. For example, customer demand for low-delay, uncongested networks will give providers an incentive to implement some form of congestion control pricing, but individual network providers will probably not choose to implement such methods unless there is coordination in standards and widespread adoption of the mechanism. We think that there is an important role for public and quasi-public bodies in designing coordinated policies and protocols for congestion control, accounting and usage-sensitive pricing. As Estrin (1989) explains: "The Internet community developed its original protocol suite with only minimal provision for resource control ... This time it would be inexcusable to ignore resource control requirements and not to pay careful attention to their specification."

One role for government is to insure interconnectivity between competing network providers. It may also be important for governments to provide the regulatory framework for in-line accounting and billing.[41] Whether protocols for actually implementing accounting and billing should be defined by a public body or an industry consortium is not immediately obvious.[42]

The history of standards for voice networks offers an interesting lesson. U.S. voice communications are now provided by a mesh of overlapping and connected networks operated by competing providers (AT&T, MCI and Sprint being the largest). This is similar to the situation we expect to emerge for data networks. However, during the decades when switching and billing standards were being designed and refined, the only significant provider was AT&T, so it could develop a single, coordinated standard that later providers adopted. International voice networks, in contrast, require interconnection and traffic handoff between various (mostly national) providers. These standards were designed and imposed by a public body, the CCITT.

A pricing standard must contain enough information to encourage efficient use of network bandwidth, and contain information for accounting and billing. A privatized network is simply not viable without such standards: work should start immediately on developing them.

The other important task for government is to estimate the public benefit from access and usage by users who might not be willing to pay their own costs, and then to design subsidies to encourage those users. We think the growth and development of the Internet will be best served if network services are priced according to cost (including congestion costs), and subsidies should be distributed so that users can pay those charges. Implementing subsidies instead by continuing to charge zero prices would give the biggest subsidies to the wrong users, would not provide useful signals to guide the use of costly resources, and would not guide investments in network expansion and upgrading. Using an efficient pricing scheme instead will encourage growth in network use and capacity, and guide resources to the highest-value uses.

Appendix 1 : Some Analytics of Pricing a Congestible Resource

The classic "problem of the commons" is that property held in common will tend to be overexploited. Each user is aware of the costs he incurs by using the common property, but neglects the costs he imposes on others. In the context of the Internet, the scarce resource is the switching capacity of the routers. When the network is highly congested, an additional user imposes costs on other users to the extent that his switching prevents or slows down switching by other users.

Efficient use of the switch capacity requires that users who are willing to pay more for access be admitted before users willing to pay less. The price for admission to the switches should reflect the social cost of an additional packet.

In this appendix we briefly examine some of the analytics of a standard (static) congestion model.[43] Arnott, Palma, and Lindsey (1990) argue that congestion models should examine dynamic microbehavior in a more detailed way. We agree, and think that modeling congestion behavior for computer networks is a promising avenue for future research; here, however, we consider the simplest case of congestion.

Suppose that a representative user has a utility function $u(x_i) - D$, where x_i is the number of packets sent by user i and D is the total delay she experiences. The delay D depends on the total utilization of the network, $Y = X/K$, where X is the sum of the x_i, representing the total usage, and K is network capacity.[44] This specification implies that if usage is doubled and capacity is doubled, then network utilization and delay remain the same.

If there is no congestion-based pricing, user i will choose x_i to satisfy the first-order condition[45]

$u'(x_i) = 0.$

The efficient utilization of the network maximizes the sum of all users' utilities, $\Sigma u(x_i) - nD(X/K)$, where the sum is from 1 to n. This yields the n first-order conditions

$u'(x_i) - (n/k)D'(Y) = 0.$

One way to achieve this efficient outcome is to set a congestion price per packet of

$$p = (n/k)\ D'(Y), \tag{1}$$

so that user i faces the maximization problem

$\max_{xi} u(x_i) - D(Y) - p\,x_i.$

The first-order condition to this problem is

$$u'(x_i) = p = (n/k)\ D'(Y), \tag{2}$$

which leads to the optimal choice of x_i. The price has been chosen to measure the congestion costs that i's packets impose on the other users.

Optimal Capacity Expansion

Suppose now that it costs $c(K)$ for capacity K and that we currently have some specific capacity. Should it be expanded? The welfare problem is

$$W(K) = \max_K \Sigma\ u(x_i) - nD(Y) - c(K).$$

Since x_i is already chosen to maximize this expression, the envelope theorem implies that

$$W'(K) = nD'(Y)(X/K^2) - c'(K).$$

Substituting from equation (1),

$$W'(K) = p(X/K) - c'(K).$$ (3)

Suppose that the marginal cost of capacity expansion is a constant, $c_K = c'(K)$. Then we see that $W'(K)$ is positive if and only if $pX - c_K K > 0$. That is, *capacity should be expanded when the revenues from congestion fees exceed the cost of providing the capacity.*

A Competitive Market for Network Services

Suppose that several competing firms provide network access. A typical producer has a network with capacity K and carries X packets, each of which pays a per-packet charge of p. The producer's operating profits are $pX - c(K)$.

Let $p(D)$ be the price charged by a provider that offers delay D. In general, if the delay on one network is different than on another the price must reflect this quality difference. The utility maximization problem for consumer i is to choose which network to use and how much to use it:

$$\max_{xi, D} u(x_i) - D - p(D) \, x_i,$$

which has first-order conditions

$$u'(x_i) - p(D) = 0,$$
$$-1 - p'(D) x_i = 0.$$

The first equation says that each user will send packets until the value of an additional packet equals its price. The second equation says that the user will choose a network with a level of delay such that the marginal value to the user of additional delay equals the marginal cost of paying for the delay (by suppliers of switching). Adding up this last first-order condition over the consumers yields

$$n = -p'(D) X.$$ (4)

A competitive producer offering delay $D(Y)$ wants to choose capacity and price so as to maximize profits, recognizing that if it changes its delay the price it can charge for access will change. The profit maximization problem is

$$\max_{X,K} p(D(Y)) \, X - c(K),$$

which gives us first-order conditions

$$p'(D)D'(Y)Y + p(D) = 0,$$
$$-p'(D)D'(Y)Y^2 - c'(K) = 0. \tag{5}$$

Combining these two conditions and using equation (4) gives us two useful expressions for $p(D)$:

$$\begin{aligned} p(D) &= (n/K) \, D'(Y) \\ &= c'(K)(K/X). \end{aligned}$$

Comparing the first equation to (2) we see that the competitive price will result in the optimal degree of congestion. Comparing the second equation to equation (3), we see that competitive behavior will also result in optimal capacity.

Adding Capacity

Suppose that a competitive firm must decide whether to add additional capacity ΔK. We consider two scenarios. In the first scenario, the firm contemplates keeping X fixed and simply charging more for the reduction in delay. The extra amount it can charge for each packet is

$$(dp/dK) \, \Delta K = -p'(D) \, D'(Y) \, (X/K^2) \, \Delta K.$$

With equation (5) this becomes

$$(p/K) \, \Delta K.$$

Since the firm can charge this amount for each packet sent, the total additional revenue from this capacity expansion is

$$p \, (X/K) \, \Delta K.$$

This revenue will cover the costs of expansion if

$$p\ (X/K\ )\ \Delta K - c'(K\ )\ \Delta K = [\ p\ (X/K\ ) - c'(K\ )\ ]\ \Delta K\ \geq 0,$$

which is precisely the condition for social optimality given in equation (3).

In the second scenario, the firm expands its capacity and keeps its price fixed. In a competitive market it will attract new customers due to the reduction in delay. In equilibrium this firm must have the same delay as other firms charging the same price. Suppose that in the initial equilibrium $X/K = Y$. Then the additional number of packets must satisfy $\Delta X = Y \Delta K$. It follows that the increase in profit for this firm is given by

$$pY\ \Delta K - c'(K\ )\ \Delta K = [\ p\ (X/K\ ) - c'(K\ )\ ]\ \Delta K.$$

Again we see that capacity expansion is optimal if and only if it increases profits.

The relationship between capacity expansion and congestion pricing was first recognized by Mohring (1962) and Strotz (1978). Recent general results can be found in Arnott and Kraus (1992a,b).

Appendix 2: A Hypothetical One-Node Backbone with Smart Market

Implementing any pricing scheme for backbone services will require changes to user applications, host operating systems, and router algorithms. Very little work has been done on the software and protocol changes necessary to support efficient pricing.[46] To illustrate the types of changes that will be necessary, we shall briefly describe how our smart market might be implemented in a very simple case.

Consider a simple network fragment: two host machines, each with multiple users, each connected to a separate local area network. The two LANs are connected by a backbone with a single switch (which admittedly doesn't have much work to do!). Users have applications that send packets to each other. How would the smart market work if users are sending each other a steady flow of packets that is sufficient to cause congestion at the switch if all packets were admitted?

User Application

Suppose user 1 on machine 1 (u_{11}) is sending e-mail to user 1 on machine 2 (u_{12}). u_{11} needs to be able to set her bid (maximum willingness to pay) for the packets that make up her e-mail message. However, she prefers not to think about a bid for every message since she usually puts the same, very low priority price on e-mail. Thus, the e-mail software needs to provide hooks for a user to set a default bid price, and to override the default when desired.

User System

The host machine must handle some new tasks through systems software. First, the e-mail is packetized with one new piece of information loaded into the header: the bid price.[47] Also, since this is a multiuser machine and the network only recognizes machine (IP) addresses, not user names, the host machine must create a record in an accounting database that records the user name, number of packets sent, and the packet identification number. It is not possible to record the price for the packets yet because of the design of the smart market: the user specifies her maximum willingness to pay, but the actual price for each packet may (and typically will) be lower. However, since the TCP protocol offers positive acknowledgment of each packet, the acknowledging packets that are returned can contain the actual price charged so that the host database can record user-specific charges.

Local Area Network

It may be desirable to implement some hooks in the local organization network, before the packet reaches the backbone.[48] For example, organization policy may want to impose a ceiling on bids to restrict the maximum price that users volunteer to pay. Also, billing from the backbone provider may be only to the organization level since the IP address of host machines identifies only a station, not the responsible users. It may be that backbone providers will provide bills that itemize by host IP address; the organization may want to record packets sent by each host, as well as the price extracted from the acknowledgment return.

In this example we assume that the local network is not imposing its own charges on top of the backbone charges. If local pricing is desired to allocate locally congested resources (as we suspect it often will be for large organizations), the tasks identified below for the backbone must also be carried out by the LAN.

Backbone

As a packet reaches the backbone router, its bid price is compared to the current smart market price for admission. If the bid is too low, a message (presumably implemented in the ICMP protocol) is returned to the user with the packet number, user's bid and the current price. If the bid exceeds the admission price, then the packet is admitted and routed.

Every packet is checked for its bid, but to control the transactions costs of pricing, accounting, and billing we assume that only 1 of every N packets is sampled for further processing. A copy of the header of the sampled packets is diverted to a separate CPU, where it is used for several functions.

One task is to update the state of demand on the backbone. Packets with bids come in over time; it will be necessary to aggregate packets over some window (the width of which could be time- or event-driven) to construct the "current" state of demand. When a newly sampled packet arrives, it is added to the history window of bids, and a stale bid is removed.[49]

The sampled packet is logged to the accounting database: the current price times N (since the packet represents on average $1/N$th of those sent by a particular user) and the billing identification information. Periodically the backbone provider will prepare and deliver bills.

Periodically the smart market price would be recalculated to reflect changes in the state of demand. A new price might be event-driven (e.g., recalculated every time a new Nth packet arrives, or less frequently) or time-driven (e.g., recalculated every T msecs). The new price would then be sent to the gatekeeper subsystem on the router, and in a network with multiple nodes possibly broadcast to the other nodes.[50]

"Collect Calls": Pricing Proxy Server Packets

We have assumed so far that the originator of a packet is the party to be billed. Many of the most important Internet services involve packets that are sent by one host at the request of a user on another host. For example, ftp file transfers and gopher information services take this form; these are currently the first and seventh largest sources of bytes transferred on the NSFNET backbone (Braun and Claffy, 1993). Clearly most services will not offer to pay the network charges for any and all user requests for data. We need something like collect calls, COD, bill-to-recipient's-account, or all of the above.

There are at least two straightforward methods to charge the costs back to the responsible party. A traditional approach would have users obtain accounts and authorization codes that permit the proxy server to use an external billing system for charges incurred by user requests; this is the way that many current commercial information services (e.g., Compuserve) are billed.

However, the growth of the Internet has been fueled by the vast proliferation of information services. It is implausible to think that a user would be willing to obtain separate charge accounts with every service; it would also be inefficient to have the necessary credit and risk management duplicated by every proxy server provider. A more advanced method that fits in well with the scheme we have described is to allow for billing directly back to the user's backbone usage account.

To implement a system of bill-to-sender would require some further work, however. The user's application (client software) would presumably have to allow the user to specify a maximum price for an entire transaction that could be included in the request for service, since it will often be impossible to anticipate the number of packets that are being requested. The server could then send the packets with a flag set in the packet header that indicates the charges are to be levied against the destination IP address, not the source. However, to make such a system feasible will require authentication and authorization services. Otherwise, unscrupulous users could send out packets that were not requested by the recipients but charge them to the destination address; likewise malicious pranksters could modify their system software to generate forged requests for data that is unwanted by but charged to another user.[51]

Acknowledgments

Jeffrey MacKie-Mason was visiting the Department of Economics, University of Oslo when this paper was completed. We wish to thank Guy Almes, Eric Aupperle, Hans-Werner Braun, Paul Green, Dave Katz, Mark Knopper, Ken Latta, Dave McQueeny, Jeff Ogden, Chris Parkin, Scott Shenker and Paul Southworth for helpful discussions, advice and data. We are also grateful to James Keller and Miriam Avins for extensive, helpful editorial advice.

Notes

[1] Most users of the NSFNET backbone do not pay a pipeline fee to ANS, the service provider, but instead pay for a connection to their "regional" or mid-level network, which then is granted a connection to the NSFNET.

[2] In addition, a new alliance called CoREN has been formed between eight regional networks and MCI. This represents a move away from the traditional backbone structure towards a mesh-structured set of overlapping interconnections.

[3] Some telephone lines are multiplexed, but they are synchronous: $1/N$th of the line is dedicated to each open circuit no matter how lightly used that circuit is.

[4] Some interactive terminal programs collect keystrokes until an Enter or Transmit key is struck, then send the entire "line" off in a packet. However, most Internet terminal sessions use the telnet program, which sends each keystroke immediately in a separate packet.

[5] Some packet-switching networks are "connection-oriented" (notably, X.25 networks, such as Tymnet and frame-relay networks). In such a network a connection is set up before transmission begins, just as in a circuit-switched network. A fixed route is defined, and information necessary to match packets to their session and defined route is stored in memory tables in the routers. Thus, connectionless networks economize on router memory and connection set-up time, while connection-oriented networks economize on routing calculations (which have to be redone for every packet in a connectionless network).

[6] Dynamic routing contributes to the efficient use of the communications lines, because routing can be adjusted to balance load across the network. The other main justification for dynamic routing is network reliability, since it gives each packet alternative routes to their destination should some links fail. This was especially important to the military, which funded most of the early TCP/IP research to improve the ARPANET.

[7] Routing is based on a dynamic knowledge of which links are up and a static "cost" assigned to each link. Currently routing does not take congestion into account. Routes can change when hosts are added or deleted from the network (including failures), which happens often with about 2 million hosts and over 21,000 subnetworks.

[8] "Kbps" is thousand (kilo) bits per second; "Mbps" is million (mega) bits per second.

[9] While preparing the final manuscript we repeated our delay experiment for 20 days in October-November 1993. The range in delay times between Ann Arbor and Norway was then 0.153 seconds and 0.303 seconds.

[10] In a postal service most of the cost is in labor, which varies quite directly with the volume of the mail.

[11] The regional network providers generally set their charges to recover the remainder of their costs, but there is also some subsidization from state governments at the regional level.

[12] This, of course, represents only backbone costs for NSFNET users. Total costs, including LAN and regional network costs, are higher.

[13] Since packet size has been slowly increasing, the amount of data transported has increased even more.

[14] A NOC monitors traffic flow at all nodes in the network and troubleshoots problems.

[15] We estimated costs for the network backbone only, defined to be links between common carrier Points of Presence (POPs) and the routers that manage those links. We did not estimate the costs for the feeder lines to the mid-level or regional networks where the data packets usually enter and leave the backbone, nor for the terminal costs of setting up the packets or tearing them apart at the destination.

[16] We use the term bandwidth to refer to the overall capacity of the network to transport a data flow, usually measured in bits per second. The major bottleneck in backbone capacity today is in fact switch technology, not the bandwidth of the lines.

[17] The high maximum delay for the University of Washington at 4PM is correct, but appears to be aberrant. The maximum delay was 627 msec; the next two highest delays (in a sample of over 2400) were about 250 msecs each. After dropping this extreme outlier, the University of Washington looks just like UC Berkeley.

[18] Note that the Claffy et al. data were for the old, congested T1 network. We reproduce their figure to illustrate the time-of-day variation in usage; the actual levels of link utilization are generally much lower in the current T3 backbone. Braun and Claffy (1993) show time-of-day variations in T3 traffic between the United States and three other countries.

[19] We should also note that our experiment underestimated the delay that many applications might experience. We were sending probes consisting of a single

packet. Some real data flows involve hundreds or thousands of packets, such as in terminal sessions, file transfers and multimediatransmissions. For these flows, periodic delays can be much longer due to the flow-control protocols implemented in the applications.

[20] An "ms" or millisecond is one one-thousandth of a second.

[21] The compound growth rate in bytes transported has been 5.8% per month from March 1991 to September 1993, and 6.4% per month from September 1992 to September 1993. This probably underestimates growth in Internet usage because traffic on other backbone routes has been growing faster.

[22] In 1986 the NSFNET experienced severe congestion and there was some experimentation with routing based on the IP precedence field and the type of application. When the NSFNET was upgraded to T1 capacity, priority queuing was abandoned for end-user traffic.

[23] Enforcing externally determined priorities may be impossible anyway since bytes are bytes and it is difficult to monitor anything about the content of a data stream.

[24] A vigorous, one-minute phone call on a digital network today utilizes about 60 x 64K/8 bytes of network throughput capacity, but only 1 accounting record. This much information would require roughly 2500 average-sized IP packets, each potentially with its own accounting record if full packet accounting were required.

[25] The most obvious example is to have the billing information transmitted, and the bank account debited, through the network rather than through off-line printed bills and checks written several weeks later.

[26] See Claffy, Braun, and Polyzos (1993) for a detailed study of sampling techniques for measuring network usage.

[27] COMBits has been plagued by problems and resistance and currently is used by almost none of the mid-level networks.

[28] In fact, many of the mid-level regional networks are government agencies, and they charge prices to connect organizations to their networks.

[29] Food stamps are an example of such a scheme. The federal government more or less ensures that everyone has sufficient resources to purchase a certain amount of food. But food is priced so that given one's wealth plus food stamps, the consumer still must decide how to allocate scarce resources relative to the costliness of providing those resources. The government does not guarantee unlimited access to foodstuffs, nor to all varieties of caloric substances (alcoholic beverages are not eligible).

[30] Furthermore, in the pricing scheme we propose, users willing to tolerate delay when the network is congested would face a usage price close to or equal to zero.

[31] The fees for some providers are dramatically lower due to public subsidies.

[32] Customers generally also pay a monthly "local loop" charge to a telephone company for the line between the customer's site and the Internet provider's

"point of presence" (POP), but this charge depends on mileage and is generally set by the telephone company, not the Internet provider.

[33] One complication in implementing packet pricing is dealing with the difference between packets *sent* and packets *received*. The former will be greater than or equal to the latter due to dropped packets, which becomes important especially during periods of congestion.

[34] More traffic is generated by file transfers, but this reflects fewer users sending bigger data streams (files vs. e-mail messages).

[35] In future work we will investigate how a profit-maximizing or welfare-maximizing provider of network access might use price discrimination in connection fees.

[36] It is hard to see how absolute guarantees *can* be made on a connectionless network. However, there have been proposals to provide hybrid networks, with some connection-oriented services in parallel to the connectionless services. Connection-oriented services are well-suited for delivery guarantees.

[37] Of course, in real-time operation, one would presumably cumulate demand over some time interval. It is an interesting research issue to consider how often the market price should be adjusted. The bursty nature of Internet activity suggests a fairly short time interval. However, if users were charged for the congestion cost of their usage, it is possible that the bursts would be dampened.

[38] In technical terms, our mechanism can be viewed as an auction where the n highest bidders gain access at the $n + 1$st highest price bid, otherwise known as a Vickrey auction.

[39] With bursty traffic, low-priority packets at "peak time" might experience only moderate delays before getting through. This is likely to be quite different from the telephone analogue of making customers wait until after 11PM to obtain low-priority, low-rate service. The average length of delays for low-priority traffic will depend on the average level of excess capacity in the system. One advantage of our scheme is that it correctly signals the efficient level of capacity to maintain.

[40] We don't discuss the mechanics of the billing system here. Obviously, there is a need for COD, third-party pricing, and other similar services.

[41] A recent Congressional bill submitted by Representative Boucher to begin implementing the NREN requires uniform protocols for interconnection between providers. It is not clear whether Congress will also mandate uniform standards for providing management information like accounting data.

[42] The current standards body for the Internet is the Internet Engineering Task Force (IETF), which is a voluntary, loosely-knit organization run by network specialists from industry, academia and other interested groups.

[43] The treatment is intended for economists; it is probably too terse for non-economists.

[44] We could also make the utility of packets depend on the delay by writing utility as $u(x_i, D)$. We choose the additively separable specification only for simplicity.

[45] We assume that the user ignores the fact that his own packets impose delay on his own packets; we can think of this effect as being built into the utility function already. There is no problem in relaxing this assumption; the calculations just become messier.

[46] A draft technical report has proposed some semantics and a conceptual model for network usage accounting, but this has not become a standard, nor does it deal with billing or cost allocation; see Mills (1991). See Braun and Claffy (1993) for a detailed discussion of some of the problems facing usage accounting.

[47] It would be natural to use the priority field to contain the bid price.

[48] In practice there may be several levels of interconnected network between the user and the backbone: departmental, organization, regional, national. What we say here about a single local network should generally apply at each such level.

[49] The market algorithm would account for the fact that each packet was a representative for N other packets assumed to have the same bid.

[50] We comment below on some of the issues for implementing a smart market in a multiple node environment.

[51] There may also be a way to steal network services by having them billed to another user, but we haven't figured out how to do that yet.

References

Almquist, P. (1992). Type of service in the internet protocol suite. Tech. rep. RFC 1349, Network Working Group.

Arnott, R., de Palma, A., and Lindsey, R. (1990). Economics of a bottleneck. *Journal of Urban Economics, 27*, 111–130.

Arnott, R., and Kraus, M. (1992a). Financing capacity on the bottleneck model. Technical Report, Department of Economics, Boston College.

Arnott, R., and Kraus, M. (1992b). Self-financing of congestible facilities in a dynamic environment. Technical Report, Economics Department, Boston College.

Bohn, R., Braun, H.-W., Claffy, K., and Wolff, S. (1993). Mitigating the coming Internet crunch: Multiple service levels via precedence. Technical Report, UCSD, San Diego Supercomputer Center, and NSF.

Braun, H.-W., and Claffy, K. (1993). Network analysis in support of internet policy requirements.Technical Report, San Diego Supercomputer Center.

Claffy, K., Braun, H.-W., and Polyzos, G. (1993). Application of sampling methodologies to wide-area network traffic characterization. Technical Report CS93-275, UCSD.

Claffy, K. C., Polyzos, G. C., and Braun, H.-W. (1992). Traffic characteristics of the T1 NSFNET backbone. Technical Report CS92-252, UCSD. Available via Merit gopher in Introducing the Internet directory.

Cocchi, R., Estrin, D., Shenker, S., and Zhang, L. (1992). Pricing in computer networks: Motivation, formulation, and example. Technical Report, University of Southern California.

Estrin, D. (1989). Policy requirements for inter administrative domain routing. Technical Report RFC1125, USC Computer Science Department.

Faulhaber, G. R. (1992). Pricing Internet: The efficient subsidy. In B. Kahin (Ed.), *Building Information Infrastructure.* McGraw-Hill Primis.

Gerla, M., and Kleinrock, L. (1988). Congestion control in interconnected LANs. *IEEE Network*, 2(1), 72–76.

Group, I. A. W. (1992). Usage reporting architecture. Tech. rep., Internet Engineering Task Force. Draft.

Kahin, B. (1992). Overview: Understanding the NREN. In B. Kahin (Ed.), *Building Information Infrastructure.* McGraw-Hill Primis, NY.

Kleinrock, L. (1992). Technology issues in the design of NREN. In B. Kahin (Ed.), *Building Information Infrastructure.* McGraw-Hill Primis.

Krol, E. (1992). *The Whole Internet.* O'Reilly & Associates, Inc. Sebastopol, CA.

MacKie-Mason, J. K., and Varian, H. (1993). Some economics of the internet. Technical Report, University of Michigan.

Mohring, H., and Hartwize, M. (1962). *Highway Benefits: An Analytical Approach.* Northwestern University Press, Evanston.

Prue, W., and Postel, J. (1988). A queuing algorithm to provide type-of-service for IP links. Technical Report RFC 1046, USC Informational Sciences Institute.

Roberts, L. G. (1974). Data by the packet. *IEEE Spectrum*, XX, 46–51.

Ruth, G., and Mills, C. (1992). Usage-based cost recovery in internetworks. *Business Communications Review*, xx, 38–42.

Shenker, S. (1993). Service models and pricing policies for an integrated services internet. Technical Report, Palo Alto Research Center, Xerox Corporation.

Smarr, L. L., and Catlett, C. E. (1992). Life after Internet: Making room for new applications. In B. Kahin (Ed.), *Building Information Infrastructure.* McGraw-Hill Primis.

Strotz, R. (1978). Urban transportation parables. In J. Margolis (Ed.), *The Public Economy of Urban Communities.* Resources for the Future, Washington, DC.

Waldspurger, C. A., Hogg, T., Huberman, B. A., Kephart, J. O., and Stornetta, W. S. (1992). Spawn: A distributed computational economy. *IEEE Transactions on Software Engineering*, 18(2), 103–117.

Wilson, R. (1989). Efficient and competitive rationing. *Econometrica*, 57(1), 1-40.

Service Models and Pricing Policies for an Integrated Services Internet

Scott Shenker

Introduction

In the next five years, the Internet will undergo significant technical changes. These will probably include dramatic increases in bandwidth[1] on the backbone transmission links, better physical access from homes and businesses, and a more sophisticated network architecture. Internet policies are also likely to change; these policy changes will probably include allowing more public access, increasing privatization of service provision, reduced or at least modified government subsidies, and new pricing schemes. These policy and technical changes will reinforce each other: some forthcoming technical developments will enable or force the Internet community to contemplate new policy options; some policy choices will dictate certain technical design choices.

Many current workstations and personal computers can transmit and receive audio and video signals. As a result, multimedia teleconferencing applications and other forms of remote multimedia communications are becoming increasingly common. In recent years, many researchers have been investigating ways to provide *integrated services*—essentially, the ability to carry video and voice as well as data—in packet networks. This integration is not just a matter of increased speed; instead, integration will require a major change in the basic network architecture. This paper introduces policy-makers to the technical aspects of integrated services, and explores the impact this technical development will have on pricing policies. This paper does not address the technology, economics, or policies of the Internet in a comprehensive manner, but rather focuses on the specific topic of integrated services.[2]

The first section of this paper explains why the integration of services requires a new network architecture. In essence, this is because simultaneously delivering adequate service to video, audio, and data in the current Internet architecture would require a prohibitive amount of bandwidth. This section also describes the service requirements of various applications such as video, voice, and data, and then briefly sketches an appropriate service model. The next section discusses how the integration of services, combined with increased public access and privatization, will affect pricing policies. In particular, I argue that an integrated services Internet must employ per-user, quality-of-service–sensitive, and usage-based pricing policies. The final section discusses some important steps along the path to the future integrated services Internet.

Integration of Services

Background

Since 1985, the speed of the Internet's backbone links[3] has increased by roughly three orders of magnitude (from 56 Kbps to 45 Mbps), and in the next decade is likely to increase by another two orders of magnitude. Similarly, since 1985 the number of sites and hosts has increased by several orders of magnitude (from roughly 50 and 1000 respectively to over 10,000 and 1,000,000 respectively). Moreover, in the next decade many if not most homes will likely have some access to the Internet or an equivalent network. This astounding growth in both speed and size was achieved without changing the basic network architecture. The Internet's basic network architecture, as embodied in the underlying TCP/IP [25,26] protocols, has remained virtually unchanged since its inception; this is a powerful testimonial to the robustness of the original design. However, a recent flurry of research activity has focused on building integrated services packet networks[4] or ISPNs. Such networks represent a major departure from the basic network architecture currently used in the Internet.[5]

The search for a new network architecture is driven by the emergence of a new generation of computer-based applications that make extensive use of the network. These applications include multimedia teleconferencing, remote video, computer-based telephony, computer-based fax, telemetry, remote visualization, virtual reality, and many others. It is widely expected that many future remote business, scientific, and social interactions will utilize such tools to enhance the quality of communication and to reduce the need for co-location. These applications require very different Qualities of Service (QoS) from the network.[6] For instance, a casual telephone conversation requires relatively little bandwidth, and can tolerate occasional dropped packets,[7] but is rather intolerant of network-induced delay.[8] A video connection used for remote control of an experiment requires a relatively high bandwidth rate, cannot tolerate any dropped packets, and also needs low delay. A video broadcast of a lecture requires a relatively high bandwidth rate, but can tolerate a few dropped packets and some delay. Bulk data transfers, such as computer-based fax, file transfer, and electronic mail, do not have an intrinsic bandwidth rate; they use as much bandwidth as is available to minimize the transfer time. These bulk data transfer applications can tolerate high delays for individual packets, but are sensitive to the loss of many packets. The current Internet architecture cannot efficiently support this emerging generation of applications, because it cannot simultaneously meet all of their service needs unless the network is extremely overprovisioned (i.e., the average utilization is quite low and so all applications receive good service).[9]

Our current telecommunications infrastructure handles different applications on separate networks: the telephone network carries voice and fax traffic; the cable TV network carries broadcast video; the Internet and other similar data networks carry data traffic. As computers begin supporting many video, voice, and fax applications, separate networks might be developed to support these different applications. However, a network offering an integrated set of services seems more attractive. It would be extremely awkward to implement multimedia applications across several different networks, and wiring buildings for multiple networks is a significant expense. These two problems could be resolved by combining the networks where they enter the office or home. A more fundamental advantage of a single integrated services network is that it uses bandwidth more efficiently[10] than a collection of separate networks. Segregating network traffic by application type leads to a substantial loss of efficiency.

Thus we have a formidable technical challenge: to build a single network architecture that can meet the service needs of the emerging generation of applications. To support these applications the network must accommodate extreme variations in delay and bandwidth requirements. Packet-switching, as used in the Internet, is widely regarded as the technology of choice to meet this challenge.[11] Its principle advantage is that it allows statistical multiplexing to occur on a packet-by-packet level, and thus wastes no bandwidth.[12] The Internet, and most other data networks, employ a first-in-first-out (FIFO) packet scheduling algorithm; that is, the first packet to arrive at a network switch is the first one sent. Such scheduling algorithms cannot provide different service to different clients, such as low delay to one client and high delay to another. Thus, to provide a variety of qualities of service, the network must employ nontrivial packet scheduling algorithms.[13] Incorporating these algorithms into high-speed switches is one of the technical hurdles facing designers of ISPNs.

Service Model

The set of services offered by the network is called the service model. The service model is embodied in the service interface, which allows users to request various qualities of service from the network. This service interface plays a key role in network design, because it regulates the interaction between applications and the underlying network and keeps the two cleanly separated. A network can employ any technology that supports the service interface; similarly, any application that expresses its needs through the service interface can use the network. A stable service interface allows rapid technological improvements in both applications and network technology, without the need for coordination.

The service interface is embedded within applications; it is thus very hard to change without disrupting service to current network clients. Thus, the price for quick progress in applications and networks is that the service interface must remain stable. Because the service interface is essentially a particular parameterization of the service model, the service model must also remain stable.

ISPN designers face the question: What set of services should an ISPN offer? The answer should be based on conjectures about future application and institutional requirements, as well as technical feasibility. For designers, the basic technical assumption is that the more closely aligned the service model is to the needs of applications, the more efficient the network will be. Before addressing application and institutional service requirements in detail, it is useful to provide some context by first reviewing the service offerings of the current telephone network and the Internet.

The telephone network is a circuit-switched network. Phone calls require an explicit preallocation of resources while the connection is being established. Calls are blocked if sufficient resources are not available. The service model for ISDN telephone service is the delivery of data at a fixed bandwidth with a fixed delay; all data arrives at the receiver a fixed time after it was transmitted. For the purposes of this discussion, this can be considered one kind of bounded-delay service.

The telephone network serves one application, spoken voice conversation.[14] Specific data rates and delays were chosen to accommodate speech production and recognition. The performance of a phone call is independent of the speed of the underlying phone lines. In case of overload, excess calls are blocked, rather than allowing all calls to connect and delivering degraded service to them all.

Data networks such as the Internet are quite different. The most obvious difference is that data networks are typically packet-switched rather than circuit-switched. In addition, there is no explicit call set-up, no preallocation of resources, and no admission control;[15] the network offers only best-effort service. This means that the network attempts to deliver packets as quickly as possible, but makes no guarantees about delivery and delays. The switches typically use the FIFO packet scheduling algorithm and thus deliver the same quality of service to all applications. Since there is no admission control, the network cannot prevent overloads by refusing service. When the network is overloaded, delays increase and packets are dropped.

Thus, the telephone network and the Internet provide very different service models. The best-effort service model is scaleable; it adapts to whatever bandwidth is available. Programmers rarely build real-time requirements, or even specific time-scales, into software.[16] As machines speed up, the program works better; if system performance degrades, the program still works, just not as quickly. This is the appropriate service model for traditional computer-based applications, such as Telnet, FTP, and electronic mail, that also improve with better service (more bandwidth and/or less delay), and degrade gracefully with deteriorating service (less bandwidth and/or more delay). This scalability is amply verified by the fact that this application family has remained relatively unchanged even though network speeds have increased by several orders of magnitude since their introduction.

Applications such as voice conversations or video transmissions are not scaleable; they have some fundamental bandwidth and delay requirements.[17] Their performance does not improve greatly if their service requirements are exceeded, but does quickly degrade if their requirements are not met. The best-effort service model, with its inability to provide any assurance about the quality of service, is obviously inappropriate for this class of applications. Applications such as video and voice are better served by service models that resemble the telephony service model with its bounded delays and fixed bandwidth.

One problem shared by the Internet and telephony service models is that they do not offer different services to different applications. Any ISPN must overcome this limitation by allowing applications to specify their requirements through a service interface that offers a wide variety of services. Several prototype ISPNs are in operation,[18] but the designers have not reached a consensus on the appropriate service model; in fact, there is strenuous disagreement about several fundamental issues. There is, however, one point of widespread agreement—the service model should be more varied, or richer, than the current telephony and Internet offerings, and should combine these paradigms by offering (1) quantitative delay bounds and (2) several levels of best-effort service. The remainder of this section describes one such proposed service model[19] (see References [1,2,29] for a much fuller exposition).

The service model is based on the requirements of applications and institutions. Applications can be roughly divided into those that are elastic or scaleable, and those that are real-time. Elastic applications adjust easily and flexibly to delays in delivery; that is, a packet arriving earlier helps performance and a packet arriving later hurts performance, but there is no set need for a packet to arrive at a certain time. Typical Internet applications are elastic in nature, and the Internet service model has performed well for them. Thus, for elastic applications we propose a service model consisting of several classes of best-effort service. These classes allow applications to indicate their relative sensitivity to delay so that the network can distinguish between the delay requirements of, for example, interactive burst transactions (e.g., Telnet and X-protocol), interactive bulk transfers (e.g., FTP), and asynchronous bulk transfers (e.g., electronic mail and fax).

Real-time applications have more stringent requirements. Some real-time applications are playback applications (see Figure 1). In these applications, the source digitizes some signal and transmits it over the network; the data packets are delivered to the receiver with varying delay; the receiver buffers the data and plays the signal back at some specified moment; this moment is called the playback point and is the generation time plus some essentially fixed offset delay. Data that does not arrive at the receiver before its playback point cannot be played back on time; it is of essentially no use. To choose a reasonable value for the offset delay, an application needs some a priori characterization of the maximum delay; this could either be provided by the network in a delay bound, or through the observation of the delays of earlier packets. While our discussion has treated the offset delay as essentially fixed, in reality the application can slowly adjust its offset delay during use as its estimate of the maximal packet delays change.

Delay can affect the performance of playback applications in two ways. First, the value of the offset delay (which is determined by predictions about the future packet delays) affects the interactive nature of the application. Applications vary greatly in their sensitiv-

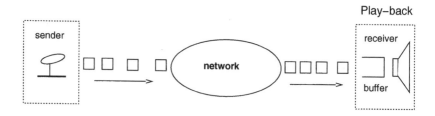

Figure 1 Playback Applications. The receiver plays the data back at the playback point, which is the sum of the generation time and the offset delay.

ity to this offset delay. Some playback applications, in particular those that involve interaction such as a phone call, are extremely sensitive to this delay; transmissions of a movie or lecture are less sensitive.

Second, the signal becomes degraded when packet delays exceed the offset delay. Applications vary greatly in their sensitivity to late packets. We can divide these playback applications into those that are tolerant of occasional dropped or late packets, and those that are not. Intolerant playback applications require an absolutely faithful playing back of the original data, either because the hardware or software is unable to cope with missing data, or because the users are unwilling to risk missing any data. On the other hand, users of tolerant applications, as well as the underlying hardware and software, are prepared to accept occasional losses of data. Most casual telephone conversations are tolerant, since human speech tends to be redundant and, if necessary, users can request that the other participants repeat the missing parts of the conversation. It is important to note that the distinction between tolerant and intolerant applications is not just a function of the software and hardware involved but also depends on the needs of the users themselves.

In essence, the performance of elastic applications is more closely related to the average delay of the packets, whereas the performance of real-time applications is more closely related to the maximum delay of the packets. Best-effort service produces reasonable values for average delays but, because the service has wide variations in delay, the maximal delays are intolerable. To keep the maximal delays within a reasonable range, real-time applications need a service with a bounded delay. For intolerant applications, the service model we propose is a firm worst-case bound on delay; this bound should not be violated as long as the network switches and links function properly. Tolerant applications do not need such a reliable bound; for these applications the service model we propose is a loose bound on delay that incorporates predictions about the aggregate traffic load; this bound will occasionally be violated when the predictions are wrong.

Future video and audio applications will likely be playback applications,[20] and we conjecture that the vast majority of real-time traffic will be produced by such playback applications. Thus, we expect that our real-time services will fit the needs of most future real-time applications. The taxonomy of applications, and the relevant service offerings, is depicted in Figure 2.

Services for both tolerant and intolerant real-time applications involve admission control; before commencing transmission, applications must request service from the network. This service request consists of a traffic descriptor, in which applications specify their traffic load, and a QoS descriptor, in which applications specify the desired quality of service. We envision employing a traffic descriptor that specifies bandwidth and burstiness. After receiving a service request, the network decides whether or not to accept the request based on whether or not it can deliver the desired QoS. In contrast, there is no admission control for the best-effort service classes. Thus, the predominant failure mode for real-time service is that requests can be blocked, and for best-effort service that best-effort packets can be dropped. Most failures should be suffered by users who indicate—in return presumably for cheaper service—that they are willing to experience a higher failure rate. Thus, the service model incorporates the notions of preemptable packets—the first packets discarded when the network is overloaded[21]—and preemptable connections, which are terminated when incoming connections would otherwise be blocked.

These best-effort and real-time service offerings are designed to meet application requirements. Institutional requirements are less frequently discussed. Currently, many private firms partially bypass

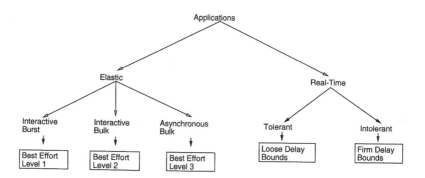

Figure 2 Application Taxonomy: application classes and associated service offerings.

the regular phone system and lease lines directly for their own internal computer and telephone networks. Leased lines are the telecommunications equivalent of buying wholesale, and the need to lease will likely persist. However, such bypass is harmful to an ISPN because it reduces the revenue stream and prevents the network from taking full advantage of the increasing returns to scale of statistical multiplexing. For an ISPN to remain economically viable, it should keep bypass at a minimum by offering firms a service which is at least equivalent to and preferably superior to directly leasing lines.

One possibility would be to offer virtual leased lines consisting of a long-term reservation of real-time service with some bounded delay and fixed bandwidth. This service would be essentially equivalent to directly leasing a line. In order to make the virtual leased line service more attractive than directly leasing lines, two problems common to both virtual leased lines and direct leased lines must be addressed. First, leasing a virtual line leads to inefficient use of bandwidth because the network's QoS scheduling mechanism is circumvented; not all packets sent over this real-time channel need the real-time service. For instance, if a firm leases a real-time line but uses it mostly for file transfer or electronic mail traffic, the internal network switches would schedule the traffic as if it needs the real-time bounded delay service when in fact it needs much less stringent service. Second, such a line cannot be shared by several entities in a controlled way without the firm exercising its own scheduling at the entrance to the connection. This is especially important if several divisions of a firm, or departments of a university, choose to jointly lease some bandwidth and want to ensure that every entity gets its fair share when the link is fully loaded.

We propose a modified virtual leased line service that allows link-sharing through the specification of a hierarchy of link ownership shares. For instance, a link could be shared by several universities; these shares could be split between their various academic departments; these shares in turn could be split among the staff and students of the department, so that finally each individual in the department would have his or her own individual share. In addition, this modified virtual leased line service would offer the QoS service classes discussed above, so that the service needs of the packets are revealed to and utilized by the network in the packet scheduling algorithm. Thus, real-time requirements will always take precedence over elastic ones, but admission control will ensure that every entity gets its share of the bandwidth. Such a service would meet the needs of institutions better than direct leased line service because of its more efficient use of bandwidth and more flexible sharing options.

Thus, our proposed service model incorporates two kinds of real-time service, several classes of best-effort service, and a modified virtual leased-line service. This service model is designed to meet the needs of the entire spectrum of future Internet applications. Of course, a period of experimenting and rethinking will be needed before the field reaches—if it ever does—a consensus on the appropriate service model for an ISPN; while we expect the general form of the eventual service model to resemble our proposal, there will likely be important differences in the details.

Efficiency

Our case for the desirability of ISPNs is based largely on the efficient use of the network bandwidth, a notion explored in this subsection. Efficiency is not measured by link utilization or some other network-related quantity; instead, efficiency must be connected to the performance of applications using the network. The following model provides such a notion of efficiency. Consider some network with a set of clients. Let s_i denote the network performance delivered to client i; s_i describes all the relevant service parameters (such as bandwidth, delay, etc). Assume that every network client's degree of satisfaction with its service is expressed by some function $V_i(s_i)$; this function quantifies how much money the client would be willing to spend for such service. The network has a finite capacity, and so only certain s are feasible; let F denote the feasible set of service allocations. A measure of the efficiency of some service allocation s is just the sum $V_{total}(s) = \sum_i V_i(s_i)$. The most efficient feasible service allocation $s \in F$ is the one that maximizes $V_{total}(s)$. The service interface and the underlying packet scheduling algorithm determine the feasible set of allocations.

This formulation of efficiency reveals two problems with offering a variety of qualities of service. First, not every client gains directly from the resulting increase in efficiency; that is, $V_{total}(s^1) > V_{total}(s^2)$ does not imply that $V_i(s_i^1) > V_i(s_i^2)$ for all i. Efficiency in heterogeneous networks is gained by shifting resources from applications that are not extremely performance-sensitive to those that are; the performance-sensitive clients gain from using more sophisticated scheduling algorithms, but the less performance-sensitive clients lose. Considering only network service, the increase in efficiency benefits only the performance-sensitive applications and in fact harms the less performance-sensitive applications. Why should users of less performance-sensitive applications be in favor of richer service models?

Second, in order to achieve efficiency, clients must request the appropriate service for their application. High-quality service should only be requested by users of performance-sensitive applications. This raises an important incentive issue: if efficiency depends on the truthful revelation of preferences, but the less performance-sensitive clients lose when they reveal their lack of performance sensitivity, what will motivate clients to reveal their preferences honestly?

Careful pricing of network services provides a solution to both of these problems. Pricing can provide the appropriate incentives to clients to reveal their service requirements honestly. Pricing can also spread the benefits of the increased efficiency to all clients.

Clearly, the network should charge less for low-quality service than for high quality service. More specifically, the pricing scheme should be designed so that the increase in quality of service outweighs the increase in cost for performance-sensitive applications, and the decrease in cost outweighs the decrease in quality of service for the less performance-sensitive applications. In this case, when both the cost and quality of network service are considered, all application classes benefit from the increased efficiency of ISPNs. Furthermore, such a pricing scheme will provide the proper incentives so that only users of performance-sensitive applications will request high-quality service; then the selfish choices of individual clients will allow the network as a whole to achieve optimal efficiency.[22] We return to the issue of pricing below.

Policy Developments and Pricing Schemes

Much of the design and prototyping of ISPNs takes place in research settings that are quite insulated. In particular, for the various testbed networks where these designs are or will be tested, the test user community is small and cooperative, the designs are determined more by technical factors than market pressures, and network service is free. However, in the Internet, or in any other similar public network, these conditions will no longer hold. In particular, users will be charged, either directly or indirectly, for network service. In this section, I discuss how the integration of services, along with the policy developments of public access and privatization, determine the form of the pricing schemes.

Public Access

With the rapid fall of policy and technical barriers, access to the Internet is becoming much more widespread; within the next decade, a sizable fraction of homes may have Internet access. A dramatic increase in the Internet user population would have several important ramifications. First, once a home consumer standard is widely adopted, there is tremendous pressure for it to remain stable. Thus, once Internet usage becomes a staple for many American families, the service interface and other network protocols will become even harder to change than they are now (and they are already quite difficult to change). It is extremely important that the networking community make the right technical decisions about the proper service interface now.

Also, once artificial access restrictions are lifted, the Internet will no longer have a small, technically knowledgeable, and very cooperative user community. As with other widely-used public facilities, informal enforcement of behavioral norms is unlikely to be sufficient to ensure socially desirable behavior; not all network clients will truthfully reveal their service preferences, unless it is in their own interest. One cannot rely on policing for this, so pricing will have to provide incentives for proper network usage.

Privatization

In the future, multiple private carriers will compete to offer network services, perhaps much as we now have multiple long-distance phone companies. While the issue of competition raises many issues, here I discuss only that of reselling bandwidth. Assuming that the principle of common carriage[23] applies to these networks (there are those that doubt the viability of this principle; see [21]), then a firm can purchase network service from one provider and resell it to others. There is nothing intrinsically wrong with reselling; in some sense it is simply the transfer of marketing responsibilities. However, reselling can result in decreased efficiency when the service requirements of the traffic are not accurately represented. For example, buying real-time service in bulk and then reselling this service to elastic traffic leads to inefficient use of the network; a different allocation of service—giving the bulk elastic traffic best-effort rather than real-time service—would produce a higher total level of satisfaction. Thus, for a pricing scheme to encourage efficient allocation of resources, such reselling must not be profitable.

Our modified virtual leased line service proposal discourages the mislabeling of service needs since it allows users to buy in bulk and still utilize the QoS service classes; the network is presented with each packet's true service needs and can schedule the packets accordingly. However, other factors besides pricing and the service model can influence the profitability of reselling. In a connection-oriented technology, such as ATM, if connection set-up involves substantial delays then there will be strong market pressure to resell service from pre-set-up connections to clients with intermittent traffic needs. Thus, if ATM and other similar technologies are to avoid being primarily a leased-line service, they must provide rapid connection establishment.

Pricing

With widespread competition among network service providers, pricing schemes will likely lead to a high degree of efficiency because providers must guard against new competitors with more efficient schemes. Thus, we will assume that network efficiency is an important pricing goal.[24]

There are a wide variety of pricing policies. The granularity of the pricing policy can vary by what is priced—access, connections, packets, etc.—and by how charges are identified—by institution, user, application, etc. This is not a question of who pays the bill (in many cases that will be the institution), but rather how detailed the bill should be.

There is tremendous pressure to offer access-based pricing schemes; that is, to charge only for the size of the access link.[25] This has two important advantages: it is technically easy (in fact, it is currently the predominant charging scheme in the Internet) and predictable.[26] However, in a network with a nontrivial service model, to achieve efficiency the pricing scheme must (1) provide incentives for users to specify the appropriate service class and (2) ensure that reselling is not profitable. Access-based pricing fails to meet either requirement.

To provide incentives for appropriate service requests, the network must tie costs to the individual clients who make the QoS choices, and must also price the various services differently. Pricing based exclusively on access charges does neither. These requirements are met by QoS-sensitive pricing schemes that charge for both the establishment of the reservation or connection and its duration.[27]

Furthermore, access-based pricing makes reselling profitable, since a firm should attempt to sell all of its unused capacity. This reselling problem persists even when the pricing scheme includes charges for individual connections. For example, if I establish a video connection with a reserved bandwidth of 100 Mbps, but my video source has an average bandwidth of 10 Mbps (and a peak rate of 100 Mbps), then if I am charged for 100 Mbps I should resell the remaining 90 Mbps. I would make sure that my packets get priority when my video surges to the peak rate, and thus the service I actually sell is not real-time but best-effort. To ensure that such reselling is not profitable, the pricing policy should also be usage-based; that is, my cost should not be based only on the size of my access pipe, my QoS, and my connection parameters, but also on my actual usage; the per-packet charge must be greater than what I can resell the best-effort service for. Thus, in addition to the access charge, the appropriate pricing scheme for real-time connections is a QoS-sensitive multipart tariff with a charge for the establishment of the reservation, a charge for the duration of the reservation, and a charge for the actual usage of the reservation. For best-effort traffic, a QoS-sensitive per-packet charge is appropriate.

Such a scheme would impose severe accounting requirements on the underlying network architecture. There is almost no accounting infrastructure currently in place. For the kind of QoS-sensitive and usage-based pricing advocated here, the network needs an accounting infrastructure that can record individual packets and assign their costs to the appropriate clients. The network and the operating system of the host would have to cooperate to identify individual users (or perhaps applications) as the responsible entities. It is not clear where this division of labor should split; in the ATM context, the network would most likely assign the charge to a VCI (virtual circuit identifier) and the operating system would be responsible for associating each VCI to a user or application. The network accounting infrastructure must be built into the underlying network protocols, which must support some degree of authentication so that charges are not misassigned. While the integration of services is a fashionable topic in academic research circles, accounting and authentication are not.[28] If we are to succeed in building an integrated services Internet, we must address these problems.

The fact that users will generate costs based on their network usage (even if they themselves don't pay the bill) will be a dramatic shift away from the recent trend in computer systems to hide the underlying technology from users. Operating systems will need to account for network usage, and user interfaces will need to inform users about the charges their actions are incurring. Again, little work has been done in this area, but it must be if an integrated services Internet is to be widely used.

One objection is that a highly detailed pricing scheme will create huge transaction costs. However, there are two aspects to these anticipated transaction costs: accounting (collecting data and computing the amount to be charged) and billing (sending out bills, handling incoming envelopes, cashing checks, etc.). My uninformed guess is that the cost of doing the accounting is significantly smaller than the cost of the actual billing; our proposal necessitates detailed accounting, but for commercial customers the billing should be done at the institutional level, not sent to the individuals users, and so the billing costs for commercial users will be low. Thus, at least in the beginning when most users of the Internet are commercial or academic, not residential, the billing overhead may be manageable. In any case, I conjecture that a network that provides a variety of qualities of service must have detailed pricing because, despite its cost, such pricing is likely to be more cost-effective than doing without a QoS mechanism.

Next Steps

An efficient integrated services Internet must offer a rich service model that combines real-time service, best-effort service, and a modified virtual leased line service. Moreover, such a service model will only be used efficiently if it is combined with a usage-based and QoS-sensitive pricing scheme. However, the current Internet has neither a rich service model nor an accounting infrastructure capable of supporting sophisticated pricing schemes. What are the critical next steps that will take us from the current Internet to our vision of the future Internet?

First, and most importantly, the Internet must adopt standards that mandate a full accounting infrastructure and a rich QoS service interface. Such a radical change in the Internet would have been difficult enough in the Internet's infancy, when technical decisions were made by a rather small and cohesive technical community. In the current environment, changing the Internet's basic architecture is especially problematic. Because the government no longer plays a significant role in determining the Internet's architecture, the companies who produce network equipment and the consumers of this equipment must reach a consensus on this architectural transformation. Managing this transition will be the ultimate test of the Internet's organizational coherence.

Second, since the cost of usage will become important, operating systems and user interfaces need to be modified so that users are more aware of their network usage and its cost. Organizations will feel comfortable with usage-based pricing only when users are familiar with network costs and can make informed decisions. Most organizations can handle usage-based phone charges because users understand the pricing structure and are able to control their own costs effectively; we need to create a similar situation in the Internet.

Finally, while it may lead to inefficiencies in the short term, the pricing structure should accommodate users who require either a fixed-fee cost structure or extremely inexpensive service. There are important user communities, such as schools and libraries, where the variability in usage-based costs would cause extreme difficulties. We must find ways to accommodate these communities.[29] There are also likely to be many potential users who, at competitive prices, could not afford even the most basic level of Internet access. However, if we expect the Internet to become an important part of our telecommunications infrastructure, we must strive for universal access either through price regulations or user subsidies.

Acknowledgments

The ideas in this paper were developed through many hours of discussion with my colleagues David D. Clark, Deborah Estrin, Bryan Lyles, David Sincoskie, and Lixia Zhang. Furthermore, the service model presented here represents joint work with David D. Clark and Lixia Zhang. In addition, I would like to thank Hal Varian, Jeff MacKie-Mason, Vint Cerf, Steve Deering, Padmanabhan Srinagesh, and Abel Weinrib for helpful discussions. However, not all of the discussants agree with everything written here, and all errors or misconceptions in this draft are solely the responsibility of the author.

Notes

[1] Bandwidth is the amount of data a link can move per unit time, and is the usual measure of capacity of a link.

[2] References [7,19,21,30,31] provide more general treatments.

[3] The figures cited in this paragraph and the next were taken from Reference [31]. We adopt their terminology, in which Internet refers to Arpanet but not to Milnet.

[4] The term "integrated services packet networks" is not completely standard.

[5] For a discussion of such research efforts, see [1, 2, 8, 9, 10, 12, 13, 14, 15, 16, 17, 18, 20, 22, 23, 27, 29, 32, 34, 35].

[6] It is perhaps useful to clarify that networks such as the Internet are packet-switched: transmissions of data from one site to another are broken up into many small packets of data and each packet is transmitted separately. The network switches (also called routers or gateways) determine the route each packet travels to its final destination, where the packets are reassembled into the original data. The bandwidth requirement of an application is determined by the rate at which these packets are transmitted (and their size). The delay referred to below is the time taken by these packets to traverse the network.

[7] Human speech is quite redundant and human conversation has a built-in recovery mechanism, so occasional dropped packets have little ill effect.

[8] We discuss the delay requirements of such applications in great detail below.

[9] Such inefficiency is only a problem if bandwidth continues to be the scarce commodity in networks. Some, such as in [11], maintain that all-optical networks will soon make bandwidth plentiful and switching resources scarce. I disagree and think that bandwidth will continue to be scarce, but this paper is not the place to debate this point.

[10] Efficiency is measured by the total application performance achievable on the network for a given amount of bandwidth; see the section on "Efficiency" below for a more precise definition.

[11] See MacKie-Mason and Varian, in this volume, for an introductory presentation. ATM is also a packet-switching architecture. The Internet uses a connectionless packet-switching architecture, while ATM is a connection-oriented packet-switching architecture. While the technical community is in agreement that for today's transmission technologies packet-switching is the correct choice, there is still an active debate about the relative merits of connection-oriented and connectionless packet-switching architectures.

[12] Statistical multiplexing occurs when several entities with variable resource demands share a single resource. The aggregation of these multiple demands has a lower variance than the individual demands, and so the resource is used more efficiently. Packet-switched networks can share on a packet basis, whereas circuit-switched networks can only share at the less efficient level of circuits.

[13] There has been much research in the past few years designing and analyzing these packets scheduling algorithms. See [2, 5, 10, 12, 13, 14, 18, 20, 22, 27, 32, 35] for some examples.

[14] I will ignore fax, as this is in some sense a data application that has been overlaid on the phone network because of its ubiquitous connectivity.

[15] That is, applications need not ask the network's permission before sending data.

[16] In fact, one of the important paradigms of computer software design is to abstract away performance issues by using concepts such as virtual processors, virtual memory, and abstract machines to organize programs.

[17] The bandwidth requirements can be modified by the encoding algorithm, but that entails a change in the signal quality. Also, we will be more specific about the lack of scalability later in this section.

[18] The networks cited in [10,17,18,20] are examples of operating prototypes; the design my colleagues and I work on is operational on DARTnet, an ARPA-funded T1 testbed linking roughly a dozen industrial and academic research sites.

[19] There are other aspects to the service model that are not addressed here (such as policy routing, multicast, etc.); this discussion is restricted to services relevant to packet scheduling. The inclusion of other services only strengthens the argument.

[20] Current video and audio applications on circuit switched networks do not fit this model, since there is no jitter in the network delays; however, the video and audio applications in use on the Internet today, such as vat and nv, do fit this model.

[21] See [24] for an example of how this might work.

[22] See [33] for a discussion of such priority pricing and [3,4] for an application of these ideas to networks. For a more theoretical treatment of incentive issues and efficiency, see [28].

[23] Common carriage is the requirement that networks provide service to all customers on an equal footing. In particular, common carriage means that networks cannot refuse to sell service to competitors.

[24] MacKie-Mason and Varian, in this volume, discusses these efficiency issues in much greater detail.

[25] Most pricing schemes will include at least some charge for access; I use the term access-based pricing to refer to pricing schemes which only charge for access.

[26] While predictable costs are indeed desirable, in many facets of life such as utility and phone usage we have adjusted quite well to variable costs. However, both the newness of the basic technology and the rapidly changing usage patterns, in addition to the historical legacy of access-based pricing, contribute to the rather vocal demand for predictable costs in networking.

[27] These might most naturally be called connection charges, but to avoid the possible confusion because often access charges are called connection charges,

we will adopt the term reservation charges.

[28] Reference [6] is one of the few contributions in this area.

[29] This could involve using other forms of incentives to control network usage, or merely accepting the inefficiencies that result when the proper incentives don't exist.

References

[1] R. Braden, D. Clark, and S. Shenker. Integrated Services in the Internet Architecture: an Overview. Request For Comments 1633, Information Sciences Institute, University of Southern California, July 1994.

[2] D. Clark, S. Shenker, and L. Zhang. Supporting Real-Time Applications in an Integrated Services Packet Network: Architecture and Mechanism. *Proceedings of SIGCOMM 92*, pp 14–26, 1992.

[3] R. Cocchi, D. Estrin, S. Shenker, and L. Zhang. A Study of Priority Pricing in Multiple Service Class Networks. *Proceedings of SIGCOMM 91*, pp 123–130, 1991.

[4] R. Cocchi, S. Shenker, D. Estrin, and L. Zhang. Pricing in Computer Networks: Motivation, Formulation, and Example. *IEEE/ACM Transactions on Networking*, 1(6), pp. 614–627, 1993.

[5] A. Demers, S. Keshav, and S. Shenker. Analysis and Simulation of a Fair Queueing Algorithm. *Journal of Internetworking: Research and Experience*, 1(1), pp. 3–26, 1990.

[6] Deborah Estrin and Lixia Zhang. Design considerations for usage accounting and feedback in internetworks. *ACM Computer Communication Review*, 20(5), pp. 56–66, 1990.

[7] G. Faulhaber. Pricing Internet: The efficient subsidy. In B. Kahin, ed., *Building Information Infrastructure* (New York: McGraw-Hill, 1992).

[8] D. Ferrari. Client Requirements for Real-Time Communication Services. *IEEE Communications Magazine*, 28(11), 1990.

[9] D. Ferrari. Distributed Delay Jitter Control in Packet-Switching Internetworks. *Journal of Internetworking: Research and Experience*, 4(1), pp. 1–20, 1993.

[10] D. Ferrari and D. Verma. A Scheme for Real-Time Channel Establishment in Wide-Area Networks. *IEEE Journal on Selected Areas in Communications*, 8(3), pp. 368–379, 1990.

[11] P. Green. The Future of Fiber-Optic Computer Networks. *IEEE Computer*, 24(9), pp. 78–89, 1991.

[12] S. J. Golestani. A Stop and Go Queueing Framework for Congestion Management. *Proceedings of SIGCOMM 90*, pp. 8–18, 1990.

[13] S. J. Golestani. Duration-Limited Statistical Multiplexing of Delay Sensitive Traffic in Packet Networks. *Proceedings of INFOCOM 91*, 1991.

[14] S. J. Golestani. A Framing Strategy for Congestion Management. *IEEE Journal on Selected Areas in Communications*, 9(9), pp. 1064–1077, 1991.

[15] R. Guérin and L. Gün. A Unified Approach to Bandwidth Allocation and Access Control in Fast Packet-Switched Networks. *Proceedings of INFOCOM 92*, 1992.

[16] R. Guérin, H. Ahmadi, and M. Naghshineh. Equivalent Capacity and Its Application to Bandwidth Allocation in High-Speed Networks. *IEEE Journal on Selected Areas in Communications*, 9(9), pp. 968–981, 1991.

[17] J. Hyman and A. Lazar. MARS: The Magnet II Real-Time Scheduling Algorithm. *Proceedings of SIGCOMM 91*, pp. 285–293, 1991.

[18] J. Hyman, A. Lazar, and G. Pacifici. Real-Time Scheduling with Quality of Service Constraints. *IEEE Journal on Selected Areas in Communications*, 9(9), pp. 1052–1063, 1991.

[19] B. Kahin. Overview: Understanding the NREN. In B. Kahin, ed., *Building Information Infrastructure* (New York: McGraw-Hill, 1992).

[20] C. Kalmanek, H. Kanakia, and S. Keshav. Rate Controlled Servers for Very High-Speed Networks. *Proceedings of GlobeCom 90*, pp. 300.3.1–300.3.9, 1990.

[21] E. Noam. The Impending Doom of Common Carriage. Preprint, 1993.

[22] A. Parekh and R. Gallager. A Generalized Processor Sharing Approach to Flow Control—The Single Node Case. *IEEE/ACM Transactions on Networking*, 1(3), pp. 344–357, 1993.

[23] A. Parekh. A Generalized Processor Sharing Approach to Flow Control in Integrated Services Networks. Technical Report LIDS-TR-2089, Laboratory for Information and Decision Systems, Massachusetts Institute of Technology, 1992.

[24] David Petr, Luiz DaSiliva, and Victor Frost. Priority discarding of speech in integrated packet network. *IEEE Journal on Selected Areas in Communications*, 7(5), pp. 644–656, June 1989.

[25] J. Postel. Internet protocol. Request For Comments 791, Information Sciences Institute, University of Southern California, August 1981.

[26] J. Postel. Transmission control protocol. Request For Comments 793, Information Sciences Institute, University of Southern California, September 1981.

[27] H. Schulzrinne, J. Kurose, and D. Towsley. Congestion Control for Real-Time Traffic. *Proceedings of INFOCOM 90*.

[28] S. Shenker. Efficient network allocation with selfish users. In P. J. B. King, I. Mitrani, and R. J. Poole, eds., *Proceedings of Performance 90* (Amsterdam: North-Holland, 1990), pp. 279–285.

[29] S. Shenker, D. Clark, and L. Zhang. A Scheduling Service Model and a Scheduling Architecture for an Integrated Services Packet Network. Preprint, 1993.

[30] M. Sirbu. Telecommunications Technology and Infrastructure. *A National Information Network*, Institute for Information Studies, 1992.

[31] L. Smarr and C. Catlett. Life after Internet: Making room for new applications. In B. Kahin, ed., *Building Information Infrastructure* (New York: McGraw-Hill, 1992).

[32] D. Verma, H. Zhang, and D. Ferrari. Delay Jitter Control for Real-Time Communication in a Packet Switching Network. *Proceedings of TriCom 91*, pp. 35–43, 1991.

[33] Robert Wilson. Efficient and competitive rationing. *Econometrica*, 57(1), pp. 1–40, 1989.

[34] L. Zhang. A New Architecture for Packet Switching Network Protocols. Technical Report LCS-TR-455, Laboratory for Computer Science, Massachusetts Institute of Technology, 1989.

[35] L. Zhang. VirtualClock: A New Traffic Control Algorithm for Packet Switching Networks. *ACM Transactions on Computer Systems*, 9(2), pp. 101–124, 1991.

Pricing and Competition Policies for the Internet

Michael A. Einhorn

Introduction

The Internet is in the middle of an important transition. From a research network that provided e-mail, remote log-in, and file transfer to university computers, policy-makers now envision extending the Internet to elementary and secondary schools, libraries, and hospitals. Eventually, the Internet backbone may provide comprehensive broadband connectivity throughout the United States.[1]

Policy makers and network operators face three key issues in the upcoming years:

1. What network services will be offered and how should they be priced?

2. How can competition be encouraged and interconnection facilitated?

3. How should subsidies for schools, libraries, hospitals, and other customers be structured?

This paper addresses these concerns. It concludes that:

• Future Internet uses will require higher reliability, which may necessitate traffic control during busy hours. Users should be able to reserve bandwidth for specified periods, but instantaneous arrangements should be available for short-run applications as well. Service offerings should vary by bandwidth, hours of use, and allowance for delay and loss.

- Competition among network providers can drive down prices, encourage speedy investment, and stimulate innovative service offerings. Open interconnection between independent networks may expedite this.

- Subsidies can be used to help increase Internet access among K-12 schools, libraries, and possibly hospitals. Subsidy dollars should flow from general tax dollars rather than from other Internet users. These dollars should be earmarked exclusively for interconnecting targeted users and passed directly to whatever network provider offers interconnection.

Network Services and Prices

The Internet is a packet-switched network that originally supported three data services for researchers: remote log-in, file transfer, and e-mail. These applications functioned reasonably well despite occasional delays and packet loss; network congestion was no serious problem. Each Internet customer paid hookup and flat-rate monthly charges; minutes-of-use were sometimes billed as well.

The network has recently incorporated several important new capabilities. Distributed search and retrieval tools (e.g., Gopher, Veronica, Archie, WAIS, and World Wide Web) now expedite data retrieval for researchers. Real-time audio and video broadcast and multicast have been practiced and are rapidly developing. Problematically, network congestion now sometimes arises on many popular servers.

In a packet switched network, disjoint packets of signal information are routed simultaneously over several alternative channels; routing of each packet is governed by control algorithms that determine the instantaneous least-cost option. Depending upon the dynamic configuration of channel uses, packets may or may not arrive at their receiving host in proper sequence. Nodal receivers then are needed to store (or *buffer*) incoming packets for eventual playback to the receiving host; individual message packets that arrive at a node after the message has been played are discarded. While a user of a congested circuit switch simply grabs capacity that another prospective user cannot use at all, users of congested packet switches create traffic delays (or fluctuations in arrival time called jitter) that distort transport and playback time for all users.

When congestion is not significant on packet networks or when network uses can tolerate loss, delay, and jitter, these usage costs are zero. Since economically efficient prices should reflect associated costs, efficient usage prices are zero as well.[2] However, with the advent of asynchronous transfer mode (ATM) switching and broadband transport, the Internet will soon support a wider variety of voice, data, and image applications, including high-speed facsimile, remote video, multimedia conferencing, data fusion, remote X-terminals, visualization, and virtual reality. These applications could benefit users of all types, and should be encouraged if Internet users are to have the powerful state-of-the-art capabilities of other data networks. However, the new applications tolerate less delay and packet loss and require considerably more bandwidth.[3] Much as postal customers do now, future Internet users will want to choose among several gradations of priority and quality. Transmission speeds and quality will become increasingly important; if users cannot have a high-quality video conference over the Internet, they will find another venue. Therefore, it is economically efficient to charge users for the cost of reliably and speedily transmitting their packets, which is reflected primarily in the need for faster additions of transport capacity.

A reasonable strategy for Internet service pricing is priority pricing, which is used by postal and natural gas providers.[4] There are several reasonable proposals for priority classifications.[5] *Guaranteed service* would provide certain packet deliverability or guaranteed delay bounds; *predicted service* would provide delivery with possible delays or packet losses of predictable magnitude; *link-sharing* service would allocate bandwidth to a group of users with specified rules for sharing; and *datagram* service would make no quality commitment except best effort using first-in first-out dispatch.[6] Guaranteed service seems necessary for certain real-time uses, such as video, that cannot tolerate delay or packet drop and that require large amounts of bandwidth. Certain kinds of predicted service could be useful for voice, which can tolerate some packet drop, or data, which can tolerate some delay.[7] Datagram service may be perfectly satisfactory for many non-urgent uses of e-mail, file transfer, and remote log-in.

In a related paper in this volume, MacKie-Mason and Varian suggest that real-time prices can be used to efficiently allocate capacity on a packet-switched Internet link.[8] Prospective system users would indicate the value they place on a service by encoding a bid price on each outgoing packet; packets would be admitted up to the point where bid price equals marginal congestion cost, and all admitted packets would pay the lowest accepted bid price.

In addition to priority service, certain applications (for instance, corporate or academic video conferences) may require reserving bandwidth some days, weeks, or even months before anticipated deployment in order to permit appropriate user planning and coordination. By contrast, medical users may need instant access to large blocks of bandwidth to meet emergency needs. These types of arrangements are now in use for space rental on satellites.[9] Internet users will probably need a similar variety of reservation periods and usage intervals.

Given the complexity of user needs and the evolution of transport technologies, it is impossible to specify in advance what precise menu of service offerings is appropriate. Network providers with more service classes might better distinguish differences in consumer values, but would probably use more router energy and network capacity in administration and billing. In designing its service menu, each provider must balance the benefits and costs of increasing service diversification. A wise strategy would allow competing providers to ascertain consumer demands and provide needed services on a level playing field; together, decentralized research, decision-making, interaction, and luck may achieve what central planning cannot.

The Role of Competition and Interconnection

Users and providers of Internet services must collectively determine whether network provision will be regulated (and protected) to some degree in order to promote a broader social objective, such as universal service. The AT&T breakup illustrates the choice and its consequences.

As formalized in the Kingsbury Agreement and the Communications Act of 1934, the government granted AT&T 19 regional monopolies on the provision of local service and access and a national monopoly on long-distance service and equipment interconnection; the company agreed to minimize interconnection and local usage prices to encourage universal subscription.[10] Monthly interconnection charges were set well below the actual cost of the copper wire needed to provide service. To recover the resulting revenue shortfall, long-distance prices were set considerably above actual costs, which continually decreased due to improvements in switching and transport technologies.

This pricing policy would have been sustainable indefinitely if long-distance service had not been opened to competition. However, the Federal Communications Commission (FCC) and the U.S. Department of Justice came to view the telephone monopoly as inefficient and anticompetitive and saw competition an appropriate means to discipline market power. Consumers were allowed to use non-Bell equipment and long-distance service; subsidies from long-distance callers that were recovered for the local exchange were reduced. Consequently, long-distance prices declined and local rates increased. Long-distance telephone service was transformed from a protected monopoly to a more competitive industry.

The potential benefits of Internet competition are profound. First, competition forces service prices closer to efficient levels based on marginal cost. Second, competition and open interconnection generally encourage more service and product offerings; specialized providers may serve niche markets. Third, competition encourages network managers to adopt speedily the most efficient technologies to keep up with or gain advantage over competitor abilities. Finally, a monopoly that behaves inefficiently can sometimes be punished by the entry of a new competitor. Therefore, the mere *threat* of competition may deter price increases. This entry threat may be particularly significant in Internet provision; i.e., because the fiber capacity of the three major long-distance networks is well beyond present needs, new transport providers can rent dedicated lines from these companies.[11]

Interconnection in Practice

To intensify competition and encourage entry, interconnection between networks should be as open as possible, particularly for those networks that receive government financial support. A provider that could hinder a rival's ability to interconnect could substantially increase the rival's costs of reaching the access point of a long-distance backbone and consequently its prices. Therefore, a regional network has an advantage in attracting new subscribers if it can deny local rivals least-cost access to its existing subscriber base.

The High Performance Computing and Communications Act of 1991, S. 272, states:

The Network shall be established in a manner which fosters and maintains competition within the telecommunications industry and promotes the development of interconnected high-speed data networks by the private sector ... The Network shall be phased into commercial operation as commercial networks can meet the needs of American researchers and educators.

However, Alison Brown, the Director of OARNET (one of NSF's regional networks), in the same year distinguished network practice from legal theory:

The Internet currently has a high level of technical interoperability but at present has virtually no basis for using each others' facilities... and there is certainly no set of economic agreements in place which are comparable to those worked out by the phone companies.[12]

The state of interconnection between subsidized providers and commercial data networks now appears to be mixed. Interconnection disputes have arisen between commercial providers and the high-speed backbone that is now administered by Advanced Network Services (ANS)/Merit. Interconnection difficulties also have appeared between commercial and regional networks.

The problem may emerge more profoundly later in 1994, when ANS grants are eliminated but grants to regional networks continue.[13] The NSF's Solicitation 93-52 of May 6, 1993 invited proposals for provider organizations for one Very high-speed Backbone Network Service (155 Mbps), a set of Regional Networks to serve end users, a Routing Arbiter to direct network traffic, and one or more manager organizations to arrange for and oversee Network Access Points (NAPs), where the high-speed backbone may interconnect with Regional Networks or intermediary Network Service Providers.[14] Total NSF funding for all awards will be $18 million over four years.

In the solicitation, "existing and/or realigned regional networks are invited to propose how they will meet the interregional connectivity needs of their client/member organizations." The NAP solicitation specified three priority locations—California, Chicago, and New York—and five desirable locations—Atlanta, Boston, Denver, Texas, and Washington, D.C.; specific sites will be selected by the provider. Proposed NAPs can be local area networks, metropolitan area networks, or an ATM switch; providers must operate NAPs at the same speeds as the networks to which they are attached, upgrade capacity as network usage requires, develop necessary attachment policies, and propose fair and equitable pricing arrangements.

On May 27, 1993, the distinction between regional and backbone provider blurred. Eight subsidized regional networks—BARRNet, CICnet, MIDnet, NEARnet, NorthWestNet, NYSERNet, SURAnet, and WestNet—announced the formation of the Corporation for Regional and Enterprise Networking (CoREN) to expedite interconnection. They chose MCI as their backbone provider. By handling large amounts of Internet traffic, the CoREN backbone may achieve substantial operation economies and may bill regional affiliates efficient internal transfer prices for transport service provided.[15]

While it has great potential for operating efficiencies, the resulting scenario nonetheless is problematic: the government will subsidize eight regional networks that transmit signals through a very high-speed backbone, but backbone interconnection rights for other networks might be limited. Possible problems might be resolvable by instituting more NAPs and specifying bilateral interconnection rules. NSF then may need to continually evaluate network performance and develop formal ways of arbitrating interconnection disputes.

Interconnection Prices

Since network congestion is not now a significant problem and marginal usage costs are basically zero, two interconnecting networks now may install and share the cost of the gateway routers that serve as their bridge without having to assess positive usage charges for traffic moving in either direction. However, pricing for interconnection will need to become more complicated if congestion arises in the future. For example, to reach an interregional backbone, Network A may wish to interconnect with Network B at the nearest possible gateway—a computer center located on a university campus. However, because the proposed interconnection strains the capacity and threatens the reliability of network B, network B may suggest a more remote interconnection point. Network A protests, citing the higher costs needed to reach the latter point. Either interconnection point then imposes a cost on one network provider that the other fails to consider.

Unless the relevant costs of contending interconnection sites can be balanced, the resulting outcome can be seriously inefficient. In resolving disputes, informed arbitrators may attempt to determine the relevant costs and mandate the more efficient solution.[16] Alternatively, if interconnection prices can be based on marginal cost (as competition would tend to provide), interconnecting providers themselves may choose the most efficient option without need for administrative mandate.

Nonprofit Users and Network Subsidies

A laudable ideal is to interconnect every school, hospital, and library to the emerging national broadband information network to permit voice communication, high-speed data transfer, animated imaging, and videoconferencing. Subsidies could legitimately be used to lower prices to these nonprofit users.

An important policy question concerns whether subsidies to support nonprofits should be paid to users directly or to the network providers that serve them. Secondly, policy makers must determine how to generate the necessary subsidy dollars.

Who Gets Paid?

Subsidies paid directly to each user, regardless of its choice of network provider, would empower the customer to deploy the best possible network arrangement for its particular needs. Competition would be even-handed and new providers could enter the market and compete without disadvantage. By contrast, directly subsidizing a small group of chosen producers could unfairly disadvantage rivals and generate serious anticompetitive advantages and inefficiencies.

However, there are practical difficulties with direct user subsidies that should not be ignored. Administrative costs may increase seriously if subsidies or vouchers are allocated to every U.S. school, hospital, or library, rather than to a considerably smaller group of network providers. This administrative problem becomes even more complicated if the amount paid to each institution is based upon the number of students, doctors, users, or host computers on its premises; this would require extensive monitoring and verification. Finally, many K-12 schools, libraries, and hospitals are not administratively equipped to write grant applications to secure necessary funding.

A reasonable alternative to paying subsidies to end-users or choosing favored network providers would establish direct grants for *any* network provider that interconnects with a target user. Dollar amounts for each interconnected target would depend upon the amount of transport capacity provided to it. Subsidy allocations would change as target customers come on-line or add capacity; target customers who switch network providers would carry their subsidy credits with them.[17]

Who Pays?

A second question involves whether subsidies should be financed through higher prices that other Internet users pay or through general tax dollars.

Higher usage prices passed on to other Internet users might be popular among non-users, who avoid payments as long as they stay off the Internet. However, present business and university users benefit little from most K-12 school, library, and hospital interconnections; it therefore does not seem fair or wise that existing users should bear this subsidy burden. Indeed, subsidy-laden prices may induce business users to find alternative network configurations to avoid higher prices.[18]

Much like the nation's military system, K-12 schools, libraries, and hospitals are public goods with social benefits that accrue to the entire nation. As we accept the notion that schools and libraries should be financed through general taxes, taxpayers who pay for books, buildings, and staffs for schools and libraries should also pay for their Internet interconnection. Hospital costs are appropriately recovered from patient fees and insurance companies.

Conclusion

The Internet has been so successful that it is difficult, without balking, to advocate restructuring the whole system in the manner suggested. However, if the Internet were to continue until 2000 to provide principally e-mail, remote log-in, and file transfer, fewer would consider it the great success that it is now. When we consider what the network has the potential to become, we can appreciate more why the reforms advocated here are necessary.

Acknowledgments

The views expressed in this paper are those of the author and not those of the U.S. Department of Justice. I have benefited from talks with Rick Adams, Miriam Avins, Vint Cerf, Sperry Kaylor, James Keller, Leonard Kleinrock, Sunni Lotta, David Lytel, Dick Mandelbaum, Terry McGarty, Mahal Mohan, Cindy Mills, Aaron Nabil, Bob Pepper, Glenn Ricart, Padmanabhan Srinagesh, Scott Shenker, Bill Schrader, Hal Varian, Bill Washburn, Al Weiss, Greg Werden, Stephen Wolff, and especially Robert Kahn.

Notes

[1] Since 1985, the Internet has grown from a network of 50 sites and 1000 hosts to one that comprises 13,000 sites and 2,000,000 hosts; network traffic has increased a hundredfold and backbone speeds have increased from 56 Kbps to 45 Mbps, with 1 Gbps envisioned by the year 2000 or sooner.

[2] Assuming that customer subscription is not sensitive to increases in prices, access prices can be used to recover needed revenues. If both access and usage are price-sensitive, both usage and access prices may be distorted from related costs if revenue recovery is deficient under marginal cost pricing. See William J. Baumol and David Bradford, "Optimal Departures from Marginal Cost Pricing", *American Economic Review*, Vol. 60, No. 2, June 1970.

[3] For example, voice applications need modest bandwidth and permit some packet loss, but require low delay; data applications permit more delay but less loss; videoconferencing and animated imaging might require more bandwidth, low loss, and low delay.

[4] See Robert Wilson, "Efficient and Competitive Rationing", *Econometrica*, Vol. 57, No. 1, February. For packet network applications, priority pricing contrasts favorably with time-of-use and peak load pricing; see C. Parris and D. Ferrari, "A Resource Based Pricing Policy for Real-Time Channels in a Packet-Switching Network", International Computer Science Institute, Berkeley, California, 1992.

[5] D. D. Clark, S. Shenker, and L. Zhang, "Supporting Real-Time Applications in an Integrated Services Packet Network: Architecture and Mechanism", *Proceedings of SIGCOMM*, 1992; D. D. Clark, S. Shenker, and L. Zhang, "A Scheduling Service Model and a Scheduling Architecture for an Integrated Services Packet Network", Palo Alto Research Center, Xerox Corporation, Palo Alto, California, unpublished manuscript, 1993.

[6] Scheduling algorithms have been devised to enable this selection of services; see D. Ferrari and D. C. Verma, "A Scheme for Real-Time Channel Establishment in Wide-Area Networks", *IEEE Journal on Selected Areas in Communications*, Vol. 8, No. 3, 1989. Admission control rules can be used at routers to ensure that low-priority packets do not interfere with service guarantees made to other users; see D. W. Petr, L. A. DaSilva, and V. S. Frost, 1989, *IEEE Journal on Selected Areas in Communications*, 7(5): 644–656; L. Zhang, 1991, "VirtualClock: A New Traffic Control Algorithm for Packet Switching Networks", *ACM Transactions on Computer Systems*, 9(2): 101–124. D. Ferrari, A. Banerjea, and H. Zhang, "Network Support for Multimedia: A Discussion of the Tenet Approach", International Computer Science Institute, Berkeley, California, 1992, sets forth a protocol suite for real time applications; D. Estrin and L. Zhang, "Design Considerations for Usage Accounting and Feedback in Internetworks", *ACM Computer Communication Review* Vol. 20, No. 5, 1990, discusses important accounting and metering issues.

[7] Permissible delay and drop limits are quite technical. The research cited above discusses some appropriate parameters.

[8] MacKie-Mason, J., and H. Varian, 1993, "Some Economics of the Internet", Dept. of Economics, University of Michigan, Ann Arbor, Michigan, unpublished manuscript.

[9] Satellite space is often available on long-term leases so that, for instance, cable television companies can rent space for three to five years. Space also is made available for shorter-run applications that may or may not be anticipated; for example, ABC can reserve capacity months in advance to broadcast the World Cup, or minutes in advance to broadcast from an earthquake site. Finally, capacity rights made available through long-term contracts can be traded in spot markets to meet immediate short-run needs. Both firm and interruptible usage rights are made available to interested users in gas and electricity transport as well.

[10] The company also agreed to interconnect non-Bell local companies to its long-distance network.

[11] Alternatively, one network provider can act as a market coordinator by foregoing operations, consolidating power as a buying coop, and taking competitive bids from prospective providers to operate franchises for a designated period of time; see R. Mandelbaum and P. Mandelbaum, "The Strategic Future of the Mid-Level Networks", in B. Kahin, ed., *Building Information Infrastructure* (New York: McGraw Hill, 1992).

[12] Alison Brown, Letter to members@farnet.org, March 1, 1991.

[13] In addition to NSF subsidies, state money is often forthcoming; e.g., Colorado Super Net, Texas' THENET, and North Carolina's CONCERT are all state-funded.

[14] National Science Foundation, 1993, "Network Access Point Manager, Routing Arbiter, Regional Network Providers, and Very High Speed Backbone Network Services Provider for NSFNET and the NREN(SM) Program", Washington, DC.

[15] A transfer price is the usage charge that two integrated company divisions (in this case CoREN and its regional networks) charge one another for usage. Ideally, transfer prices should be equal to the marginal cost.

[16] If administrators choose the high-cost alternative, the two parties may be able to negotiate—with mutual gain—a less costly alternative.

[17] This is akin to voucher plans for K-12 education, which allow parents to freely choose schools for their children. State money flows directly to chosen institutions based on enrollment totals; parents may switch schools and carry voucher credit with them.

[18] Strategic routing through real and virtual networks now occurs frequently in voice telephony, where long-distance companies and large users avoid surcharges on switched minutes by directly interconnecting with one another or by leasing special access lines that pass through the central offices without being switched. These arrangements often arise simply to avoid access charges, but they pass the revenue burden to smaller users, who cannot profitably bypass the switch. If subsidies are funded through user taxes, similar behavior can be expected on the Internet.

Network Analysis Issues for a Public Internet

Hans-Werner Braun and Kimberly C. Claffy

Introduction

While initially conceived as a dedicated communications research facility for the United States federal government, today's Internet carries traffic from many more constituencies. As the number of client networks of the Internet rises to tens of thousands with millions of users world-wide, the image of a ubiquitous network, relying on globally shared resources, has already become a reality. A key characteristic of the Internet is that its constituent networks do not simply pay for a service from a transit provider, but rather contribute network resources, ranging from vast national and international backbones to regional transmission services to local network services within individual campuses and companies. Such pooling of resources raises the issue of resource and cost allocation. In the early days of the Internet, when one or a few U.S. government agencies assumed the financial burden of building and maintaining the transit network infrastructure, there was little controversy over proportioning of costs. However as the number of federal, academic, and commercial entities increases, equitable resource allocation dominates many discussions of Internet development. Usage policy considerations, e.g., acceptable use guidelines of mission-oriented agencies, complicate the discussions further.

Cost allocation and policy considerations in the Internet require models different from those used by phone companies in the past, where end-users pay their service provider directly and service providers use among themselves a settlement process that is largely transparent to the end-user. Impediments to using such a model, for example in the U.S. portion of the Internet, include the current funding framework, where major government agencies fund significant fractions of the infrastructure based on often abstract goals, such as fostering scientific research. Many times these goals in turn impose specific criteria for transmitted traffic, resulting in Acceptable Usage Policies (AUPs) for the network. An example is the NSFNET backbone,[1] one of the Internet's core networks. The United States National Science Foundation (NSF) pays for this network in line with its objective to foster research and education, and requests that traffic using the NSFNET support NSF programmatic requirements.

Other U.S. federal agencies provide even more restricted network services: e.g., NASA, DOE and DoD each maintain a dedicated network in direct support of their missions. Other organizations, such as commercial entities within the U.S. or the pan-European EBONE network, provide unrestricted transmission service for any legal traffic from any paying customer.

With today's large number of service providers, many of which are competitors, the ad hoc interconnection approach (or *Reach-As-Far-and-As-Fast-As-You-Can* paradigm[2]) used thus far has begun to break down. For example, during the recent establishment of a major multi-service-provider interconnection facility, or Network Access Point (NAP), in early 1993, some service providers who wished to protect their own assets and marketing opportunities refused to connect without clearly articulated interconnection policies. Such market-based and political issues transcend the technical conceptualization of the NAP environment and hinder further evolution of more extensive international interconnection points.

This *Reach-As-Far-and-As-Fast-As-You-Can* paradigm sufficed for the initial development phase of the Internet, but as the network matures out of a research community and into one of operational and often commercial service providers, new constraints emerge. Specifically, we must consider how the Internet differs from the other major communications industry: telecommunications. Several aspects of the Internet render imprudent the borrowing of procedural mechanisms from the telecommunications industry: individual bandwidth demand is constantly and rapidly increasing; an increasing number of service providers must cooperate to provide resources; and finally, end-users are often those who develop the multi-protocol technologies to advance it, and they want to see new technologies deployed far sooner than traditional telecommunications carriers have ever imagined. Combined with the demand for ever increasing bandwidth, predictability, and ubiquity, the resulting environment requires service providers to rapidly adapt to new technologies and user needs and to support an ever-increasing number of constituents. The complexity of the Internet system means that network policies must be clear, implementable, and verifiable.

In this paper we describe the importance of network analysis in support of these policy considerations and evaluate a number of examples. We begin with a description of the current U.S. Internet environment, the range of clients from which it aggregates traffic, and the multiple levels of *granularity* at which one can investigate it. We then offer examples of analysis of currently collected operational statistics. We use NSFNET backbone data to depict traffic flowing from NSFNET-connected countries into and out of the United States. We then describe how a mechanism within the communication protocol of the network allows rough analysis of the type of service of traffic crossing the NSFNET backbone. These data support our hypothesis that, in the face of the current evolution of global information infrastructure, vastly expanding both in ubiquity and sophistication of applications, Internet policy considerations and network analysis must begin to interact in new ways. In particular, as the scale of, access to, and commercialization of the Internet broadens, cost allocation among shared resources will require the development of new models of resource and cost allocation to accommodate the wide range of players and services.

As the network aggregates traffic among an increasing number of clients, each with increasing bandwidth and service requirements, greater understanding of resource consumption is critical to engineering network evolution. Network analysis is the vehicle to develop these models, which must cover: attribution of resource consumption; traffic profiling (e.g., bursty vs. continuous); performance metrics; service models; and verifiable product quality.

We emphasize that upgrading the architecture to support these and other analysis tasks will require significant change in community mindset toward network analysis. Current Internet service providers have relatively small systems and typically scarce resources (funding) for anything but the operation and short-term extension of their environment. Analysis is often limited to watching rough link utilizations metrics and trying to upgrade infrastructure ahead of imminent demand. However, the size of the system is beginning to transcend the threshold for which such an approach is possible. System survivability in the face of its unrelenting growth will require in-depth analysis of network flows, a resource-intensive undertaking that will not come from armchair efforts.

The Current Internet Environment

The U.S. component of the Internet currently consists of a three-level hierarchical architecture. National backbones are attached to mid-level networks,[3] which are attached to local sites. Similar architectures have evolved in other areas of the globe, perhaps most visibly in Europe, where the EBONE supports communication among participating countries.

Figure 1 depicts several logical levels of the U.S. portion of the Internet.[4] Components at each layer are typically operated and managed by autonomous organizations, each with its own rules and policies.

Aggregation Granularity

Network traffic on the Internet consists of an aggregation of individual connections. Those connections can be described as flows, from a variety of perspectives in *flow granularity*: between end-systems or users; between IP network numbers, which aggregate many end-systems; between entry/exit points of a network. At a very coarse flow granularity one can describe or model traffic as a flow matrix among countries participating in the Internet and analyze the impact of such flows on major constituent networks such as the NSFNET backbone. At the other extreme of granularity, one may attribute network usage to individual users, applications of the user, or more abstract definitions, for example, transmission of a

Braun and Claffy

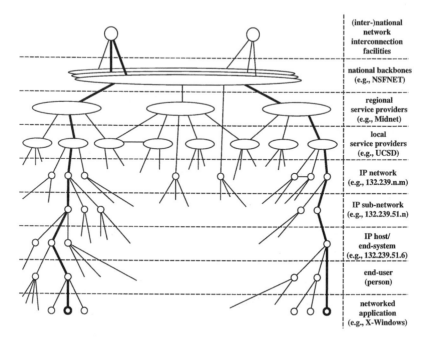

Figure 1 Model of U.S. Internet Interconnectivity Architecture.

high volume packet video stream. Intermediate granularities of service aggregation include traffic flows by multibackbone environment (e.g., those of different agencies), single backbone at large, backbone node, external interface of a backbone node, backbone client service provider, Administrative Domain, IP network number, and individual hosts. A single user or application might straddle several hosts, network numbers, or other aggregation mechanisms. The flow specification also defines the granularity at which one can audit traffic characteristics, and the ideal specification depends on the application of the data, e.g., network planning, accounting, flow control, statistical reports. As the complexity of such possible questions continues to grow, the ability to account for fine-grained flows, especially for real-time needs, easily exceeds the capabilities of available Internet technology.

The issue of granularity is critical for implementing mechanisms for cost allocation and accounting. As accounting matures, it may eventually be used for billing purposes, at which time the developed accounting models must accurately reflect network usage at whatever level of aggregation the billing mechanisms use.

A prerequisite to equitable cost allocation and accounting is a secure mechanism for the attribution of consumption of network resources, a difficult task in globally shared datagram infrastructures. Today's service providers typically focus on operational and near-term engineering. As a result, operationally collected statistics are generally geared toward day-to-day operations and management, such as indicators of real-time utilizations and outages. However, as the Internet grows in geographic and functional scope, the requirements for statistics reporting grow more complex, and the Internet community must define an appropriate structure for information about dynamic consumption of network resources. For example, a service provider would find it hard to attribute Internet usage to individual users with current technology because of the underlying datagram service, as well as the heavy aggregation of many users via multiple service providers.

Since most IP networks[5] are connected to the Internet via intermediate service providers, an alternative is a hierarchical model of attribution, where higher-level providers attribute resource consumption to intermediate providers, who in turn attribute consumption among their clients. In some cases of provider/client accounting a simple accounting model of aggregated packet/byte flow counters at service interfaces may suffice. An example is a private company connected to a transit network service provider. The company may choose not to take the effort to recharge individual departments; indeed such detailed billing may cost more company resources than the connection itself. It may instead just pay network costs from a specific network budget. This model assumes that volume sufficiently defines traffic exchange.

Most situations are not so simple. Often attribution to service providers will require measuring traffic volume not just as total packets traversing an interface, but according to the source and/or destination as well as type of each packet. Current network instrumentation for collecting such data on the NSFNET backbone supports only the granularity of individual clients (identified by IP network numbers). However, one could group multiple IP network numbers into their associated Administrative Domain. Many wide area network infrastructures must rely on sampling to determine traffic flows [4]. The NSFNET T3 backbone is an example of such an infrastructure; the next section discusses the impact of sampling on flow assessment capabilities.

Effect of Sampling on Assessing Accuracy of Traffic Locality

The National Science Foundation requires its backbone service provider to furnish an account of how many bytes and packets each IP network sends to other IP network destinations.[6] For performance reasons, the T3 backbone routers only sample every 50th packet. Thus these net-to-net matrices, collected and stored in fifteen-minute increments, are incomplete. Achieving accurate network number matrices via sampling is difficult, since more than 21,000 networks were exchanging traffic via NSFNET as of February 1994 and the number is rapidly growing. Particularly for a fifteen minute interval, the sampling cannot accurately reflect actual net-net usage.

For example, the sampled net-to-net matrix for December 1992 accounted for communication between 1,378,065 network pairs. For 281,680 (19.8%) pairs, the sampling mechanism only captured 1 packet. There is no way to know whether that pair exchanged only 1 packet, which just happened to be a in the 2% that were sampled, or 1 million packets, of which only 1 happened to be sampled.

Such difficulties of sampling will affect short-term needs such as billing and to a lesser extent longer-term needs such as capacity planning. The granularity of the required accounting flow, the time over which sampling can occur, and the required accuracy of traffic attribution are all factors that constrain sampling policies. For example, accounting by source or destination is more feasible than by network pair due to the smaller number of categories into which data is distributed. Collecting data for long enough intervals to bring the error margin down to an acceptable level is also an alternative, but the definition of "acceptable" may depend on the use of the data, e.g., billing likely requires greater accuracy than capacity planning. Network pair matrices could be important if there is an uneven cost distribution based on distance, link utilization, or value added services (e.g., commercial data base access).

Assessment of International Flows

Aggregation in time or in space may increase the accuracy of sampled statistics. This section presents examples of statistics on international traffic flows across the NSFNET backbone for a week in February 1993. These statistics are of particular interest to national or international policy makers who want to attribute consumption of network resources to individual countries to evaluate cost-sharing models. Figure 2 is a matrix of the volume of traffic exchanged by each country during the first week of February 1993. We created this matrix from operationally collected data sets for the NSFNET backbone, which include source-destination matrices by network numbers. We exclude the United States as its traffic volume dwarfs those of the other countries. Table 1 provides figures for relative proportions of traffic by country.

This data also allowed us to explore aspects of the data such as those in Table 1, which shows for the entire month of February 1993 the asymmetries in traffic volume by direction and average packet size by country. The sixth column in Table 1 provides an indication of the asymmetry with which countries utilize the backbone; this column shows the ratio of bytes received from the backbone to the number of bytes sent into the backbone. Figure 3 plots these ratios, along with the traffic volume each country sent into the backbone, for this first week of February 1993. The other graphs in this section also reflect the same period.

The distribution of packet sizes among countries provides an indication of the payload per packet each country is getting from the network. The last three columns in this table show the average packet size (in bytes) sent to and received from the backbone, and the ratio of the two values, for the month of February 1993. Most countries had an average packet size sent of under 90 bytes, while the average sizes of packets received from the backbone is substantially larger. We hypothesize that these countries are likely requesting bulk traffic from U.S. sites.

Some European countries received particularly large packets. In particular, Luxembourg's average packet size sent to the backbone was 41 bytes, and its average packet size received from the backbone during February 1993 was 514 bytes (almost twice that of the number two country, Korea!). Of course the traffic volume of

Braun and Claffy

Table 1 Traffic to and from NSFNET backbone per country for February 1993 (Data source: nis.nsf.net: *pub/nsfnet/statistics*)

Country	Country code	Existing networks	% of total bytes into NSFNET	% of total bytes from NSFNET	Bytes ratio from/to bb	Mean packet size inbound	Mean packet size outbound	Ratio to/from NSFNET
United States	US	4170	90.89	80.93	0.89	195	NNN178	0.91
Canada	CA	289	1.64	4.51	2.76	110	NNN276	2.51
United Kingdom	GB	214	0.64	2.01	3.12	112	NNN254	2.27
Australia	AU	171	0.88	1.19	1.35	172	NNN238	1.38
Germany	DE	297	0.71	1.89	2.68	151	NNN324	2.15
Sweden	SE	67	0.60	1.02	1.69	153	NNN193	1.26
Switzerland	CH	58	0.77	0.75	0.97	201	NNN190	0.95
France	FR	291	0.73	1.17	1.59	230	NNN276	1.20
Finland	FI	59	0.79	0.50	0.63	257	NNN138	0.54
Netherlands	NL	96	0.54	0.70	1.31	180	NNN258	1.43
Taiwan	TW	73	0.23	0.58	2.49	121	NNN250	2.06
Norway	NO	38	0.20	0.53	2.65	105	NNN221	2.10
Italy	IT	116	0.18	0.67	3.73	96	NNN309	3.20
Japan	JP	189	0.24	0.46	1.92	145	NNN262	1.81
Austria	AT	59	0.13	0.41	3.24	103	NNN279	2.72
Mexico	MX	19	0.07	0.21	2.77	78	NNN196	2.51
Denmark	DK	7	0.28	0.27	0.93	313	NNN213	0.68
Singapore	SG	16	0.06	0.33	5.42	75	NNN329	4.38
Israel	IL	22	0.07	0.30	4.51	96	NNN303	3.15
Hong Kong	HK	8	0.04	0.29	7.99	60	NNN349	5.83
Korea	KR	30	0.04	0.24	5.83	84	NNN355	4.22
Spain	ES	29	0.03	0.13	4.47	84	NNN322	3.84
New Zealand	NZ	38	0.02	0.10	4.29	76	NNN304	4.00
Brazil	BR	38	0.02	0.10	5.27	70	NNN290	4.15
Belgium	BE	11	0.03	0.11	3.64	116	NNN313	2.70
South Africa	ZA	32	0.03	0.11	3.53	123	NNN320	2.61
Czecho-slovakia	CS	35	0.02	0.09	4.50	78	NNN341	4.36
Chile	CL	9	0.02	0.06	2.62	103	NNN253	2.46
Puerto Rico	PR	3	0.02	0.03	1.94	80	NNN171	2.15
Ireland	IE	16	0.01	0.06	5.11	78	NNN273	3.51
Poland	PL	19	0.01	0.04	4.81	67	NNN244	3.62
Portugal	PT	26	0.02	0.04	2.48	152	NNN284	1.87
Greece	GR	11	0.01	0.04	5.88	71	NNN188	2.64
Hungary	HU	8	0.01	0.02	3.17	80	NNN262	3.26
Venezuela	VE	5	0.00	0.02	3.43	73	NNN194	2.65

Iceland	IS	5	0.01	0.01	2.11	109	NNN181	1.69
Slovenia	SI	6	0.00	0.01	5.77	56	NNN305	5.46
India	IN	2	0.00	0.01	5.27	57	NNN112	1.96
Thailand	TH	3	0.00	0.01	2.65	62	NNN178	2.85
Luxembourg	LX	4	0.00	0.02	17.62	42	NNN514	12.31
Argentina	AR	1	0.00	0.00	2.13	77	NNN131	1.70
Estonia	EE	3	0.00	0.01	7.39	63	NNN294	4.69
Malaysia	MY	3	0.00	0.00	5.42	66	NNN318	4.81
Ecuador	EC	10	0.00	0.00	3.96	66	NNN203	3.08
Croatia	HR	2	0.00	0.00	2.70	70	NNN141	2.03
Tunisia	TN	1	0.00	0.00	2.78	74	NNN196	2.64
Latvia	LV	1	0.00	0.00	5.13	55	NNN194	3.56
Cyprus	CY	6	0	0	5.03	61	NNN184	3.00
Kuwait	KW	1	0	0	3.15	53	NNN114	2.15
Costa Rica	CR	1	0	0	12.62	58	NNNN90	1.56
Turkey	TR	5	0	0	3.46	276	NNN159	0.58
Cameroon	CM	1	0	0	NA	NA	NNNN40	NA

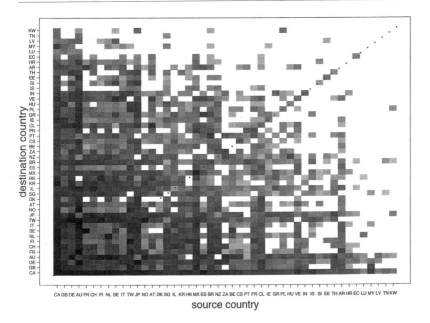

Figure 2 Intensity of Traffic Exchanged between Non-U.S. Countries during 1–7 February 1993.

Luxembourg and many other countries is relatively low, as is the number of IP network numbers (Luxembourg had only four). Germany was notable during this month for having a relatively large number of networks with rather large outbound NSFNET packets; these packets are more efficient than the inbound packets in terms of payload. A few countries send traffic to the backbone via large packets; we assume the top networks in that category are major FTP data sources.

We explored traffic shifts between the United States and specific countries via the NSFNET backbone. (On several occasions the NSF has needed such analyses of traffic volume exchanged among countries, often to address policy and funding related questions relative to global interconnectivity.) Figure 4 shows for the first week of February 1993 the bidirectional flow of traffic between the United States and three countries in different time zones, Japan, Mexico, and Great Britain. The impact of the time zones is quite visible in relationship to the flows of traffic volume; traffic tends to peak during the business hours of the particular country.

Figure 5 depicts the ratios of inbound to outbound NSFNET backbone traffic. Over the seven-day period almost all countries received more bytes from the United States then vice versa, though the discrepancies vary dramatically. The data indicate that asymmetry is a long term effect; in shorter periods, for example two-hour intervals, traffic flow into the U.S. is sometimes higher.

The NSFNET backbone network functions as a switching hub among many countries. While the reachable countries typically exchange the bulk of their NSFNET traffic with the U.S., a large fraction often goes to other countries via the U.S. In fact, many countries use the backbone for their own domestic communications. Figure 6 shows the extent to which countries were using the NSFNET backbone for domestic communications, both in terms of absolute volume and in relationship to the overall traffic those countries exchanged with the NSFNET.

Domestic communication through the NSFNET backbone may be a result of multiple connections between some country and the United States, and it is addressed on a case-by-case basis by the constituents of the connections. In many cases the magnitude of this kind of traffic is quite low relative to the traffic exchanged with the United States. In other cases this kind of traffic appears during

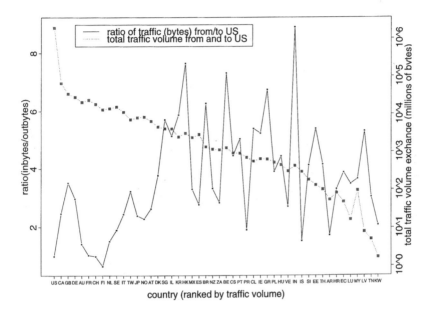

Figure 3 Intensity of Traffic Exchanged between Countries during 1–7 February 1993.

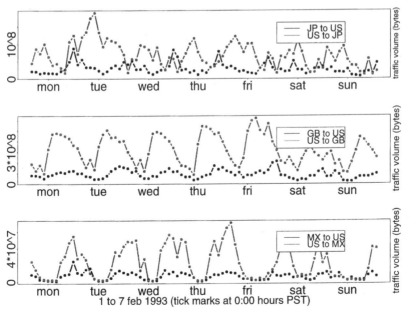

Figure 4 Traffic Exchanged from Japan, Mexico, and Great Britain to the United States, 1–7 February 1993.

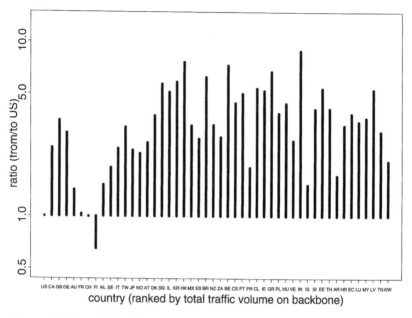

Figure 5 Ratio of Traffic Volume from/to the United States through the NSFNET Backbone.

startup phases, i.e., before final routing architectures for the interconnections are in place. As such, the intra-country traffic via the United States is in many case more of a political and administrative issue than a technical one.

Such attribution of international traffic flows is rapidly becoming an important issue as the mechanism of splitting the costs evenly between the two end-point countries of a connection breaks down. Several recent international connection scenarios have required the reevaluation of this current model of interconnection. Since all international networking resources contribute to the quality of the global Internet, including the emergence of major international data servers which source huge amounts of traffic to the global Internet community, better instrumentation will be necessary to assess the service qualities and network impact of such resources.

Application Diversity

The increasing variety of network applications further complicates a description of traffic. A reasonable model of flow attribution

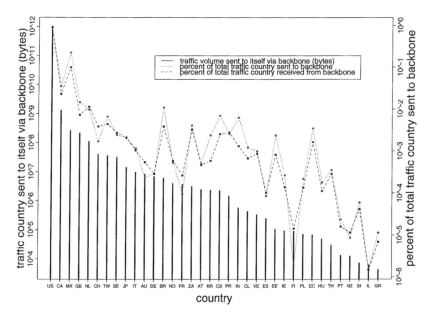

Figure 6 Traffic from Countries to Themselves through the NSFNET Backbone.

among specific sites must describe the service carried. For example, one may want to assign financial or political responsibility for file transfer traffic volume to the destination site, and assign responsibility for electronic mail to the source site. Unfortunately, currently collected data does not allow the simultaneous attribution of traffic type and geographic distribution. Claffy *et al.* [2] provides a description of the limitations of the current methodology used to track the traffic cross-section. In this section we provide only a brief summary.

Most applications on the NSFNET are built on top of the Transmission Control Protocol (TCP) or the User Datagram Protocol (UDP). Both TCP and UDP packets use port numbers to identify the Internet application that each packet supports. Each TCP or UDP header has two 16-bit fields to identify the source and destination *ports* of the packet. Originally, the Internet Assigned Numbers Authority (IANA) at ISI (Information Sciences Institute, University of Southern California), on behalf of DARPA, administered a space of 1 to 255 as the group of port numbers assigned to specific applications. For example, telnet received port assignment

23 [9]. To open a telnet connection to a remote machine, the packet carries the destination IP address of that machine in its destination IP address field, and the value of 23 in the destination port field.[7]

During the early years of the TCP/IP-based Internet, particularly in the early eighties, Unix developers injected a bit of anarchy into the IANA system when they unilaterally began using numbers between 512 and 1024 to identify specific applications. For example, they used port 513 for rlogin. Eventually network users started to use numbers above 1024 to specify more services, extending the lack of community coordination. In July 1992 [9], the IANA extended the range of port assignments they manage to 0-1023. At this time, they also began to track a set of registered ports within the 1024-65535 range. IANA does not attempt to control the assignments of these ports; they only register port usage as a convenience to the community [9]. Figure 7 presents a schematic of the port number categories discussed.

These port numbers are the only mechanism through which the NSFNET can monitor statistics on the aggregated distribution of applications on the backbone. Specifically, Merit (and now ANS) collects port-based information in the ranges 0-1023, 2049 (for NFS) and 6000-6003 (for X-window traffic). Merit/ANS categorizes packets into these ports if either the source or destination port in a given packet matches one of these numbers. However, even within this range, not all ports have a known assignment, so packets using undefined ports go the *unknown* port category [11].

Figure 8 uses this data to classify the proportion of packet traffic on the network by category since August 1989. This figure illustrates the difficulty in tracking changes in the cross-section of NSFNET traffic.[8] In this figure, "non-TCP services" corresponds to applications using a transport protocol other than TCP or UDP; the "other TCP services" to non-standard or not well-defined ports. Both of these categories have grown much larger over the years, reflecting an increasingly multi-application environment and the diminishing ability to track individual new applications using non-standardized ports. In fact, "other TCP services" has been, as of November 1992, the largest single category of packet-traffic on the backbone, as the number of type of non-standard applications

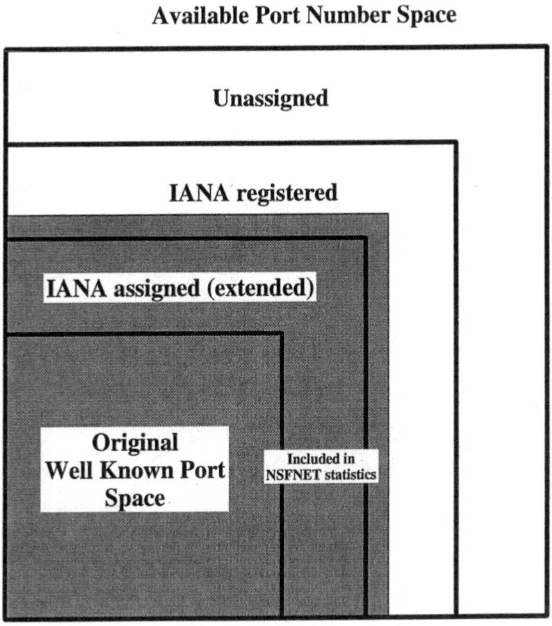

Available Port Number Space

Figure 7 Descriptive Categories of Port Numbers.

proliferate, collectively using substantial bandwidth. Because the port numbers are not standardized for anyone except the end site using them, the traffic volume growth for such applications is difficult to track; most statistics collection mechanisms can only attribute traffic to well-known port numbers, making attribution of more than the base services (telnet, ftp, etc.) nearly impossible.

Impact on Accounting and Pricing

In this section we discuss several problems related to accounting and pricing as the network evolves from a research environment with relatively narrow scope to a more commercialized environment that will eventually render data networks more of a utility, similar to the water, electric power, and telephone systems.

Comparison to the telephone infrastructure illuminates the difficulty of network usage accounting in an environment that aggregates datagram traffic among many end users and their

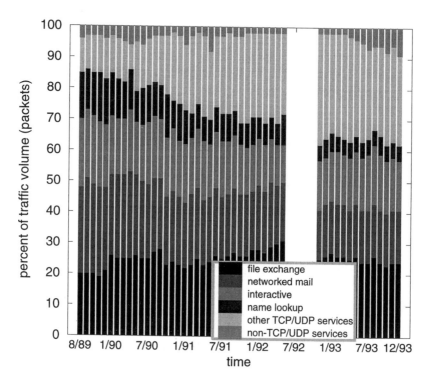

Figure 8 Distribution of the Number of Packets Offered into NSFNET Backbone by Application. Data source: Merit/NSFNET operations.

applications. When providing dedicated circuits or services to a single client, verifying the delivery of the promised product is straightforward.[9] In contrast, a network provider in the Internet environment promises a customer a probability of service rather than a dedicated and constantly verifiable physical pipe. It is difficult to verify the promised level of service to any given customer. The evaluation of network performance and integrity of services becomes even more complicated when a virtual network service is mapped into a larger physical infrastructure, such as ANS's provision of the virtual NSFNET backbone via its larger physical infrastructure, or Sprint's provision of international bandwidth for NSF via its rich network infrastructure.[10] As IP providers continue to expand across existing infrastructures, it will be imperative to find mechanisms to differentiate service components and performances and to assure clients that they are receiving contracted network services.

A further complication arises because charging by traffic volume per source does not always charge the beneficiary of a service. Shaping charging policies thus demands consensus on accounting conventions and the distribution of benefits not only across transactions but also within the transactions themselves, such as the relative costs and benefits to the end points of the transactions. Unfortunately, statistics collection mechanisms, e.g., at service interfaces, inhibit the attribution of traffic to the transaction-*requesting* country; one can only attribute the traffic volume according to its physical source and destination countries. This distinction is important in the Internet: the generator of a connection may not be the entity benefiting from the transaction. For example, charging for File Transfer Protocol (FTP) services based on the specific flow of IP packets from source ports to destination ports would be unacceptable to most sites that sponsor FTP-servers, which respond to requests for data with their own requests to transmit the data. End-point accounting was not a goal in the initial design of the FTP protocol, and retrofitting it for a market-based environment will be challenging at best.

Proposed Pricing Models

Research in network pricing for computer and other network infrastructures has led to several possible models of billing. We discuss some of the models recently proposed in the literature, and then discuss how current Internet infrastructure and its instrumentation constrain the viability of these models.

The telephone network offers several models for billing, and even offers customers options. Possible billing options include a flat service charge (typically for unlimited service within a local area), or a base price for a certain number of local calls plus an incremental charge for any calls above that limit. Long-distance telephone service billing is typically completely measured according to individual calls.

Applying telephone service billing models to the Internet imposes several difficulties since the Internet has far greater, and ever-increasing, functionality and diversity. Currently, some larger institutions lease bandwidth from a network service provider in the form of dedicated circuits for Internet services. For example, a company might pay for a T1 line from Alternet and using any amount up to the T1 limit. This model of bulk bandwidth distribution is not appropriate for the vast majority of the Internet community, whose traffic could not justify the expense of a leased line.

Categories of service that may require different billing policies include: information retrieval; real-time video; conferencing; multicasting; non-real-time messaging; low-priority bulk transfer; and distributed computation. Classification of traffic will rely on whether it is priority, standard, or deferrable, and might also extend to distributions of low-level traffic characteristics such as packet length histograms and burstiness profiles. The impact of time of day and time zone differences on network contention also require consideration.

Cocchi [5, 6] used computer simulations to show that in a network with multiple service priorities, it is possible to set prices so that users of every application type are more satisfied with the combined cost and performance than they would be with flat pricing. Thus a priority pricing scheme is always achievable that will enhance total community utility.

Parris and Ferrari [8] offer a scheme for real-time pricing in computer networks that allows users to reserve resources. It is based on charging per real-time channel based on the resources reserved, including the type of service, time of day, and channel lifetime. For computational feasibility, the authors assume a homogeneous network and reduce their analysis to a single network node. We do not know if it is possible to scale their scheme to the multiple, very heterogeneous nodes, of the Internet. A bigger obstacle is that it is not possible to reserve resources in the current Internet.

MacKie-Mason and Varian [10] offer an alternative model of real-time Internet pricing. Their model addresses the inability to predict in advance the optimal price of network service based on internal congestion, which is a short-term, bursty, and unpredictable phenomenon in most parts of the Internet. They propose a two-component pricing scheme: a flat connection charge, based on characteristics such as the type of customer or size of bandwidth, and a per-packet congestion charge assessed during times of network congestion.

The congestion-based charge would vary minute-by-minute to reflect the current state of the network contention. Each packet would have a "bid" field in the header that would indicate how much the sender is willing to pay. The network would admit all packets with bids over the current cutoff amount, equal to the marginal congestion costs imposed by a packet.

Similar to the Parris scheme, this scheme would require a separate pricing and queuing "auction" to occur at each network router. The authors claim that their model, drawn from other economic applications of network pricing and applied to the Internet, has the long-term advantage that properly set congestion prices are the appropriate prices for valuing capacity expansion. In other words, efficient pricing of network congestion in the short run, with investment of resulting revenue in capacity expansion, provides the optimal investment in future capacity.

Current Instrumentation

Unfortunately, current instrumentation will constrain the feasibility of implementing aspects of several proposed pricing models. Schemes that require each router to assess instantaneous congestion state and recompute and attribute charges would likely interfere unacceptably with packet-switching performance. Network congestion often modulates within sub-seconds, although in many cases it lasts and blocks network resources for minutes or even longer.[11] It is unlikely that short term pricing recomputation could keep up with the frequency of these changes in congestion.

Proposals of dynamic adaptation of pricing strategies to the existing network situation are attractive, but several obstacles will render such schemes difficult to implement in the existing architecture:

- overhead in the router
- difficulty with broad acceptance by users due to:
  - inability to independently verify billing;
  - unpredictability of the actual networking cost;
  - cost increases due to other clients using the network

Some feel that the end user should not need to worry about congestion in real time. Real-time contention for network services is the responsibility of the service provider, who must base available resources on long-term planning. Long-term planning may create fluctuations in use that would suggest graded pricing schemes through the day, similar to telephone service rates. The user can predict and, perhaps more important, independently verify such payment schemes. Real-time pricing adjustments based on network resource contention would result in network providers being attracted to a semi-congested state of their network, as it would drive up the price of network access to the network customer. Furthermore, the price a client has to pay would depend on the demand of networking resources by other network clients.

Thus in our opinion allocation of the task of pricing to external systems will have far more auspicious effects on overall network stability. Routers may be able to supply statistics and reallocate bandwidth among multiple prioritized queues, but it is critical to save router cycles for switching. Pricing schemes based on hourly or daily fluctuations in utilization are more feasible, predictable, and verifiable, than rapid price recomputation.

Regardless of the pricing scheme, billing models amenable to implementation will have to deal with constraints of current network instrumentation. NSFNET, which is typical of most wide-area Internet service providers, can currently keep measurements of raw volume (bytes), transactions (packets), or both (packets and payload). The mechanism for these measurements is the SNMP protocol at network interfaces, which cannot attribute the traffic to packet type or geographic source or destination. The NSFNET does collect a flow matrix by network number for traffic crossing the T3 NSFNET backbone, but the cost of collecting and computing the matrix prevents the complete collation of traffic; the computation must rely on only sampled packets. Attributing individual network numbers to other granularities, such as network external interfaces, Administrative Domains, or sub-service providers may allow for a greater accuracy of the collected statistics information. Such aggregation would allow the backbone provider to assess separate charges to these administrative entities, which would perform their own accounting to redistribute the cost.

The NSFNET backbone project also provides a distribution of ports as described above. There are two clear problems with the current implementation of this mechanism. First, the service classes include only conventional Internet application categories such as interactive, file transfer, and transactions. It is difficult to track other service categories, including the new continuous video/voice traffic type. A second difficulty relative to the NSFNET data is that the collation of this distribution is decoupled from the traffic flow matrix described above, and thus one cannot attribute a packet of a particular service category to a specific end network. Currently there is a recognized need within the NSFNET as well as other service providers to address both of these issues, but solutions will require community agreement on standards of accounting for various service qualities and standard procedures and tools for accounting analysis. Port information may be one criterion, but precedence and geographic source and destinations may suffice.

Capacity Planning

The issue of unknown applications is not by itself necessarily as disturbing as the dramatically changing nature of the newly introduced traffic. The recent deployment of prototype packet video and audio applications bodes ominously for an infrastructure not able to preferentially deal with certain traffic. This section describes the dangers of our increasing inability to monitor traffic type in a "high-end" Internet.

Today's Internet is based on a datagram architecture which aggregates traffic flows, typically with no admission control. Most entrance points into transit networks cannot gracefully control the flow of traffic from clients into the network. Like cars on a busy and uncontrolled highway ramp, a heavy inflow can create serious resource starvation. Typically neither the equivalent of traffic lights to block further flow into the network nor notifications to the traffic source exist in today's Internet. End systems can thus unfairly monopolize available bandwidth and cause significant congestion in the larger network.

During the life of the 56 Kpbs NSFNET backbone in the mid-1980s, congestion developed to a dangerous degree, and in response the NSFNET engineers deployed an emergency measure to provide certain interactive network applications, specifically Telnet, preferential treatment. The priority service prototyped in the Fuzzball-based 56 Kbps backbone in 1986 queued traffic based on both the IP precedence field and the interactivity, i.e., human sensitivity to response time, of the protocol.[12] The emergency measure to classify applications into service types, and priority queuing of traffic based on type and IP precedence value, addressed real-time service contention, allowing interactive users to continue working under highly network congested circumstances.

When the NSFNET was upgraded to T1 capacity, offering a 24-fold bandwidth increase and a richer topology, the designers did not re-introduce the priority queuing for end-user traffic. The new infrastructure used multiple queues only to differentiate between user traffic and network management traffic. An overabundance of bandwidth, with a bulk rather than per-volume payment scheme, rendered superfluous the use of multiple queues. The NSFNET project partners bore all the costs of maintaining the bandwidth ahead of demand. The subsequent upgrade to the T3 network further exemplified this method of coping with network congestion.

However, software developers continue to build network applications that can consume as much bandwidth as network engineers provide. In particular, applications using packet voice and video are not "bursty," like more conventional applications such as file transfer and electronic mail, but rather require continuous delivery of large amounts of traffic in "real-time," and continuously consume significant fractions of the available bandwidth. Usage of such applications will not scale in the current Internet, where uncontrolled continuous resource consumption from only a few clients will consume all available resources. Many thousands of simultaneous point-to-point flows multiplex on top of a typical current 45 Mbps "high speed" connection, most of them of very short duration. A network would be able to support far fewer simultaneous flows if the majority of those flows were of continuous point-to-point multimedia profiles, e.g., video.[13]

It is difficult to overestimate the dramatic impact such real-time applications will have on the Internet fabric. No other phenomenon could more strongly drive the research community to outfit the network with admission control as well as accounting and billing. Prerequisite to accounting and billing instrumentation will be a more accurate model for the attribution of resource consumption, derived from how particular applications affect network performance. Such a model may have to reliably attribute applications or traffic profiles to clients if multiple levels of services exist.

While performance optimization and accounting considerations are the dominant motivation for the establishment of various traffic priorities and types, network engineers must incorporate the burden of this additional complexity into a longer term view. It will be a challenge for a multi-provider infrastructure to remain robust in the face of—or even take advantage of—a greater number of possible traffic profiles based on an increasing range of diversity in service quality categories. A range of service providers, from local companies or campuses to international backbone service providers, will thus find it critical to stay aware of both short and longer term fluctuations in flows within the increasingly dynamic infrastructure. Longer term trends in flows can enable network providers and designers to plan or improve various aspects of the network, including topologies, application profiles, and underlying transmission technologies. Consideration of such flows requires the definition of a granularity model, as with the accounting case, but will also require greater focus on the traffic type and characteristics, including perhaps service categories based on traffic priorities, service quality, and application distribution.

A final consideration is accommodation of the diverse interests of network funding agencies, such as the NSF, that aim to encourage the development, deployment, and use of advanced, network-transparent applications on the network. An accurate assessment of traffic profiles could demonstrate to what extent the infrastructure supports advanced applications, which could thus motivate planning for a higher performance network. An example might be a high-volume image rendering software package that routinely and transparently executes some software module on a remote supercomputer before locally displaying resulting data. Performance profiles and resulting accounting characteristics for such applications will differ from those used for more conventional networking applications.

Summary

In the face of today's critical point in the evolution of global information infrastructure, Internet policy considerations and network analysis must interact and support each other. In particular, network analysis can offer insight into service categories relevant to accounting and policy considerations in network environments ranging from local to global scope. Results of traffic matrices by country have already proven useful to the U.S. NSF to illustrate international exchange of traffic among its constituents. In addition to quantifying network flows by various degrees of granularity, it will also be important to quantify and validate performance. As the threshold of high performance continues to expand into high volume real-time applications and advanced distributed computing paradigms, mechanisms to verify performance over shared infrastructures will be essential to clients and funding agencies.

Network analysis methodologies will also have obvious value for the integration of Internet accounting and billing mechanisms. As the functional and geographic scope of network performance continues to diversify, so does the financial structure of the Internet. Currently a transitional and confusing blend of public and private funding sources, some of which impose usage policies on critical pieces of the infrastructure, this structure can intimidate potential service providers and end-users. Creative and innovative developments in network analysis, with feedback to the developers of network policy, may dispel fears that a concerted effort between public and private networking efforts is not possible. On the contrary, such collaboration can enhance rather than retard Internet evolution.

Acknowledgment

The authors acknowledge support from the National Science Foundation for studying engineering and architectural issues of the National Research and Education Network.

Notes

[1] The "NSFNET backbone" now refers to a virtual backbone service, i.e., a set of services provided across the ANSnet physical backbone. In this paper we refer to the "T3 NSFNET backbone" with the understanding that we are referring to a service provided to NSF, not a dedicated NSFNET infrastructure.

[2] Mandelbaum, in [12], also refers to this as the "throw me a line" approach.

[3] Mid-level networks have also been called "regionals," reflecting their geographical span, but we will use the term "mid-level" to reflect their hierarchical position in the architecture.

[4] The actual implementation of all the connections forms a much more complex framework, and Internet interconnectivity is evolving in different ways in different areas of the world.

[5] An IP network typically aggregates computers at a location, such as a university campus or company.

[6] ANSnet collects these statistics using custom-designed software, the ARTS (ANSnet Router Traffic Statistics) [1] package, based on experience gained from the NNStat software [3].

[7] In the case of telnet, the packet uses some arbitrarily assigned source port that has significance only to the originating host. Often these "return address ports" have values greater than 1000.

[8] The categories in these figures correspond to:

• File exchange: FTP data and control (TCP ports 20, 21)

• Mail: SMTP, NNTP, VMTP, UUCP (TCP ports 25, 119, 175, 540)

• Interactive: telnet, finger, who, login (TCP ports 23, 79, 513, UDP port 513)

• Name lookup/DNS: (UDP port 53, TCP port 53)

• Other TCP/UDP services: all TCP/UDP ports not included above (e.g., irc, talk, X-windows)

• Non-TCP/UDP services: Internet protocols other than TCP or UDP (e.g., ICMP, IGMP, EGP, HMP)

Note that Merit began to use sampling for this collection on the backbone in September 1991. In November 1991 traffic migration to the T3 backbone began; the majority of the links had migrated by May 1992, and in November 1992 the T1 backbone was dismantled. For June to October 1992 no data was available for either the T1 or the T3 backbone.

More detailed distribution of traffic by port on the NSFNET backbone is available via ftp from nis.nsf.net and shows some indication of the growing range of applications. For example, several Internet resource discovery services (WAIS, WWW, gopher, prospero, mosaic [7]) have experienced tremendous growth in volume since their deployment, filling a significant void in network services.

In addition to resource directory services, other applications are gaining a greater proportion of network bandwidth: MUD (Multi-User Domain), a distributed electronic role playing environment; X11, or X-windows, for remote graphical displays across the network; and, more recently, packet video and audio. Many of these applications use multiple TDP/UDP port numbers or port numbers not centrally coordinated and often unknown to the anyone but the end site using them.

[9] Perhaps a greater problem is that in the Internet a "single client" is often not well defined.

[10] NSF funds Sprint, via the International Connections Manager (ICM) cooperative agreement, for components of its international connectivity to NSF clientele in other nations.

[11] Congestion manifests itself via queue growth in routers that do not have the local CPU capacity or external bandwidth to handle all received network traffic. As a router could starve more and more for resources under congestion, the contention might intensify sufficiently to consume all available buffer storage for additional packets. Alternatively, packet contention for processing via the CPU could consume all CPU resources, leaving the processor incapable of handling additional traffic.

[12] NSF based these categories on experiences and user feedback during the course of the NSFNET backbone project.

[13] Even a "small" 100 Kbps video flow would use up 1/450 of a T3 connection.

References

[1] ANS. ARTS: ANSnet Router Traffic Statistics software, 1992.

[2] T. Asaba, K. Claffy, O. Nakamura, and J. Murai. An analysis of international academic research network traffic between Japan and other nations. In *Inet '92*, pp. 431–440, June 1992.

[3] R. T. Braden and A. DeSchon. NNStat: Internet statistics collection package. Introduction and User Guide. Technical Report RR-88-206, ISI, USC, 1988. Available for anonymous ftp from isi.edu.

[4] K. Claffy, H.-W. Braun, and G. Polyzos. Application of sampling methodologies to wide-area network traffic characterization. In *Proceedings of SIGCOMM '93*, September 1993.

[5] R. Cocchi. *Pricing in multiple service class computer communication networks.* Ph.D. thesis, University of California, Berkeley, 1992.

[6] R. Cocchi, D. Estrin, S. Shenker, and L. Zhang. Pricing in computer networks: Motivation, formulation, and example. Technical report, University of California, Berkeley, 1993.

[7] P. B. Danzig, K. Obraczka, and S.-H. Li. Internet resource discovery services. Technical report, University of Southern California, March 1993.

[8] C. Parris and D. Ferrari. A resource-based pricing policy for real-time channels in a packet-switching network. Unpublished paper, University of California, Berkeley, International Computer Science Institute, ICSI TR 92-018, 1992. Available via anonymous ftp from tenet.icsi.berkeley.edu (directory / pub/papers).

[9] J. Postel and J. Reynolds. Assigned numbers. RFC 1340, 138 pages, July 1992.

[10] J. MacKie-Mason and H. Varian. Pricing the Internet. Technical report, University of Michigan, May 1993.

[11] Network information services, February 1993. Data available on nis.nsf.net: /nsf/statistics.

[12] R. and P. Mandelbaum. The strategic future of mid-level networks. In Brian Kahin, ed., *Building Information Infrastructure*, 1992.

Contributors

George Baldwin (George_Baldwin@Monterey.edu) is on the Planning Faculty at California State University, Monterey Bay.

Lewis M. Branscomb (lewisb@ksgrsch.harvard.edu) is the Albert Pratt Public Service Professor at Harvard University. He is Director of the Program on Science, Technology, and Public Policy at Harvard's John F. Kennedy School of Government and is Principal Investigator of the Information Infrastructure Project.

Hans-Werner Braun (hwb@cs.ucsd.edu) is with the Applied Network Research Group, San Diego Supercomputer Center.

Richard Civille (rciville@clark.net) is Executive Director of the Center for Civic Networking, a nonprofit organization dedicated to the application of information infrastructure to community and economic development.

Kimberly C. Claffy (kc@cs.ucsd.edu) is with the Applied Network Research Group, San Diego Supercomputer Center.

Daniel Dern (ddern@world.std.com) is an Internet analyst and writer. He is the author of *The Internet Guide for New Users* and *The Internet Business Handbook.*

Michael A. Einhorn (einhorma@justice.usdoj.gov) is an economist with the Antitrust Division of the U.S. Department of Justice.

Samer Faraj (samer@bu.edu) is a doctoral student in MIS at Boston University.

Miles Fidelman (mfidelman@civicnet.org) is President of the Center for Civic Networking, a nonprofit organization dedicated to the application of information infrastructure to community and economic development.

Cliff Figallo (fig@well.sf.ca.us) is a networking consultant living in the San Francisco area. He served as Director of the Whole Earth Lectronic Link from 1986 until 1992.

Carole Haywood is with RAM Mobile Data, Inc.

Carol Henderson (cch@alawash.org) is the Executive Director of the Washington Office of the American Library Association.

Beverly Hunter (bhunter@bbn.com) is Educational Strategist in the Educational Technologies Department at Bolt Beranek and Newman, Inc. Previously she was Program Director for Applications of Advanced Technologies in science education at the National Science Foundation.

Brian Kahin (kahin@harvard.edu) is Adjunct Lecturer in Public Policy and Director of the Information Infrastructure Project in the Science, Technology, and Public Policy Program at the John F. Kennedy School of Government, Harvard University. He is also General Counsel for the Annapolis-based Interactive Multimedia Association.

James Keller (keller@ksgrsch.harvard.edu) is a Research Associate and Coordinator of the Information Infrastructure Project in the Science, Technology, and Public Policy Program at the John F. Kennedy School of Government, Harvard University.

Frederick D. King (phred@access.digex.net) is Electronic Services Librarian at the University of Maryland University College.

Jeffrey K. MacKie-Mason (jmm@umich.edu) is Associate Professor of Economics and Public Policy at the University of Michigan, Ann Arbor.

Terrence P. McGarty (mcgarty@delphi.com) is Chairman and CEO of The Telmarc Group, Inc.

Frank Odasz (franko@bigsky.dillon.mt.us) is Director of Big Sky Telegraph, Western Montana College of the University of Montana. For free access to BST, telnet to bigsky.dillon.mt.us or 192.231.192.1, or dial-in at 406-683-7680; type bbs at login.

Scott Shenker (shenker@parc.xerox.com) is with the Palo Alto Research Center, Xerox Corporation.

Lee Sproull (lsproull@acs.bu.edu) is Professor of Management at Boston University. She is currently undertaking a program of research on electronic groups sponsored by The Markle Foundation.

Hal R. Varian (Hal.Varian@umich.edu) is the Reuben Kempf Professor of Economics at the University of Michigan, Ann Arbor.

Index